The Doctor with Two Heads

THE
DOCTOR
WITH
TWO HEADS
and Other Essays

GERALD
WEISSMANN

Alfred A. Knopf New York 1990

Grateful acknowledgment is made to the following for permission to reprint previously published material:

Carcanet Press Limited: Extracts of the poetry of John Cornford are taken from *John Cornford: Collected Writings*, edited by Jonathan Galassi. Reprinted by kind permission of Carcanet Press Limited.
Harcourt Brace Jovanovich, Inc., and A. M. Heath & Company Limited: Excerpts from "Why I Write" in *Such, Such Were the Joys* by George Orwell. Copyright 1953 by Sonia Brownell Orwell and renewed 1981 by Mrs. George K. Perutz, Mrs. Miriam Gross, Dr. Michael Dickson, Executors of the Estate of Sonia Brownell Orwell. Reprinted by permission of Harcourt Brace Jovanovich, Inc., and A. M. Heath on behalf of the Estate of the late Sonia Brownell Orwell and Secker & Warburg.
Thames & Hudson Limited: Excerpts from translation of Baudelaire's "Ragpicker" from *Absolute Bourgeois* by T. J. Clark. Reprinted by permission of Thames & Hudson Ltd.

Library of Congress Cataloging-in-Publication Data

Weissmann, Gerald.
The doctor with two heads.

1. Science and the arts.   2. Medicine and art.
I. Title.
NX180.S3W45   1990   306.4'5   89-45298
ISBN 0-394-57833-3

For my parents, Adolf and Greta Weissmann

The opposite of a true statement is a false statement. But the opposite of a profound truth may be another profound truth.

—NIELS BOHR

Contents

Acknowledgments

The editorial director of *Hospital Practice*, David W. Fisher, has been a source of encouragement and useful criticism since 1973. I thank him for having the patience to publish my nonscientific pieces with only the gentlest of corrections. Recently, Joseph Wisnovsky of *Hospital Practice* has been vetting my prose and I am most grateful. I should also acknowledge the second source of support for my amateur efforts in the arts and social sciences, New York University's Society of Fellows. This remarkable organization was started over a decade ago with the help of the NYU Humanities Council, and Leslie Berlowitz has been the principal spirit behind both groups. Many conversations begun at gatherings of the Society have ended as essays in this book. Of past and present members, I would especially like to thank Thomas Bender, Jeremy Bernstein, Robert Bernstein, Thomas Bishop, Jerome Bruner, Norman Cantor, Norman Dorsen, Thomas M. Frank, William Golden, Wassily Leontieff, Cathleen Morawetz, Richard Sennett, Frank Stella, Nicholas Wahl, and Aileen Ward. They have provided ideas or facts that only a professional can offer.

Several of these essays were written in the course of a sabbatical in 1987–8. I acknowledge the generous hospitality of Professor Sir John Vane, FRS, at the William Harvey Research Laboratories of St. Bartholomew's Hospital Medical College, and Lady Daphne Vane. Thanks are also due to the Rockefeller Foundation for its residency at the Villa Serbelloni in Bellagio, and to Roberto and Gianna Celli, who proved to be gracious and intellectual ringmasters of the study center at Lake Como. In Paris, I was helped most directly by Mme. Nadine Simone of the Musée de l'Assistance Publique, by Marianne Held, and by the well-situated private library of Mme. Arlette Gaillet. In New York, thanks are due to Annette Blaugrund and Barbara Hatcher for generous help with sources. Paula Frosch did heroic work in tracking down the illustrations. The penultimate essay in this book owes an obvious debt to Tobé and Steve Malawista. Andrew Spielman and Allen Steere were also most patient with my questions on Lyme disease.

Institutions and those who run them are usually faulted more than praised. But were the NYU Medical Center under Dean Saul J. Farber not so tolerant a place as it is, I would have been under far greater restraint with respect to academic house-keeping. Were the Marine Biological Laboratory, under Harlyn Halvorson and Prosser Gifford, not the exhilarating center of excellence that *it* is, I would have spent less time in its labs and library than on its tennis courts. The libraries of NYU, the Marine Biological Laboratory, and—especially—Woods Hole have been the source of many of the references found in this book. Secondary references are the mark of the amateur, and since we are all amateurs on playing fields away from home, I offer these without shame. I have relied most heavily on accounts of French art and culture provided by T. J. Carter, Jerrold Seigel, and Anita Brookner.

Andrea Cody and Douglas Becker have helped prepare my manuscript, offered astute and plucky advice, and worked on these essays with more care than they might seem to deserve. Without my agent, Gloria Loomis, and my editor, Elisabeth Sifton, the final version of these essays would have been far more imper-fect still, and I owe to both of them my sense of their overall form. I must once more acknowledge the extensive editing of my pieces by Ann Weissmann, who together with Andrew and Lisa Beth Weissmann is responsible for many of the warmer and more generous themes in this book. Belated thanks are also due to Professor Meyer Schapiro, who first taught me as an undergradu-ate how to look at pictures. Finally, I must gratefully acknowledge the example of my first chief of medicine at NYU–Bellevue, Dr. Lewis Thomas, who taught me not only how to write my first scientific papers but also how to listen to the words of which they were composed.

G.W.
New York and Woods Hole
Summer 1989

Introduction

The essays in this book deal with art and science, but they are not
meant to revive C. P. Snow's old squabble between the "Two Cultures." They are offered instead as a brief for the liberal imagination
filed by a friend of the court; they are not the testimony of an
expert witness. I am persuaded that nowadays we live not with two
but among a hundred—perhaps a thousand—cultures, each as differentiated and remote from the others as the many creatures of the
sea. As a winter city-dweller and summer marine biologist, I suspect
that Manhattan alone is richer in species than the bottom of oceans:
ctenophores are closer to tuna than Alistair Cooke is to Tama
Janowitz. Two cultures, indeed! No, since the cold-war days of Lord
Snow, we've let a thousand cultures bloom in the lands of the
West. We have not quite learned how to cope with their flowering.

Baubles of other lands, rhythms of other folk compete for
attention with the high art of our time in the West. We have
learned the charms of Benin masks and Shaker quilts, Dayak
chants and Zuni pots, samurai gear and the Andean flute, Indian
dances and the Grateful Dead. Malraux's museum without walls
has become a souk without borders. So rich is the polyglot feast
that we despair of taking it all in; we may become so filled by hors
d'oeuvres that we leave the meal before the main course. Science
has also burst its limits. We are taught political behavior by
students of ants and the rules of conception by lawyers in court.
We define human death by a brain-wave machine and the onset
of life by judicial appeal. We now blame each disease in the
textbook on our grandfather's genes but pardon the treason of

microbes. For every cure we effect, a new virus crawls out of the marrow to haunt us. Networks of memory and immunity intersect, and plans for their wiring resemble the Northeast power grid—or vice versa. We have, or have not, mastered superconduction and tabletop fusion, but—as in the recent Benveniste affair of alleged fraud in immunology—we won't know if the data are fudged until the editor of *Nature* sends a magician to check out the notebooks.

We have no good guide to the shift in our cultures among the experts. The prophets of Bloom and Derrida have written a dodgy scenario to follow—great poems are born in misreading, each reader decodes a new text, while a phrase is a sign with ten meanings—and the dons of DNA offer no greater consolation. Having discovered that the gears of our genes mesh quite well in reverse, they have slipped new pieces of genes into cells to control them; these nucleic-acid constructs are called—you might have guessed this from reading Roland Barthes—"antisense" strands of RNA or DNA. Their instructions are read—you'll *not* have guessed this—by blobs of proteins with "zinc fingers" or "leucine zippers." No wonder that "I have absolutely no idea what in the world *that* all meant!" can be heard as often from the scrums of molecular biology as from the covens of deconstructivists. As Orwell wrote in 1947, at the dawn of the atomic age:

> I dreamed I dwelt in marble halls,
> And woke to find it true;
> I wasn't born for an age like this;
> Was Smith? Was Jones? Were you?

Smith and Jones and you and I may do all right in a thousand cultures, but art and science require a single civilization. Its nature was defined by Cyril Connolly in *The Unquiet Grave* (1945):

> *Civilization is an active deposit which is formed by the combustion of the Present with the Past.* Neither in coun-

tries without a Present nor in those without a Past is it to
be discovered . . . and for me it can exist only under those
liberal regimes in which the Present is alive and therefore
capable of combining with the Past. Civilization is maintained by a very few people in a small number of places
and we need only a few bombs and some prisons to blot it
out altogether. [italics mine]

With its whiff of sixth-form chemistry, Connolly's definition may
strike some readers as a smug iteration of Western values: I offer
it as another epigraph for my book. Experimental art and science—
the subjects of these essays—have kinetic and political requirements.
I share Connolly's prejudice that active deposits demand liberal
regimes, and I believe that new art and new science have their
best chance in a republic of skeptics. Neither zealots of clerical
bent nor despots of secular persuasion seem to have learned the
knack of the new. In Connolly's day, Hitler, Mussolini, and Stalin
encouraged a little math and physics, a lot of awkward art, and far
too much wicked biology. In our day, ayatollahs and third-world
strongmen have dropped the math and physics. In the West, new
millennarians are ready to form barefoot battalions: the "New
Age" they await is the Age of Unreason. There are plenty of folk
about who are all too ready with more than "a few bombs and
some prisons to blot it out altogether."

In the course of writing this book, I have noted that the most
stunning confections of new art or science not only challenge the
social order but often express its highest hopes. When young
James Watson and Francis Crick built a mechanical model of
genetic material in 1953, they were realizing the reductionist
dreams of a generation of enzyme chemists and fruitfly geneticists. Ironically, that generation was displaced from the leading
edge of modern biology by one sketch, in perfect perspective,
of the double helix in *Nature.* The architecture of the gene
appeared as inevitable as the New. The dazzling revolution of
molecular biology has been led by a second generation of reduc-

tionists whose laboratories the older generation belittled for "practicing biochemistry without a license" (Erwin Chargaff). The rules were made up as they went along (DNA makes RNA makes protein), revised (RNA makes DNA makes RNA), and modified (RNA makes enzymes; RNA is an enzyme; antibodies are enzymes). Each dogma of the new biology shifted so rapidly that we might conclude that today's working hypothesis of molecular biology was summed up by Niels Bohr: "The opposite of a true statement is a false statement. But the opposite of a profound truth may be another profound truth." Sure enough, as many scientists are engaged in stitching together those strands of antisense DNA as work at the helix in the proper direction. The gods of the genes write as fluently from right to left as from left to right.

I came of scientific age just before the great triumphs of recombinant-DNA technology, and therefore much of the work in my laboratory still proceeds according to the rules of traditional biochemistry and cell biology; my essays are equally traditional and have little truck with the postmodern. I have no problem with that, as we say nowadays. When things are going well, I point to precedents: the masters of abstract expressionism and color-field painting (Robert Motherwell, Willem de Kooning, Helen Franken-thaler) didn't drop their brushes for the masking tape and Ben-Day stencils of pop art in the 1960s. On a perhaps loftier level, while the energetic Florentines of the quattrocento were discovering the power of linear perspective, their colleagues in Siena contin-ued to paint splendid panels of bravura design in the flat manner of the dead Lorenzettis. It's all a matter of perspective.

In our time, perspective has been changed by the new topol-ogy of the gene: Watson and Crick were right in there with the Florentines. Here is the operative passage of the 1953 paper in which they describe the two chains of DNA:

The novel feature of the structure is the manner in which the two chains are held together by the purine and pyrimidine bases. The planes of the bases are perpendicular to the fibre axis. They are joined together in pairs, a single base from one chain being hydrogen bonded to a single base from the other chain so that the two lie side by side. . . . One of the pair must be a purine and the other a pyrimidine for bonding to occur.

The authors close with a sentence that should be familiar to anyone with an education in science: "It has not escaped our notice that the specific pairing we have postulated immediately suggests a possible copying mechanism for the genetic material."

The architectural image of the helix dominated molecular biology for twenty years; it has recently been joined in eminence by the perfect circles of genetic recombination, by the Edmundson helical wheels of protein structure, and the linear palindromes of the genetic message. The genes click out their code letters like so many NASDAQ firms on the ticker. At our meetings these days, we see circles and helices heaving in "supercoils" from computer screens; electronic ribbons of DNA loop in three dimensions. Seeing is believing, in science as in art; it *is* all a matter of perspective.

Perspective in Florence also began with architecture, and Cennino Cennini (ca. 1400) is often credited with the opening statement of its discovery:

And everywhere in your buildings observe the following rule: the molding which you paint at the top of the buildings must slope downwards towards the background. The molding at the middle of the building, halfway up the façade, must be quite even and level. The molding limiting the building at the bottom must appear to rise, contrary to the molding at the top, which slopes downwards.

It did not escape Florentine notice that the specific technique Cennini described could apply to animate objects as well. Once they had gotten the architecture right, the figure would follow. And once flat icons became round flesh, the Renaissance was under way. Masaccio placed a three-dimensional Christ at the apex of a visual pyramid in the fresco *The Tribute Money;* the statuesque apostles form an open circle around their master. Art historians tell us that Masaccio's mural is composed according to a perfect-circle motif, a link between the new geometry and the old medieval iconography of the sphere; Brunelleschi's octagonal cupola for the *Duomo* of Florence also derives from this motif. But to me the plans for the cupola and of Masaccio's composition look like the circular maps of our proteins and our DNA transfection vectors. Both are circles of instruction: " . . . the circular plan and focus perspective, furthermore, stem from a conception of mathematical order in art and in the world. [They are] the signs of a nascent scientific understanding of the world" (M. Meiss, *The Painter's Choice*).

In the blueprints of our new science we depict arcs of manmade genes as segments inserted into the perfect circles of DNA, and I have a hunch that the cunning Florentines of the quattrocento would have known exactly what we were up to with those circular tricks. Molecular biologists have been able to fool the cell as the Florentines fooled the eye. Leon Battista Alberti, writing for his friend Brunelleschi, laid down the canon of the new art in phrases as crisp as the latest article in *Science:*

> And let the painters know that, whenever with their lines they draw contours, and with their colors they fill in the areas thus outlined, they have no other aim but to make the shapes of things seen appear on the surface of the picture not otherwise than if this surface were of transparent glass and the visual pyramid passed through it, the distance, the lighting, and the point of sight being properly fixed.

I would argue that both perspective and molecular biology are aspects of civilization in Connolly's sense: each was the active product of the Present reacting with the Past. The perfect circles of Brunelleschi and Masaccio were drafted by hands trained in the medieval circles of the *Inferno,* while the functional restraints on Watson and Crick's double helix were those of the older phage genetics. And they were both discovered in the course of what were without doubt the most liberal regimes of their time: Florence after the Black Death and the Western democracies after the Holocaust. Neither the rule of Cosimo de' Medici nor the administrations of Clement Attlee or Harry Truman were among the more repressive regimes of their day; perhaps those coincidences of meliorist politics with revolutionary art and science constitute the happiest social arrangements of all. Each was a quickening of the political spirit in the spring of the possible.

From the winter wards of Bellevue Hospital, where I work a good part of the year, the prospects for civilization as Connolly defined it seem bleak indeed. In the emergency room a few weeks ago we attended a sad, thin man gasping for breath with the infective complications of AIDS. He was a young priest with a missal tucked by the pillow of his stretcher. Since the wards were full, he had lain strapped to his rolling cot in the hallways of the holding area for almost eighteen hours. IV in place and oxygen piped into his nose, he had watched the flow of doctors and patients, cops and robbers, through the corridor. He shared a corner of that hallway with two half-draped young black women who were as crowded, sick, and frightened as he; one had been cut viciously about the face while the other had been revived from a drug overdose by means of a morphine antagonist. As I walked in with my group of medical students, we were brushed aside while a platoon of angry young "perpetrators" was hustled along in handcuffs by their guardians from Riker's Island. When the dudes had passed we proceeded to our patient. As I leaned over to listen to the priest's heartbeat with my stethoscope, he gave a pained look: "I guess it doesn't look very good for us from here."

It doesn't look very good for anyone from the emergency

room of Bellevue Hospital. The victories of humankind—the splendors of DNA and the Duomo—seem to have been won for another species on another planet. In this theater of social strife, the victims play the role of deviants: the poor are cast as feral thugs, the homeless as crazy thieves. There are few heroes and fewer heroines, save for the tireless nurses and a game house staff. As in a battalion aid station, often one simply wishes that the war outside would stop.

I have written the essays in this book convinced that, like plague and twentieth-century Fascism, these problems are *soluble* and that the key to their solution is the meliorist path of the liberal imagination. With C. P. Snow, I do not believe that "just because the individual condition is tragic, so must the social condition be. Each of us is solitary: each of us dies alone: all right, that's a fate against which we can't struggle—but there is plenty in our condition which is not fate, and against which we are less than human unless we do struggle."

The form of that struggle is reflected not by two, but by the thousand flowering cultures of our time: I would have no fewer. I have tried to describe the dandier blooms of art and science without promising anyone a rose garden. Discoveries like DNA or the Duomo make up for a lot of the wickedness we deal out to each other, and happily enough there have been other such bright spots. It is to those better moments of our kind—and not the Snows of yesteryear—that this book is addressed.

The Doctor with Two Heads

1

The Doctor with Two Heads

The Seine flows west through Paris past monuments to ineffable glory and reminders of unspeakable deeds. The river arches for about five miles through the center of the city and its banks yield views that define the official text of French history. Parisian children are taught that the towers of Notre-Dame sing the Age of Faith, while the Louvre and the Tuileries proclaim the Age of Kings. The grand dome of the Panthéon is a eulogy for the Age of Reason, and behind the Invalides flutter the flags of Napoleon's lost empire. The Eiffel Tower is an exclamation point of industrial mettle, and nowadays the victories of Foch and de Gaulle are bespoken by the Arc de Triomphe.

Strolling on cobblestones beneath weeping willows, under the arches of an ancient bridge, among fishermen, wandering lovers, and widows walking dogs, one looks up over the traffic-laden quays to see those glorious chunks of architecture against a mackerel sky. In this country of Descartes, spire and obelisk mark the distant ordinates of faith and reason. Especially after a simple five-course lunch and a liter or two of agreeable wine, the prospect of this most beautiful and horizontal of cities is enough to explain why Germans use the expression *"Glücklich wie Gott in Frankreich."* Who would not be happy as God in France? Here, from the silver river's edge, all seems *luxe, calme, et volupté.*

But from time to time the river rises. A false spring in mid-February brings weeks of warm drenching rain; the snows melt early in the east. The water turns an angry brown, and the current becomes so strong that violent froth churns at the foot of bridges. The fishermen, lovers, and widows are displaced to the stone quays which rise a full story above the normal waterside. Benches, railings, and plantings at the water's edge disappear in the flood as the Seine rises by a yard or two. The willows look like soaked spaniels. The tourist boats, the *bateaux-mouches*, can no longer slide under the arches of the Pont Marie and the expressways disappear into brown soup. Uprooted trees and sidings float downstream; errant gulls hitch rides on this flotsam to the western sea. The muddy waters strand houseboats and barges almost in midstream; riverside commerce comes to a halt. One might say that the Seine also rises. We know that there will be no flood here in the heart of the city—there has been none in this century—but can we be entirely sure?

When the river rises, the stroller or jogger is also diverted to the upper quays. Safe from the rushing waters, he finds less congenial running room: the traffic is aggressive, the pavement is fouled by dogs, a hostile concierge hoses down his shins. The dead winter sky hangs low. But the slower pace has its compensations; one has time to notice monuments to the past less imposing than the Eiffel Tower, sermons in stone less sublime than Notre-Dame. This nation of archivists and concierges has kept its ledgers. Stone tablets on quayside façades date the comings and goings of the great, their habitations are labeled as carefully as roses in the didactic Jardin des Plantes. We are informed where on the quai Voltaire lived a troubled Oscar Wilde, and where Baudelaire played with hash. Under a skylight on the quai d'Anjou, Daumier inked his stones while Courbet held court nearby. George Sand entertained Chopin on the first floor of a Left Bank hotel; down the road Borges paid a call. Science is honored as well: the statue of Lamarck (1744–1829), "discoverer of the theory of evolution [*sic!*]" sits brooding over the untidy Seine; farther up an *allée* we find Buffon (1707–88), "father of natural history," who seems to have turned his back to cope with pigeons.

The ambiguous history of Parisians between 1939 and 1945 has not escaped the mason's notice. Tucked into a cryptlike embankment at the rear of mighty Notre-Dame is the Memorial to the Deportation; the sepulcher reads: "To the two hundred thousand

French martyrs who died in the camps of deportation, 1940–1945." When the brown Seine rises, the memorial—but not the cathedral—becomes inaccessible. Notre-Dame faces the imposing Prefecture of Police and its adjacent prison of the Terror, the Conciergerie. Under German occupation the French *flics* by and large did what they were asked by their Nazi counterparts, a sort of professional courtesy among concierges. The *allemands* had help in rounding up 200,000 Frenchmen. The clandestine newspaper *Combat* reported that the German authorities "congratulate the French police, who in collaboration with the German police permitted the arrest of the guilty [*a permis l'arrestation des coupables*]."

Who were the guilty? On the walls of a Jewish welfare hostel, the Fondation Fernard Halphen on the Île St.-Louis, a tablet reads: "In memory of 112 inhabitants of this building, among them 40 children, deported and killed in German concentration camps. 1940." Beneath a similar memento to infanticide in the Marais has been added the admonition: "N'OUBLIEZ PAS!"

The French have also not forgotten their nobler half. Small marble plaques with the *tricolore* mark sites at which French Resistance fighters died in the course of the street fighting that freed Paris in advance of the Allied armies in August 1944. On the wall of the Prefecture—among the first strong points to revert to the Resistance—is fixed a marble and gold tablet:

HERE WAS RECEIVED

ON AUGUST 24 1944

FROM A LIGHT AIRPLANE

OF THE SECOND ARMORED DIVISION

THE MESSAGE OF GENERAL LECLERC

TO THE PARISIAN RESISTANCE

"HOLD ON, WE'RE COMING"

["TENEZ BON NOUS ARRIVONS"]

DROPPED BY CAPTAIN JEAN CALLET

AND LIEUTENANT ÉTIENNE MANTOUX.

KILLED ON THE FIELD OF HONOR

The battle did not really end in 1945. Fratricide came to an end only after Pierre Mendèsz-France and Charles de Gaulle pulled out of Indochina and North Africa: the last scar of self-laceration is etched on the wall of No. 25, quai des Grands Augustins: "Here lived Dr. GEORGE FULLY, member of the Resistance, deported to Dachau, man of Liberty and Justice. Assassinated June 20, 1973."

It may seem a little naive to read these quayside inscriptions as a guide to the cultural geography of two Frances: the republic of Liberty and Justice and the fiefdom of the concierge. But we have learned from the new doyens of French social thought— Foucault, Barthes, Derrida—that one can decipher the signs of a culture from the spaces assigned to words and to words that are never spoken. In this sense the apparently random inscriptions above the surging Seine might be read as a promise that *nothing* will be forgotten. Come hell or high water, Captain Callet, Dr. Fully, and the forty children from the Île St.-Louis are part of the discourse that France conducts between enlightenment and the cops.

Dr. Fully is not the only doctor remembered on the quays. There is a whole museum devoted to them on the quai de la Tournelle, close to the ritzy restaurant La Tour d'Argent. When my wife told me about the Musée de l'Assistance Publique I was pretty skeptical about the enterprise. After all, the Assistance Publique is simply the Parisian version of the Health and Hospitals Corporation of New York City: both administer the public hospitals and clinics of their city. In fact, Bellevue Hospital—where I work—and its sister institutions serve functions based on older French models, the Hôpital Dieu and the Salpêtrière, which care for the sick and the mad. I wondered what could possibly be displayed in this museum of social welfare other than the usual assortment of old microscopes, ancient ambulances, and stuffy portraits of forgotten professors.

With the quays awash, the Musée was on my new running path, and I found the familiar logo of the Assistance Publique on a blue banner that hung from a splendid seventeenth-century mansion, the Hôtel de Miramion. Needless to say, the doors were closed at eight-thirty in the morning. But mounted in an old display box to the right of the entrance was a poster that knocked my eyes out.

Brushed in acid colors, with a touch of bravura that evokes the Montmartre of Toulouse-Lautrec, the painting shows a fellow in top hat and white gown about to buzz the creamy *poitrine* of a helpless woman with an electrical gadget that could have been assembled by a junior at Bronx High School of Science. A fast reading of this sexually charged tableau might yield the message of womankind at the mercy of man and his infernal machines.

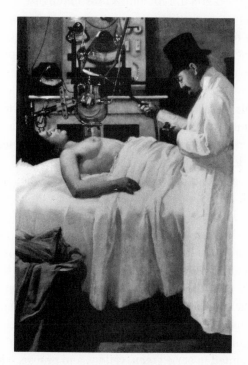

G. CHICOTOT,
The First Trial of X–ray Therapy for Cancer of the Breast.
Musée de l'Assistance Publique, Paris.

Who painted this scene, man or woman? The poster was weather-worn and I could hardly decipher the signature: CHICOTOT. Was the fellow with the top hat a doctor? If he *was* a doctor, why was he top-hatted indoors? What was a stiff devil like that doing to merit a share of quayside immortality with Dr. Fully, man of Liberty and Justice?

It took several visits, some hours in the library, and the help of Nadine Simon, curator of the Musée de l'Assistance Publique, to work it all out. The painting, signed "CHICOTOT, Georges 1907," is a self-portrait in which the doctor-painter shows himself embarked on "the first trial of X-ray therapy for cancer of the breast." It is also a smashing painting, in which the pigments splash unnatural green, red, and yellow highlights over the intricate apparatus: a postimpressionist view of new science. The canvas also fulfills the prediction of a contemporary critic, who wrote in *Le Correspondant médical*, "One sees how precious this document will be in years to come, when a writer of a future generation will trace the history of this novel form of therapy." Well, to this *"écrivain d'une génération future"* the canvas is something more; it is not only an icon of clinical research but also an emblem of the liberal, bourgeois republic of Clemenceau, the republic of doctors.

The picture can be read on several levels, but the scene is unequivocal. Dr. Georges Chicotot, head of radiotherapy at the Hôpital Broca, shows himself treating cancer with X rays. In his left hand he holds a watch to time the exposure; in his right he holds a sort of extended Bunsen burner that spouts flame from its tip. He is heating the vessel that holds the generator, the Crookes tube. The X rays are focused on the patient's breast by a glass cylinder. The ominous electrical apparatus on the mantelpiece is simply a transformer, and the two vacuum valves on either side of the tube regulate the current. The Crookes tube and its enclosing vessel are painted in eerie green, yellow, and orange. The woman, who is either sedated or oblivious, is undressed. Her corset and dress are shown on a stool at the left. She is no *jeune fille;*

a wedding ring is shown on her right ring finger. All of the composition lines of the complex painting lead to her right breast; she is a beautiful woman with a fatal disease. Chicotot does not look at her—his eyes are on the watch—but the tube in his right hand is aflame. He wears a top hat and huge apron, perhaps because—to quote a description of this work from the *Presse médicale* of 1932—"all doctors of the time were recognizable in their laboratory by their top hat [*chapeau haut de forme*] and white apron."

This picture must be the only one in the history of experimental medicine in which the doctor produced not only data but art! Chicotot was what the French call *bicéphale;* he was a doctor with two heads. In the land where the form of a hat follows the function of the wearer, he was entitled to two. An honored graduate of the École des Beaux-Arts, he won several medals for historical paintings which he exhibited at the annual Salons. His paintings were highly finished and based on an extraordinary interest in anatomy, which he had taught as a prosector in the School of Practical Anatomy. In this unique Parisian institution, young painters and doctors alike learned the disposition of muscles, tendons, and fasciae. One métier led Chicotot to the other, and he entered the École du Médicine, from which he earned his medical degree in 1899. He obtained an externship—a rare prize—and soon was launched on a career in the early days of radiology. His work on X rays at the Hôpital Trousseau gained him another medal, this time from the Academy of Medicine. Meanwhile, his paintings at the annual Salons turned more and more to medical themes, provoking *Le Correspondant médical* to claim that his gripping scenes "attracted the attention of the general public, which is fascinated by the subject of our art." They also constitute a pictorial autobiography.

A self-portrait of 1900 shows Chicotot soldering a homemade vacuum tube; he is in shirtsleeves and wears a white apron, but no top hat. In the Musée de l'Assistance Publique is another splendid Chicotot canvas of 1904: it shows a Dr. Josias inserting

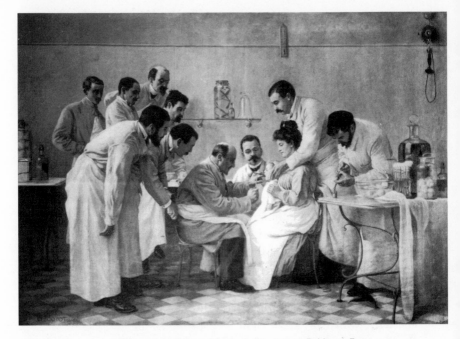

G. CHICOTOT, *Le Tubage.* Musée de l'Assistance Publique, Paris.

an airway into the throat of a small child with diphtheria. The infant is perched on its mother's lap and its head is supported by the professor's assistant. Eight other young doctors, among them Chicotot, watch the delicate maneuver. They are in street clothes, protected by white aprons: not a top hat is in sight. In 1905, Chicotot exhibited an evocative painting entitled *Autopsy: At the Dawn of the Twentieth Century.* Dr. Tollemer, a pathologist, is shown aspirating the thoracic cavity of an infant in order to establish a bacteriologic diagnosis. Chicotot has painted himself in the act of plating out the cultures. A nurse, coiffed and capped, surveys the scene. Both doctors are in white aprons; neither wears a top hat. Indeed, not one of the docs in Chicotot's paintings before 1907 wears a top hat! Nor for that matter do any of those cool, reportorial canvases sport a flash of unnatural color or hint of avant-garde brushwork. Before 1907, Chicotot was the careful observer, the *aspirant* of the Beaux-Arts, the prosector of practical anatomy. With his X-ray picture, dominated by an eerie apparatus brushed in acid colors, he moved into our anxious age of gadgets and Freud.

Top hat and bare breasts suggest the brothel, not the frontiers of medicine. How common are these images? How often did the French, whose talents with respect to the depiction of bare female flesh cannot be said to lag behind other nations, show chaps in top hats and street clothes having traffic with nudes? To answer these questions I conducted a fast field survey in the new Musée d'Orsay, which, a few laps down the quay from the *musée* devoted to the Assistance Publique, has been built in the shell of a spectacular railway station of the Belle Époque. Its fussy renovation has permitted France to empty the basements of the Louvre and to display its nineteenth-century holdings in unquestioned grandeur. I made a checklist at the Orsay of some 286 paintings, dating between 1840 and 1903. While I may have missed some—we're not talking pastels or sculpture—I was able to find 89 canvases that featured bare-breasted ladies; the search was no great hardship. Among all those paintings, those nymphs, muses, and goddesses, only three showed men in contemporary clothing in the presence of nudes.

The first is the well-known *Artist's Studio* of Gustave Courbet (1855), an allegory in which the painter shows himself in his studio surrounded by persons—real or symbolic—important to his career. In the picture, Courbet sits in a chair from which he daubs at a canvas with a long, flickering brush. He is at work on a large landscape and his back is turned on a solid, shapely nude—his muse of truth—who regards his work with adulation. Her *déshabillé* may have been the inspiration for the discarded street clothes of Chicotot's patient. Courbet sports a painter's smock: no top hat here. The rear of the studio is filled with a crowd of his friends from the *vie bohème* and the politics of the time: Baudelaire, Champfleury, Proudhon. It was Proudhon who wrote the crabby

G. COUBET, *Artist's Studio*. Musée d'Orsay, Paris.

pamphlet "The Pornocracy of Women in Modern Times" (1875) and who was persuaded that women had only two functions, that of housekeeper and that of prostitute. Proudhon's attitudes remind me of statistics presented by the cultural historian Theodore Zeldin: that in 1882 there were seven practicing women doctors in France, and in 1903 ninety-five; by way of contrast, there were 15,000 prostitutes registered in Paris alone, and between 1871 and 1903 there were 155,000 on the books; 725,000 others were arrested for practicing without a license, so to speak.

Proudhon rated the intellectual and moral value of women as one-third that of man. This paragon of French socialism formulated the principle that is so well illustrated by Courbet in the painting: "Man is primarily a force for action, woman for fascination." His pronouncements resemble those Mort Sahl parodied a century later: "A woman's place is in the oven."

The next painting to show a nude in the presence of clothed men is Manet's *Déjeuner sur l'herbe* (1863). This picnic scene might seem to be off the track of Courbet and Chicotot, but we can look at it as another example of the artist-and-model genre worked by Courbet and Chicotot. Manet shows us his model in the outdoor studio of the forest of Fontainebleau: also seated on discarded underclothing, she stares at us from the canvas. The two men neither look at nor speak to her. The artist, whose métier we know from the soft, bohemian hat he wears, grips a long cane in his hand.

The third of these paintings is more to the point. The canvas is hard to find in the quirky museum, where it is jammed into a corner of the space devoted to the arts of the Third Republic. The picture can by no means be said to make it to the finals against Courbet or Manet, and it would certainly lose in the quarterfinals to Chicotot. Painted for the Salon in 1887 by Henri Gervex, it is entitled *Avant l'opération* and shows Dr. Péan of the Hôpital

E. MANET, *Déjeuner sur l'herbe*. Musée d'Orsay, Paris.

St.-Louis at an operating table. A well-painted young woman, anesthetized and undraped from the waist up, lies before the doctors, her ginger hair spilling over the coverlets. Péan is demonstrating before five spectators the use of a new hemostat. He holds the pointed instrument over the sleeping woman. Other surgical paraphernalia lie at the head of the table. The surgeon and his assistants are in street clothes. In 1887, to quote the *Presse médicale*, one "wore the same outfit in the operating room, at the bedside, and at the autopsy table!" No top hats here, either, but a nurse is in attendance.

In fact, a second, clothed female is depicted in each of the three paintings at the Orsay. In none is the artist or doctor alone with his unclothed subject: male and female chaperones tell us that a professional interpretation is appropriate. Artist and doctor alike had access to the unclad female body, both having earned that right by long study in the prosectorium where, as in this poem by Professor J. L. Faure,

> C'est que son but est noble, et ces débris immondes
> Et ces lambeaux sanglants sont les pages fécondes
> Où l'on apprend à lire au grand livre du sort
> Et l'on connaît la vie en fouillant dans la mort.
>
> They pursue noble aims amid foul remnants
> and bloody dressings which serve as fertile texts
> from which one learns to read the great book of fate
> and to understand life from a rummage with death.

The iconography of Chicotot becomes a little clearer if we remember his standing as a *bicéphale*. We can assume that he shows himself wearing a top hat as a badge of entitlement, a sign of higher office. The hat, serving as symbolic chaperone, tells us that the doctor's tinkering is sanctioned by learning. Chicotot also wears his topper as a sign of class. Following the lead of aristocratic dandies, the bourgeoisie sprouted the *chapeau haut de forme* on all the playgrounds of the class game. At the Musée d'Orsay, I found scores of paintings in which Frenchmen are shown in toppers at the races, at balls, at assemblies, on the boulevards. If crown and scepter were the symbols of power in the Age of Kings, so top hat and cane became the objects of rank in what Roger Magraw has called the "Bourgeois Century" in France (from 1815 to 1914).

One can see in another painting at the Orsay that the successful artist as well as the successful doctor was entitled to his topper. The canvas, again by Henri Gervex, is entitled *A Session of the Jury of Paintings* and shows Gervex with other established figures of the Beaux-Arts selecting the paintings for the Salon of 1886. These doyens of fine arts are clustered around a large canvas on an easel. Most of the dozen or so of these experts—all in

H. GERVEX, *A Session of the Jury of Paintings*. Musée d'Orsay, Paris.

top hats, worn indoors—have raised their canes in approval; they are giving the official "thumbs-up" sign in the arena of Salon painting. Gervex, the *chef des artistes*, seems to be telling us that when painters have arrived they put behind them the things of childhood. Top-hatted, they raise canes.

Early in the nineteenth century, "anyone who could afford to pay for his own funeral" was considered a bourgeois, but as industry spread and the tribe increased, other descriptions applied. The French sociologist Édmond Golot summarized a major requirement: "A bourgeois had to be able to perform his job in bourgeois costume, so that manual or dirty physical work was unacceptable." Only painters and doctors were permitted to be seen in the alternative costume of smock or white apron.

The historian Jerrold Seigel reminds us in *Bohemian Paris* that when Rodolphe laments over his dead Mimi in Henri Murger's *Scènes de la vie de Bohème*, he cries, *"O ma jeunesse! C'est vous qu'on enterre"* ("O my youth! It is you that I bury.") We might say that Chicotot's canvas is an active lament for his youth as he realizes he is no longer the young *aspirant* but now a *chef du service*. His top hat signals good-bye to his bohemian past. Doctors and painters alike were expected to have passed through a bohemian phase of training, a youthful fling at eccentric dress. Murger, who in 1849 introduced the legend of bohemia to our culture, defined its limits as "bordered on the North by hope, work and gaiety, on the South by necessity and courage, on the West and East by slander and the hospital." Atelier and hospital were the stage sets of bohemian theater.

The yearly hospital balls were as frisky, bawdy, and reckless as those held by the artists. But in their mature years, doctor and artist alike willingly assumed the symbols of bourgeois achievement: top hat and cane. In his X-ray picture, Chicotot shows himself not as a bohemian, but as the mature medical scientist, admitted as by segneurial right to the intimacy of an unchaperoned woman. He does not require a chaperone because his rank and profession (hat and paraphernalia) place him *hors de passion*. He has passed the rites of study and apprenticeship and with Bunsen burner in hand can make the woman better. Perhaps he can bring this Mimi back to life! This rescue fantasy of oncology without mutilation makes an uncomfortable picture, charged as it is with Freudian images and touched by death. One also senses in this farewell to bohemia a painterly homage to a new, freer art, ablaze with the colors of the fauves and the broader highlights of postimpressionism.

Alfred Delvaux explained the need of the mature bourgeois for his alter ego, the younger bohemian: "Because he started out by being you before becoming himself, because he had a heart before he acquired his tummy, because he had debts before he had bonds, because he had long hair before he had a trimmed lawn, because he had a mistress before he had a wife. He is a conclusion to a book of which you [the bohemian] are the preface." This sympathetic view of the dialectic between bourgeois and bohemian might go far to explain why accountants from Teaneck and underwriters from Greenwich rise from their expensive seats in standing applause as Victor Hugo's revolutionaries wave the *tricolore* over the Broadway version of *Les Misérables*.

Many paintings, the *Arnolfini Marriage* by Jan van Eyck for example, are signs of a contract between the persons depicted. We could say that Chicotot's painting constitutes not only a contract between doctor and patient, but also an uneasy compact between the two Chicotots: between the young bohemian and the older bourgeois, between the artist and the scientist. As far as I have been able to establish, this was his last painting of note: it marked the end of his career as a *bicéphale*. The chief of radiology had displaced the painter. It is not a happy painting; the pleasures of Courbet or Manet cannot be found in this work. X-ray therapy is not foolproof as a cancer cure: oncology is not a carefree enterprise. But as Manet's good friend Émile Zola wrote in 1892: "Does science promise happiness? I do not believe so. It promises truth, and it is questionable whether one can ever be happy with the truth."

Some truths *are* happy, however. My father's old textbook from which he learned surgery, published in 1911, points out that by and large most women with breast cancer will die within two years after diagnosis. *CA*, the American Cancer Society journal, of January 1988 gives an overall five-year survival rate of more than 70 percent. Chicotot in his *chapeau haut de forme* and the other scientists of the bourgeois century played no small role in this reversal of fortune.

Zola and the democrats of the Third Republic were major champions of the new scientific medicine. In the year that Chicotot painted his X-ray picture, Georges Clemenceau was premier of France. Clemenceau and his radical republicans had come to power thanks in no small measure to their role in the vindication of Alfred Dreyfus. The Dreyfusards, among them Zola, Drs. Naquet and Colin, and most experimental scientists, grouped themselves around the Ligue des Droits de l'Homme. Their secular, anti-military sentiments were based on the firm conviction that social and scientific progress were linked. Zola, who had used the experimental method outlined by Claude Bernard as his model for "The Experimental Novel," wrote a medical novel entitled *Le Docteur Pascal*. The hero is patterned on many of the clinical investigators whose names we now know by their eponyms: Gilles de la Tourette, Babinski, Charcot. Zola summed up the scientific faith of the era:

> I believe that the future of mankind lies in the progress of reason through science. I believe that the pursuit of truth through science is that divine ideal to which man should aspire. I believe that all is illusion and vanity which is not among the treasures of verifiable truth that must be slowly acquired. I believe that the sum of those truths which are bound to increase continually will eventually give man incalculable power and equanimity, if not happiness.

Clemenceau was a doctor, and had begun his political career as mayor of Montmartre; his convictions were forged in the crowded clinics of the very poor. Unlike the professors of the hospitals, the doctors on the front lines of Paris medicine in the clinics of the Assistance Publique were on the lowest rungs of the top-hat ladder. Zeldin quotes a Dr. V. Macrobius [*sic*] who in 1889

> protested against the ridiculous fee of one franc per annum paid for working in the medical service for the indigent, objecting to doctors being pushed to the very bottom of the social ladder and ironically declaiming: "We do not dispute the first rank to the magistrature, clergy or army. Nor do we wish to place ourselves on the same level as engineers, actors, painters, architects or sculptors. We ask only that we may occupy a middle rank, more or less: we would like, for example, to be classed between the solicitor and the photographer."

In or out of power, the party of Clemenceau had the support of many such doctors: ten of the thirty-four deputies with whom the radical republicans began in 1876 were physicians. Together with other anticlerical, antimilitary liberals they started treating illnesses of the body politic. They successfully mandated universal education, introduced divorce, separated church and state, and extended suffrage beyond the propertied classes. They also fought the battle of Dreyfus against the combined forces of the Church, the army, and an intransigent right.

The bourgeois, ameliorationist reformers of the Third Republic were attacked by populists of the right and of the left. National socialism of the anti-Marxist kind was a French invention, and Proudhon was its prophet. The line extends through Louis-Ferdinand Céline to the *flics* of the occupation. Aristide Bruant, singer, man of politics, and *fin de siècle* rabblerouser, attacked the bourgeoisie from the left, running for office with the promise to fight "all the enemies of capitalistic feudalism and cosmopolitan Jewry." From the right, Drumont complained in his *La Libre Parole* (June 25, 1895) that "besotted by the prostitute, robbed by the Jews, menaced by the workers, the Voltairean and masonic bourgeois begins to perceive that he is in a bad way. . . . And all the corruptions he has sown are rising up like the avenging furies to push him into the deep."

The brown waters of the raging Seine have always been there to overflow the borders of reason. On my desk is a copy of *Le Petit Journal* of February 27, 1898. Its red-white-and-blue cover shows a heroic Major Henry—the Oliver North of the Dreyfus Affair—confronting Lieutenant Colonel Picquart, the archivist whose evidence was to vindicate Dreyfus. Major Henry flings down the gauntlet: "You have lied!" he tells Picquart. The text describes Henry as "brave and loyal, a child of *real people*, a simple soldier; and now despite courage, energy and devotion to country forced to respond to the likes of Lieutenant Colonel Picquart." When the Dreyfus verdict was reversed, Clemenceau and the republic of doctors made Picquart their minister of war.

Dr. Chicotot and his top hat, Dr. Clemenceau and Lieutenant Colonel Picquart remind one that *bourgeois*—noun or adjective—need not be pejorative. Jean Rostand has quipped that scientific research is the only form of poetry that is supported by the state. The poetry of French clinical research was supported by the bourgeois republic and opposed by its enemies on the right and left. Unfortunately, the republic of doctors with two heads, the meliorist brotherhood of the bourgeoisie, was laid low by the epidemic of nationalism that broke out in 1914. Clemenceau was no exception, and Chicotot served voluntarily as a combat officer, although exempt from service for reasons of age and profession. There have been no *bicéphales* of Chicotot's measure in France ever since.

Running toward the statue of Lamarck, nowadays, one trots along the allée Claude Bernard, which is lined by early-blooming forsythia. Crossing the wide boulevard in back of the Jardin des Plantes, one arrives at the great, domed Salpêtrière, a world center of neural science and healing. In the fourth courtyard of this monument to sound reason and fit architecture is the Charcot

T. ROBERT–FLEURY, *Dr. Pinel Unchaining the Mad.*
Bibliothèque Charcot, Collection Hospital, Paris.

Library. At its entrance is a huge, realistic tableau painted by
Tony Robert-Fleury in 1876. It shows Dr. Pinel in revolutionary
hat and cane presiding over the unchaining of the mad. The central figure is a beautiful, partially clad young woman with the
detached look of the very lost. A few other women lie about,
some in Salon poses of the chronically distraught. Wardens are
in the process of breaking the chains: gratitude and justice are
the message of the canvas. The young woman in the center of
the painting is posed in a gesture that reappears at the Musée
d'Orsay, where a slick marble statue by Ernest Barrias (1895)
shows another beautiful young woman lifting her veil to display
her *poitrine.* The statue is entitled *Nature Unveiling Herself
to Science.*

In the course of the bourgeois century men of Liberty and
Justice were in no doubt that when Nature was revealed to Science
she would turn out to be beautiful and just, that when the chains

L. E. BARRIAS, *Nature Unveiling Herself to Science*.
Musée d'Orsay, Paris.

of the concierge were struck, the tablets over the hospitals of the land would read LIBERTÉ, EGALITÉ, FRATERNITÉ.

Emerging from the Salpetrière, one comes to the quays again, where a school bus discharges a score of school children off to frolic in the Jardin des Plantes. Oblivious to the river, which poses no threat, their happy faces bespeak the new Paris of many races; their parents have come from North Africa, from Haiti, from Vietnam and the Ukraine, as well as from the Île-de-France. In fluent French that any Anglophone would envy they chirp the sweet noises of fraternity. They are the end to which the better France has always been devoted. They are heirs to the republic that signs itself—as in the March 1944 issue of the Resistance journal *Combat médical*—"We, doctors of the National Movement against racism and those who have never before been committed to the battle. All victims of the Germans are victims of racism: young Frenchmen threatened by deportation or persecuted Jews will find in us an ally. That is why we join forces with all those of the Resistance to hasten the day of victory when our land will be free."

2

Titanic *and* Leviathan

Why upon your first voyage as a passenger, did you yourself
feel such a mystical vibration, when first told that you and
your ship were now out of sight of land? Why did the old
Persians hold the sea holy? Why did the Greeks give it a
separate deity, and own brother to Jove? Surely this is not
without meaning.

HERMAN MELVILLE, *Moby-Dick*

We had almost forgotten that *Atlantis II* was returning to Woods
Hole that morning when the buzz of helicopters overhead reminded
us. Woods Hole is but one of several villages in the township of
Falmouth, on Cape Cod, and the whole seaside community was
expected to turn out. From the windows of the laboratory we
could see the ship approaching less than a mile offshore. The July
sky was cobalt, the sea a Prussian blue, and the sun sparkled on
whitecaps in Vineyard Sound. It was nine-thirty on the clearest
morning of summer. The research vessel was headed home in
triumph after its second voyage to the wreck of the *Titanic*.
Above, the ship was circled by a corona of helicopters and photo
planes; on the water, a flotilla of powerboats and racing sloops
kept pace.

In shorts and lab coats we rushed down the stairs to cross
Water Street in order to be on the WHOI dock when the *Atlantis
II* pulled in at ten. "WHOI" is the acronym for the Woods Hole
Oceanographic Institution, the youngest of the three scientific

installations that share the harbors of our small village. The others are the Marine Biological Laboratory, or MBL, and the U.S. Bureau of Commercial Fisheries and Aquariums. The three institutions, each eminent in its own right, tend to coexist as separate little universes. Engineering and physical sciences set the tone at WHOI, cell and molecular biology dominate the MBL, and applied ecology is the business of Fisheries. But while the professional—and, alas, the social—spheres of the three enclaves do not overlap greatly, the scientists and technicians of Woods Hole are united by perhaps the most ancient of terrestrial diseases: sea fever. Physics, biology, or ecology can well be studied under the pines of Duke or the ivy of Princeton, but folks at Woods Hole seem drawn to the seaside by the kind of urges that moved the ancients to worship a "separate deity, and own brother to Jove."

Neptune's kingdom has drawn scholars to many harbors: Naples, Villefranche, and Bermuda come to mind as other centers where marine science has flourished. But the New England shore has a special meaning for those engaged in voyages of discovery. From the landfall of the *Mayflower* at Provincetown to the triumph of the New Bedford clippers, the path to new worlds was by way of the sea. Perhaps it is no accident that the most dazzling of our epics is the tale of a Yankee in search of a whale.

> What wonder then, that these Nantucketers, born on a beach, should take to the sea for a livelihood. They first caught crabs and quahogs in the sand; grown bolder, they waded out with nets for mackerel: more experienced, they pushed off in boats and captured cod; and at last, launching a navy of great ships on the sea, explored this watery world; put an incessant belt of navigation round it; peeped in at Behring's Straits; and in all seasons and all oceans declared everlasting war with the mightiest animated mass that has survived the flood; most monstrous and most mountainous! (Melville, *Moby-Dick*)

Melville may have worked in a Manhattan counting house, but the whalers of his mind left from colder seas; Ishmael took the packet for Nantucket through the waters of Woods Hole. So too for a hundred years have marine scholars plied their craft by the shores of the Cape and its islands; the search for Leviathan—as fish, or ship, or secret of the cell—does not seem entirely preposterous there.

Our small lab in the Whitman building of the MBL is only a hundred yards or so from the main dock of WHOI, so we were there in no time at all. A good-natured crowd of visitors, tourists, and locals were milling around the gates. It turned out that passes were required, but with a neighborly gesture the guard waved us by in our MBL T-shirts. The scene on the dock was Frank Capra in a nautical setting: the crowd had clearly assembled to welcome Jimmy Stewart back to his hometown. Reporters of all shapes and sizes jockeyed for post position, television cameras were mounted on scores of tripods, Coast Guard and naval officers strutted their stripes; dockhands in cutoffs and gym shirts lugged hawsers by the pier. Assembled on a kind of grandstand were bigwigs in blazers, officials in seersucker, and the gentry of Falmouth in pink linen slacks. The Marine Biological Laboratory was represented by a packet of students and faculty from courses in physiology, embryology, and neurobiology. (The biologists, if one judged them by details of facial toilette, seemed to have strayed in from a remake of *The Battleship Potemkin*.) There were also teenagers with spiked hair and bubble gum, fresh-scrubbed wives of the ship's crew, outdoor types from WHOI and Fisheries, greasy kids from the boatyard across the street, aproned kitchen staff from the four local restaurants, firemen, and town cops.

> But to omit other things (that I may be brief) after long beating at sea they fell with that land which is called Cape Cod; the which being made and certainly known to be it, they were not a little joyful.
>
> (William Bradford, *Of Plymouth Plantation*)

The ship was now upon us. The size of a minesweeper, its silhouette in the sun displayed great winch posts at the stern. As the vessel berthed broadside, general applause and happy cheers greeted the explorers. Near the top stood the head of the expedition, Robert Ballard. He stood the height of a hero, wearing a baseball hat with the sailboat logo of the Oceanographic Institution. Next to him stood a naval officer in khaki to remind us that the Navy had supported much of this research. A platoon of oceanographers leaned against the railings of a lower deck. They were outnumbered by grinning crew members and a few lab types with round spectacles. The air rang with shouts from ship to shore and back again as friends and relatives hoisted the kind of encouraging signs that one sees at road races. Tots and schoolkids were hauled aboard as the ship made fast. Flash bulbs popped and so did the corks from sudden champagne bottles. Oceanographers soon looked like winning playoff pitchers at Fenway Park. Kisses were exchanged and animals petted. More cheers and applause. The journalists gave way: there would be a press conference a little later. It took a while for the crowd to disperse, but we didn't wait for that since the champagne was still flowing. We crossed the street and reverted to the lab, where we spent the rest of the morning watching the dissociated cells of marine sponges clump together in a test tube.

Within the week, posters appeared all over Falmouth announcing that Robert Ballard would give two lectures at the Lawrence Junior High School auditorium on August 6 for the benefit of Falmouth Youth Hockey. At these talks he would show pictures of the *Titanic* expedition before they were released to the general news media. The pictures would include footage obtained by means of novel television cameras mounted on a little robot, Jason, that had poked down the grand stairwell of the liner. My wife and I bought tickets for the first of the talks to be given at four in the afternoon, and in preparation for this event, we scoured junk shops and bookstores for literature on the *Titanic* disaster. Although it cannot be said that we stumbled across unknown masterpieces of prose, the dozen or so accounts were reasonably accurate jobs of popular history. Written at various times between 1912 and 1985, they told pretty much the same story. Their overall congruity is due no doubt to their reliance on the same primary sources, chief of which were the records of two investigative commissions, American and English.

On April 15, 1912, at 11:40 p.m., while on its maiden voyage from Southampton to New York, the largest and most luxurious ocean liner of its age struck an iceberg at latitude 41°46′ north, longitude 50°14′ west, some 360 miles off the Grand Banks of Newfoundland. By 2:20 a.m. the next morning, the ship had sunk. Only 711 out of 2,201 souls on board escaped the shipwreck. A U.S. Senate subcommittee, headed by William Alden Smith of Michigan, began its hearing on April 19 and shortly thereafter reported its findings as follows:

> No particular person is named as being responsible, though attention is called to the fact that on the day of the disaster three distinct warnings of ice were sent to Captain Smith. . . .
>
> Ice positions, so definitely reported to the *Titanic* just preceding the accident, located ice on both sides of the lane in which she was traveling. No discussion took place among the officers, no conference was called to consider these warnings, no heed was given to them. The speed was not relaxed, the lookout was not increased.
>
> The steamship *Californian*, controlled by the same concern as the *Titanic*, was nearer the sinking steamship than the nineteen miles reported by her captain, and her officers and crew saw the distress signals of the *Titanic* and failed to respond to them in accordance with the dictates of humanity, international usage, and the requirements of law. . . .
>
> The full capacity of the *Titanic*'s life-boats was not utilized, because, while only 705 persons were saved [6 died in lifeboats] the ship's boats could have carried 1,176.

No general alarm was sounded, no whistle blown
and no systematic warning was given to the endangered
passengers, and it was fifteen or twenty minutes before
Captain Smith ordered the *Titanic*'s wireless operator to
send out a distress message.

The commissioners might have noted several other factors that
contributed to the disaster. Whatever number of additional persons might have crowded into lifeboats, these had in any case
room for only about half of those aboard (1,176 of 2,201). In
addition, the two lookouts in the crow's nest had not been given
binoculars with which to spot the iceberg, and once the berg was
unavoidable, an error of navigation compounded the wreck.
Although the design of the ship was such that she probably would
have survived a head-on collision of almost any force, the first
officer swung the liner hard-a-starboard, thereby exposing a broadside target for impact.

Seventy-five years of rehashing details of the *Titanic* disaster
have not added much to this bare outline, although recent opinion has tended to lay a good share of the blame at the feet of the
owners of the White Star Line. Social critics accuse J. Bruce
Ismay and his financier, J. P. Morgan, of sacrificing safety for
speed and prudence for luxury. In contrast, amateur steamship
enthusiasts trace the ocean wreck to many individual flaws of
naval conduct, culminating in negligence by the captain of the
Californian. But if one is neither a special pleader nor a buff of
shipwrecks, the story of the *Titanic* can be read as that of a
unique, unlikely accident that was not part of a general pattern of
nautical malfeasance. Only the sentimental can derive from the
sinking ship an intimation of Western mortality: the wreck had
no immediate predecessors and no similar accident happened
again. Indeed, it is difficult to determine whether reforms insti-
tuted in response to the *Titanic* affair played a role in the remarkable safety record of ocean liners between the wars. Large ships
that were faster and more luxurious than the *Titanic* made hundreds of trips in similar waters; the *Queen Mary*, the *United*

States, the *Île de France*, and their sister ships lived out their useful lives without incident.

Nevertheless, over the years, a more or less constant set of moral lessons has been drawn from the disaster; these cautionary tales split predictably in accord with the plate tectonics of class and party. The first of these is captured in the popular image of handsome men in evening clothes awash on a tilting deck. The band plays "Autumn."

> Said one survivor, speaking of the men who remained on the ship: "There they stood—Major Butt, Colonel Astor waving a farewell to his wife; Mr. Thayer, Mr. Chase, Mr. Clarence Moore, Mr. Widener, all multimillionaires, and hundreds of other men, bravely smiling at us. Never have I seen such chivalry and fortitude." . . .
>
> But these men stood aside—one can see them!—and gave place not merely to the delicate and the refined, but to the scared Czech woman from the steerage, with her baby at her breast; the Croatian with a toddler by her side, coming through the very gate of death, and out of the mouth of Hell to the imagined Eden of America.
>
> (Logan Marshall, *The Sinking of the Titanic and Great Sea Disasters*)

This lesson—the noblesse-oblige theme—includes the story of Mrs. Isidor Straus, who returned from her place in lifeboat No. 8 to her husband, the owner of Macy's. Taking her husband's hand, she told him, "We have been living together many years. Where you go so shall I." And the magnate refused to go before the other men. Harry Elkins Widener, grandson of a Philadelphia mogul, went to his death with a rare copy of Bacon's *Essays* in his pocket; Harvard owes not only its library but its swimming requirement to his memory. Benjamin Guggenheim, the smelting millionaire, went downstairs to change into his best evening dress. "Tell my wife," he told his steward, who survived, "tell her I played the game straight and to the end. No woman shall be left aboard this ship because Ben Guggenheim was a coward."

Then there was Major Butt, aide and confidant of President Taft. Mrs. Henry B. Harris reported:

> When the order came to take to the boats he became as one in supreme command. You would have thought he was at a White House reception, so cool and calm was he. In one of the earlier boats fifty women, it seemed, were about to be lowered, when a man, suddenly panic-stricken, ran to the stern of it. Major Butt shot one arm out, caught him by the neck, and jerked him backward like a pillow. . . . "Sorry," said Major Butt, "but women will be attended to first or I'll break every bone in your body."

Whereas 140 of 144 (97.2 percent) women, and all the children in first class survived, only 57 of 175 (32.6 percent) male first-class passengers made shore. This example of social discipline served as a moral lesson for the gentry, who later went to the trenches in Flanders as if to a test match at Lord's.

The gallant behavior on the part of the moneyed class probably derived from the English code of the gentleman. On the *Titanic*, that code was honored to a remarkable degree. As the commander of the liner was going under with his ship, his last words were: "Be brave, boys. Be British!" One does not abandon the ship. That part of the legend—from out of the past, where forgotten things belong—keeps, indeed, coming back like a song. Twenty-six years after the wreck of the *Titanic*, Ernest Jones arrived in Vienna in the wake of the Anschluss and tried to persuade the aged Sigmund Freud to leave Hitler's Austria. Freud replied that he had to remain in the city where psychoanalysis was born. Leaving Vienna, he explained, would be like a captain leaving a sinking ship. Jones reminded him of the *Titanic*'s second-in-command, Lightoller, who was thrown into the water by a boiler blast. "I didn't leave the ship," he explained of his survival, "the ship left me!" Reassured by the code of the British gentleman, Freud took not only the lesson but also the Orient-Express to Victoria Station and freedom.

More recent students of the *Titanic* story have drawn a quite different set of lessons from the statistics and offer an analysis that one might call the *Upstairs, Downstairs* version of the disaster. Pointing out that the social classes were quartered on the ship as in Edwardian society at large, they find that steerage passengers fared less well than their upstairs shipmates: half as well, in fact! Of men in third class only 75 survived of 462 (16.2 percent); of women, 76 of 165 (46 percent); of children, 27 of 79 (34.2 percent). These statistics—literally the bottom line—yield another irony. Only 14 of 168 male passengers in second class, a mere 8.3 percent, survived. One might conclude that middle-class men adhered more closely to upstairs values than did the entrepreneurial folk on top deck.

Darker streaks of division mar the canvas. Many of the accounts of the time stirred up nativist sentiments, and the worst charges were leveled against dark, swarthy foreigners. Reporters grew indignant that "men whose names and reputations were prominent in two hemispheres were shouldered out of the way by roughly dressed Slavs and Hungarians." Rumors were commonplace—and have since been disproved—that violent battles took place in steerage: "Shouting curses in foreign languages, the immigrant men continued their pushing and tugging to climb into the boats. Shots rang out. One big fellow fell over the railing into the water. . . . One husky Italian told the writer on the pier that the way in which the men were shot was pitiable!"

Another rumor of the time is contradicted by later accounts: "An hour later, when the second wireless man came into the boxlike room to tell his companion what the situation was, he found a negro stoker creeping up behind the operator and saw him raise a knife over his head. . . . The negro intended to kill the operator in order to take his lifebelt from him. The second operator pulled out his revolver and shot the negro dead."

Those often-told dramas of the *Titanic* can be squeezed for the juice of class struggle, but the real fear of the time was not of social unrest. Led by the great populist William Jennings Bryan, the moralists found their true target: the enemy was luxury, luxury and speed. "I venture the assertion that less attention will be paid to comforts and luxuries and . . . that the mania of speed will receive a check," said Bryan.

Speed and comfort are among the declared goals of applied technology; those who worry about those goals—like Bryan—tend to worry about technology. For seventy-five years, those uneasy with machines have used the image of the *Titanic* to decorate the Puritan sampler that "pride goeth before a fall." The proud *Titanic* was 882 feet long—almost three football fields; contemporary illustrations show her as longer than the height of the Woolworth Building. She had a swimming pool, a putting area, squash courts, a Turkish bath, a Parisian café, palm-decorated verandas, a storage compartment for automobiles, and a full darkroom for amateur photo buffs. In the hold were hundreds of cases of luxury consignments, which ranged from thirty-four cases of golf clubs for A. G. Spalding to twenty-five cases of sardines and a bale of fur for Lazard Frères. Larder and beverage rooms stocked 25,000 pounds of poultry and 1,500 champagne glasses. This splendid, "unsinkable" hotel was powered by engines that could generate 55,000 horsepower. Rumor had it that she was not far from her maximum speed of 25–6 knots per hour when she hit the iceberg; other hearsay had it that Captain Smith was going for a transatlantic speed record. The pride of speed was blamed for the fall of the *Titanic*.

Journalists complained that "subways whiz through the tunnels at top speed; automobiles dash through the street at a speed of a mile in two minutes, and ocean liners tear through the water," but it was the clergymen who had their field day on the Sabbath after the disaster. Technological pride took a beating from the Reverend William Danforth of Elmhurst, Queens, who blamed "the age of mania for speed and smashing records. The one on whom one can fasten the blame is every man to whom all else palls unless he rides in the biggest ship and the fastest possible. He will be guilty in his automobile tomorrow." The pulpits of all denominations were united in teaching the Puritan lesson. They were hard on the pride of luxury, as manifest in the squash courts, the putting area, and the swimming pool. Had William Bradford himself been alive, he would have been the first to see the luxury steamer as "a right emblem, it may be, of the uncertain things of the world, that when men have toiled themselves for them, they vanish into smoke." The leader of the Ethical Culture Society, Felix Adler of New York, was alive enough to voice the sentiment, "It is pitiful to think of those golf links and swimming pools on the steamship which is now 2,000 fathoms deep." And Rabbi Joseph Silverman of Temple Emanu-el was of the same mind: "When we violate the fundamental laws of nature we must suffer."

In the decades since 1912, the *Titanic* has ranked high on the list of violators of fundamental law (applied-technology division). Fans of natural law put the story of the steamship right up there with the flights of the *Hindenburg* and of Icarus, the building of the Tower of Babel and the Maginot Line. Not long ago, the space shuttle *Challenger* joined those other violators. In our most recent mythology, *Challenger* and the *Titanic* have become linked in the popular mind. Both craft were the largest and fastest vectors of their kind, both were the darlings of general publicity, both carried the banners of Anglo-Saxon pride; both voyages went haywire for almost mundane reasons. In the hagiography of disaster, the binoculars absent on the crow's nest of the liner and the faulty O rings of the booster rocket have both been offered as examples of how the best of our science is in bondage to chance—or retribution.

On August 6, when we finally went to hear Ballard speak to the townsfolk of Falmouth on his discovery of the *Titanic*, I was sure that memories of the recent *Challenger* disaster were not far from the minds of many. That summer, with NASA grounded, the discovery of the *Titanic* 12,000 feet beneath the sea must have engaged sentiments in an American audience deeper than those of hometown curiosity. It seems unlikely that the community turned out in overflow numbers because of its concern for the traditional themes of *Titanic* literature. One doubts that the seats were packed with citizens who wished to hear replayed the moral lessons of noblesse oblige, the social notes of *Upstairs, Downstairs,* or the canons of technology's pride and fall. No, one might argue that the people of Falmouth went to hear the technical details of how a captain from Cape Cod tracked down the largest, most elusive object beneath the waves: *Titanic,* the Leviathan.

> For the buckling of the main beam, there was a great iron screw the passengers brought out of Holland, which would raise the beam into his place; the which being done, the carpenter and master affirmed that with a post put under it, set firm in the lower deck and otherwise bound, he would make it sufficient.   (Bradford, *Of Plymouth Plantation*)

> The whale line is only two thirds of an inch in thickness. At first sight, you would not think it so strong as it really is. By experiment its one and fifty yarns will each suspend a weight of one hundred and twenty pounds; so that the whole rope will bear a strain nearly equal to three tons. In length, the common sperm whale–line measures something over two hundred fathoms. (Melville, *Moby-Dick*)

> The echo on our sonar indicated that we were approaching bottom, at a little more than 12,000 feet. Larry released one of the heavy weights on the side of the *Alvin,* and our descent slowed. Soon in the spray of lights under the submersible, I could see the ocean floor slowly coming closer, seeming to rise toward us, rather than our sinking to it. Pumping ballast in final adjustments, Larry settled us softly down on the bottom, more than two miles below the surface.   (Robert Ballard, in *Oceanus*)

In the logbook style of his Yankee predecessors, Ballard here describes an early training dive of the deep submersible craft *Alvin*. And in this same, informative fashion, Ballard went on that summer afternoon at the junior high school to detail his two trips to the *Titanic* site. He spoke of the principles of oceanography, of the ground rules of hydrodynamics, and of how optics and sonar had been used to establish the site of the wreckage. He told us something of his decade-long career in manned submersible craft: of continental creep and hot geysers on the Mid-Atlantic Ridge. He told of the dark, sterile sea two miles beneath the surface and of the rare creatures that inhabited those depths. He acknowledged his French collaborators, without whom the wreck could not have been found, and praised the technicians of Sony who fashioned the pressure-resistant TV apparatus of the robot Jason. And then we saw film clips of the second voyage to the wreck of the *Titanic*, taken by Jason and its larger partner, the submersible Argo.

By the blue lights of Argo's cameras, we saw the decks, the winches, the bridge. The stern had become undone and the huge boilers had been scattered across the ocean floor. We saw stalagmites of rust and intact bottles of wine. We went with Jason into the cavern of the great staircase and marveled at the preservation of metalwork, silverware, and leaded glass in that cold sea. We had entered the belly of the whale.

Guided by our Ahab-Ishmael we returned to the surface as the submersibles were retrieved and stowed. Ballard suggested that these pictures tended to discount the hypothesis that the iceberg had torn a great gash in the liner's side and that instead the welds had popped from the impact. The ship's hull had cracked like a nut. But his peroration was not devoted to further anecdotes of how sad it was when the great ship went down. Ballard ended with the message he had brought to the shore for a decade: the ocean and its depths are a frontier as awesome as space itself.

When the lights came on, Ballard answered questions from his fellow townspeople. Yes, he was pleased that Congress had passed a resolution that would make the wreck site a permanent monument to the victims. No, he thought that salvage was impractical; we have better examples of Edwardian artifacts and he doubted that a few chamber pots and wine bottles would be worth the gross expense of raising the ship. Yes, the *Titanic* trip was, in part, an effort to organize support for the programs of deep ocean science.

The applause that followed was long and loud. The happy crowd, from starry-eyed teenagers to oldsters with aluminum walkers, emerged into the sunlit afternoon looking as if each had been given a fine personal present. Many of us from the Woods Hole laboratories shared that sentiment; town and gown of Falmouth had been joined in a victory celebration for science and technology. The reception of *Titanic Rediviva* reminded us that science appeals to people not only for the gadgets it invents but also for the answers it provides to the most important questions we can ask: What happens when we drown? How deep is the ocean? How bad is its bottom? How fierce is the whale?

After his first voyage, Ballard had told the House of Representatives' Merchant Marine and Fisheries Committee that he was neither an archaeologist nor a treasure hunter. "I am," he told the congressmen, "a marine scientist and explorer. I am here to point out that the technological genius most Americans are so proud of has entered the deep sea in full force and placed before us a new reality."

Influenced no doubt by Ballard's publicity on television, in newspapers, and in magazines, not all of the scientists at Woods Hole shared my enthusiasm for the *Titanic* adventure. At a number of gatherings later that summer, one heard the nasty buzzing of such adjectives as "publicity-seeking," "grandstanding" "applied," "not really basic," "developmental," and, perhaps most damning, "anecdotal." It has been no secret to the public at large since *The Double Helix* that scientists are no more charitable to each other than are other professionals; novelists, investment bankers, and hairdressers come immediately to mind. But the detractors of the *Titanic* adventure were not only upset by Ballard

per se. The naysayers also complained that technology rather
than science was becoming imprinted on the collective unconscious of television. Some of those most vexed by Ballard's
sudden prominence had themselves made major findings in the
"new reality" of genetic engineering, neurobiology, and immune
regulation. Were not their achievements also part of the "technological genius most Americans are proud of"? They argued
that their contributions to basic science will affect the world
of the future in ways more fundamental than adventures on the
ocean floor.

But that reasoning strikes me as very self-serving. Historians
of science and technology assure us that it is difficult to decide
whether public practice follows private theory or whether the
opposite is true. It is, they teach us, hard to know where technology
ends and science begins. Moreover, really important discoveries,
whether basic or applied, influence our social arrangements as
they in turn are influenced by them. Such discoveries tend to
attract attention. The Spanish court did not ignore the voyages of
Columbus, nor did Galileo fail to catch the ear of the Vatican.
Einstein's relativity was featured in headlines by *The New York
Times*, and polio was conquered in public. When one of the new
dons of DNA discovers something as spectacular as the wreck of
the *Titanic*, his lectures are likely to fill auditoriums larger than
that of a junior high school on the Cape. When she finds the
vaccine for AIDS or solves the riddle of schizophrenia, purists will
probably carp at the publicity, but I want to be in the audience to
hear her grandstanding.

> And still deeper the meaning of that story of Narcissus,
> who because he could not grasp the tormenting, mild
> image he saw in the fountain, plunged into it and was
> drowned. But that same image, we ourselves see in all
> rivers and oceans. It is the image of the ungraspable
> phantom of life; and this is the key to it all.
>
> (Melville, *Moby-Dick*)

When Ishmael—or Melville—emerged from the sinking *Pequod* to tell the story of Moby-Dick, he told us as much about the science of whales as about the descent into self. Ballard's tale of the *Titanic* is not only the story of deep ocean science but also a tale of memory, of desire, and of that search for the ungraspable phantom of life that some have called Leviathan.

3

Wordsworth at the Barbican

The Barbican Arts and Conference Centre, a glum assembly of concrete high-rises and bunkered flats, overshadows the City of London. Oldest of London's districts, the City for several centuries presented a harmonious skyline in which no structure competed for attention with the splendid dome of St. Paul's Cathedral, designed by Christopher Wren. Pierced only by the occasional steeple of one of Wren's lesser masterpieces or by a Regency cupola, the townscape remained open to the English sky and its infrequent gift of sunshine. Seen at dawn from the distance of Westminster Bridge, the City prompted Wordsworth's claim that

> Earth has not anything to show more fair:
> Dull would be he of soul who could pass by
> A sight so touching in its majesty:
> This City now doth, like a garment, wear
> The beauty of the morning; silent, bare,
> Ships, towers, domes, theatres, and temples lie
> Open unto the fields, and to the sky;
> All bright and glittering in the smokeless air.
> ("Composed upon Westminster Bridge")

That description does not apply today. Although some of the majesty remains, the grime of the Industrial Revolution, the incendiary bombs of the Luftwaffe, and the towering cranes of modern planners have turned great parcels of the City of Wren and Wordsworth into a Houston-on-the-Thames. One might, of course, argue that the modern city isn't all bad news. Whereas Earth may not have had anything to show more fair than the London of 1802, it certainly may be said now to have places to show that are cleaner and healthier: the London of 1990, for one. By my reckoning, even the grim Barbican has at least two desirable features.

First, the planners have encased a rich cluster of cultural treasures within those concrete bunkers. The Arts Centre houses not only the London Symphony Orchestra but also the Royal Shakespeare Company. There are large and small concert halls, theaters, and cinemas, two exhibition salons, art galleries, the Museum of London, a botanical conservatory, and a variety of meeting and practice rooms. This mall of culture is flanked by associated shops, pubs, and restaurants that have been neatly apportioned among the concrete piazzas and dim loggias.

The second feature is probably unplanned. No doubt on the basis of the questionable experiments of Le Corbusier in sunnier climes, modern architectural canon decrees that its megaliths be hoisted on pylons, among which the pedestrian can amble in the shade. The Barbican, no rebel against canon, has pylons aplenty. Removed from cars and commerce by empty plazas and shop-free arcades, the pedestrian can pick his way among the pylons to avoid the rain but not—alas!—the wind of London in autumn. The avid jogger soon appreciates that the dreary acreage of traffic-free Barbican is perhaps the only spot in central London where he can plod for a few miles without becoming soaked or choked.

On a recent Saturday morning, I was taking a run through the Barbican and became lost among all those pillars. Dodging the drafts, I suddenly found myself in a semicircular corridor, carpeted in red and decorated with an excess of brushed chrome. Signs informed me that I was on level six of nine levels of the Barbican, and it struck me how appropriate it was that this place, so like the one described by Dante, was divided into levels or circles rather than old-fashioned floors or stories. The corridor along which I now loped was faced on one side by glass partitions, through which could be seen the administrative offices of the Barbican. They were brilliantly lit and empty, save for one large antechamber, in which a dozen or so overtly miserable people sat waiting before a Cerberus-like secretary.

Curious as to what the action was in this belly of the cultural beast, I stopped to read a small placard on the door: "AUDITIONS THIS SATURDAY 9:30 A.M. IN ROOM B." Through the glass, I could see that the sad young people were musicians—string players in their late teens or early twenties, with damp black cases containing violins, violas, or cellos lying at their feet or across their knees. The women's wet hair was very short, the men's very long, and all fidgeted with it a good deal. Puddles collected at their feet. They did not speak to each other and assumed the expected demeanor of poor relatives about to be read out of a rich uncle's will. It was nine forty-five, and the honcho or hiring committee was clearly not on board. As the group waited, they lapsed into positions that now resembled those of outpatients at an oral-surgery clinic. They leafed glumly through damp newspapers.

Their obvious discomfort, wet locks, and clearly precarious position aroused sympathy. I recalled Anthony Powell's comment: "Reverting to the University at forty, one was reminded of the unremitting squalor of the undergraduate existence." That squalor is a function not only of means but also of ways. The young—ambitious, feisty, and filled with single-minded delight in mastery of their métier—are forced to jump through so many mazes, to wait in so many anterooms. How few, if any, of these young talents here on the block will be making a living at the fiddle or cello a decade from now! How long a road to walk for the sake of art! And the career itself: How dependent on luck, on critics, on changing musical fashion! As I was in this avuncular vein, Wordsworth sprang again to mind:

> I think of thee with many fears
> For what may be thy lot in future years.
>
> ("To H. C.")

But these charitable sentiments were erased by details of the tableau behind the glass. I noticed that the newspapers in which many of the young instrumentalists were engrossed were of the sort that even the BBC calls the "tits-and-bum tabloids": the *Daily Mail*, the *Daily Express*, the dreadful *Star*, and Rupert Murdoch's *Sun*. Difficult as it may be for an American to abandon the notion that we lead the world in trashy journalism, it must be conceded that the Brits have us beat by a country mile. Pages of scandal and acres of milk-fed flesh are served up morning and evening by these pop tabloids to support the proposition that "*The Sun* never sets on the British rear." Hurricanes may have toppled the oaks of London, the stock markets of the world may have dribbled down the drain, missile treaties may have been signed or broken, but daily the tabloids of England display on page 1 the knees of Princess Di and on page 3 the breasts of a working-class model. This mass assault on modesty, taste, and women in general seems to arouse no great protest on the part of young Albion.

The irony at the Barbican was the sight of all those would-be virtuosos of high art—those future Heifetzes, Yo-Yo Mas, Jacqueline Du Prés—digging their noses into *The Star* with its glossy shot of Marvellous Mandy's bare *poitrine*. Mandy is alleged to have "sauce! But then the magnificent 19-year-old model does come from Worcester. And when she's not posing for the cameras, there's nothing Mandy likes more than reading romantic novels and tuning-in to her favorite telly shows." How unlike the view of women from gentle Wordsworth:

> A Being breathing thoughtful breath,
> A Traveller between life and death,
> The reason firm, the temperate will,
> Endurance, foresight, strength, and skill;
> A perfect Woman, nobly planned,
> To warn, to comfort, and command;
> And yet a Spirit still, and bright
> With something of angelic light.
>   ("She Was a Phantom of Delight")

Those glorious vocables might seem more appropriate than *The Star* as morning reading for our young instrumentalists. They were, after all, about to make the most sublime noises of our civilization: Mozart rondos, Vivaldi concerti, the unaccompanied cello suites of Bach. Above their heads hung great posters announcing the masters: Rostropovich conducting Tchaikovsky, Jessye Norman singing Puccini, Itzhak Perlman playing Mozart. Oblivious to musical piety, the young paid more attention to Marvellous Mandy and her sisters of the tabloids. It struck me that only Wolfgang Amadeus Mozart might have shown the same preference.

With him in mind, the scene at the Barbican suggested other themes. Mozart, that foulmouthed angel, was the very model of an eighteenth-century Freemason. Skeptical, irreverent, without a trace of conventional piety, he anticipated not only the court manners of our John McEnroe but also the pop spirit of *The Star*. No guardian angel of Arts Centres he! How different in temperament from the CEO of English Romanticism:

> My heart leaps up when I behold
>   A rainbow in the sky:
> So was it when my life began;
> So is it now I am a man;
> So be it when I shall grow old,
>   Or let me die!
> The Child is father of the Man;
> And I could wish my days to be
> Bound each to each by natural piety.

Wordsworth, Coleridge, and Keats not only waged their Romantic revolution on behalf of "natural piety" but also presided over the expulsion of natural science from the temples of art, beginning with Isaac Newton. The English Enlightenment had been fueled by the science of Newton; the young Romantics seem to have decided that Newton himself must disappear with his Age.

In verses that require no annotation by a psychohistorian, Wordsworth recalls his adolescent self peering from a college pillow to see by moonlight:

> The antechapel where the statue stood
> Of Newton with his prism and silent face.
> (*The Prelude*, Book III)

Once Newton the father was toppled from his Cambridge plinth, a young poet might dare to put the rainbow together again. "*O statua gentilissima, del Gran Commendatore,*" with that prism in the statue's hand! This somewhat Oedipal obsession with Newtonian optics on the part of the Romantics is well described by Marjorie Hope Nicolson in her *Newton Demands the Muse*. At a memorable dinner in 1817, Keats and Wordsworth agreed that Newton was the opposition. He had destroyed all the poetry of the rainbow by reducing it to its primary colors. "Wordsworth was in fine cue," and at the end of the evening, Keats and Wordsworth joined in the toast of Charles Lamb to "Newton's health, and confusion to mathematics!" Wordsworth's verse enlarged on the theme:

> Whatever be the cause, 'tis sure that they who pry and pore
> Seem to meet with little gain, seem less happy than before:
> One after One they take their turn, nor have I one espied
> That doth not slackly go away, as if dissatisfied.
> ("Star-Gazers")

Since natural science, the realm of those who "pry and pore," can yield no satisfaction and since it reduces Nature to mathematics, why not dispense with its study once and for all?

It could be argued that in England art and science parted company somewhere between 1805 and 1820, with the Two Cultures going their separate ways ever since. It cannot be coincidental that Wordsworth and company discovered Nature, or at least the rustic landscape of England, at that moment when the Industrial Revolution was about to change that landscape forever. I have a hunch that the poet's fear of Newton followed the peasant's fear of steam. It was not a prescient vision of future Barbicans but news of a railroad through his home turf at Windermere that provoked Wordsworth to cry: "Is there no nook of English ground secure from rash assault?"

Mad William Blake joined the anti-Newtonians. He was sure that the "Epicurean" philosophies of Bacon, Locke, and Newton were responsible for the dark satanic mills that were defacing England's green and pleasant land. With his characteristic precision of thought he managed to conflate all the enemies of the Romantic movement. A few samples offered by Nicolson suffice:

Item: "The End of Epicurean or Newtonian Philosophy . . . is Atheism."

Item: "God forbid that Truth should be confined to Mathematical Demonstration."

Item: "Nature says 'Miracle,' Newton says 'Doubt.'"

Item: "The House of the Intellect is leaping from the cliffs of Memory and Reasoning; it is a barren Rock; it is also called the barren Waste of Locke and Newton."

Item: "Art is the Tree of Life, Science is the Tree of Death."

Now these unkind aphorisms may be attributed to Blake's imperfect grasp of science, but I'm afraid that the prattle continues today. Cynthia Ozick, also a great fan of the Old Testament, has told readers of *The New York Times Book Review* that art deals with the world of men, science the world of God. O Newton! Thou shouldst be living at this hour.

When I emerged from the swank bowels of the Arts Centre, the rain had stopped. Since the western terraces of the Barbican are only a hundred or so yards from the medical school I was visiting, I headed toward Charterhouse Square. St. Bartholomew's Hospital Medical College is situated at its northern side and has together with the square maintained many of the older graces of the London townscape. Brick and limestone, arch and cupola, lawns and trees are disposed in easy lines; the visual grammar is traditional. In consequence, after crossing Aldersgate Street, the busy traffic artery that separates the Barbican from this oasis of amenity, I found myself on cobblestone beneath the falling leaves. It struck me as ironic that modern science, which is thriving, was housed in conventional structures, while classical music, which is not, is played mostly in temples of confused modern design.

On the steps of the residential hall sat a group of medical students. In age, dress, and demeanor they were indistinguishable from the string players across the road. Some were waiting for the results of an exam to be posted on the bulletin board in the pharmacology building. They cannot have been reassured by the warning that accompanied an earlier posting of grades on that board: "Those with Grade D are going to have to improve their performance if they are not going to sink." The dozen or so students sat under wet leaves, hard rock came from a car radio, and several were preoccupied with Marvellous Mandy in *The Star*. A second tableau!

On this Saturday morning in London, on either side of Aldersgate Street, sat the young of the Two Cultures waiting to have their performances judged. Poised between the safety of school and the hazards of a career, they seemed to be united only by the glitter of pop and the cramps of adolescence. Wordsworth might be called the first poet of modern adolescence; indeed, I've always considered the Romantics to be the laureates of freshman passion, the troubadours of testosterone. No one has gotten adolescent angst better than Wordsworth at Cambridge:

> Examinations, when the man was weighed
> As in a balance! of excessive hopes,
> Tremblings withal and commendable fears,
> Small jealousies, and triumphs good or bad . . .
> Wishing to hope without a hope, some fears
> About my future worldly maintenance,
> And, more than all, a strangeness in the mind.
> (*The Prelude*, Book III)

Wordsworth's turmoil at Trinity, his fear for his worldly maintenance, remind one that whatever else the Romantic rebellion
accomplished, it was coincident with the gradual ascent of the
middle classes. Only an aristocracy can afford a cult of the amateur;
those who would busy themselves looking about for worldly
maintenance, who would wish to rise from mine and mill and
field, had better be very good at doing one thing. The middle
class was asked to choose art or science, and the Romantics knew
which side was theirs. By the 1840s the furrow between art and
science had deepened: Wordsworth, Keats, Coleridge, Blake, and
Lamb had succeeded in erasing the language of science from the
blackboards of culture. And on the other side of the gap, the Royal
Society began stripping its rolls of literati and amateurs. From
1847, the pattern was set that guaranteed that for over a century
no British youth has been taught *both* art and science at the
university level.

It may be a bit facile to trace the divorce in England between
the Two Cultures to the Romantic revolution. But the unity of all
cultural effort had been the unwritten rule of the Western world
from Aristotle to Maimonides, from Avicenna to Spinoza, from
the Florentine Accademia to the *philosophes*. And at the tables of
the English Enlightenment, Wren supped with Boyle; Hooke
drank with Hobbes. Nicolson's monograph has resurrected a
whole school of poetry, the "scientific" poets of the eighteenth
century, who spelled out the facts of science in the cadence of
enlightened rhyme. The poet James Thomson saw the rainbow
through the eyes of Newton:

> In fair proportion running from the red
> To where the violet fades into the sky
> Here, awful Newton, the dissolving clouds
> Form, fronting on the sun, thy showery prism,
> And to the sage-instructed eye unfold
> The various twine of light, by thee disclosed
> From the white mingled blaze.
>
> ("Spring")

The symbol of the prism posed no threat to the poets of the eighteenth century; it represented instead Enlightenment in all its radiant aspects. But Wordsworth saw the rainbow much as the ancients did and used that sign in the sky as a text for a sermon on natural piety.

I must admit that the cleavage of English science from its art in the nineteenth century has not served to diminish the vigor of either. We might in fact propose that without that sort of differentiation, we would still be back in the world of the eighteenth century. I'm clearly of two minds on this point. I wish there *were* areas of experience—other than pop culture or generational turmoil—on which the two groups of students I had seen that morning could agree. At the Barbican, in that tiresome failure of design, the theater directors were devoting their great skills to producing a cycle of Jean Genet's dramas. On the third floor of the pharmacology building at ancient Bart's, a sparkling team of scientists, led by Nobel laureate Sir John Vane, was solving the rebus of how sticky blood platelets cause heart attacks.

It is unlikely that modern drama would have differentiated to its absurdist phase, or that we could be influencing heart attacks by antiplatelet drugs, had we not first separated one art from another and one science from the next until no biologist has any idea as to what the astronomers are talking about. We have paid a heavy price for that differentiation. We have made junkyards of our cities, clowns of our rulers, gibberish of our journals, and boors of our chemists. We have made it almost impossible to hold general conversations on topics too complex for Marvellous Mandy and have reduced poetry to a hobby for professors. It is sometimes difficult to be sure what we have gained in the process— other than dramas of Genet and the discovery of how blood clots. I *am* sure that among the advantages we have gained has been a life span long enough for most of us to go expertly about any business we wish, including that of art or science. We have become not one culture, not two, but a thousand. We have become as differentiated as the tissues of our body and for the same purpose: perfection of the life *and* of the work.

Deep under the great trees of Charterhouse Square is the mass grave of 50,000 Londoners who died of the Black Death. High above the ancient grave, across Aldersgate Street, rise the towers of Barbican, where a healthy people of the thousand cultures breathe clean air and Stravinsky pulses among the pylons.

> I was the Dreamer, they the Dream: I roamed
> Delighted through the motley spectacle:
> Gowns grave, or gaudy, doctors, students, streets,
> Courts, cloisters, flocks of churches, gateways, towers.
> (*The Prelude*, Book III)

We owe to Wordsworth many towers, many walls.

4

The Treasure of Dongo

Italy has been favored with scenes of great natural beauty, to which Italians have added habitations no less pleasing to the eye than the land itself. The vernacular of their building style plays stucco and tile against rock, water, and evergreen; the most stunning arrangements of villas or villages are on rocky shores seen from on high through cypress and pine. Of all those agreeable prospects and views of shoreline bliss, the most harmonious are the ones of Lake Como from the high promontory on which the Villa Serbelloni sits.

The lake points north to the Alps in the form of an inverted Y, and the pastel villa presides over the trifurcation. Perched above the town of Bellagio, a cobbled jewel on the lakeside, the villa is wrapped in neat terraces that display a full repertoire of topiary art. A stone faun plays his flute from a mossy plinth, zinnias are splayed between trim boxwood, cotoneaster drips from the borders. By mid-autumn, the first snows of the season have frosted the great mountains that cradle the lake; at sunset the Alps in the distance blaze pink. In the park of the villa, the verticals of cypress and pine are softened by the rust and yellow of beeches; paths to the summit outlook are awash in golden leaves. Persimmons linger on the branch. The climate is so mild in this Arcadia that palm and cactus flourish next to holly and hemlock. Roses bloom in December.

From the ruins of an old tower above the villa, one can see the views that have moved visitors over the centuries and made Bellagio a way station of the Grand Tour. On the eastern shore,

Varenna shines in ocher and coral under its graceful campanile; on the west, Menaggio and Tremezzo trail their peach quays along the water. The lake trembles under a soft wind from the south, birds cry and bells toll random peals from towers in the valley. So peaceful, so unhurried a land is this that the cocks crow at noon. The scene calls to mind the description by S. N. Behrman of Max Beerbohm on the terrace of his villa overlooking a similar spectacle of Italian delight as "one who cherishes too much this evanescence, this miracle of sight and sound, to replace it with the vulgar self-assertion of work."

The work of the Villa Serbelloni is that of art and scholarship. The Rockefeller Foundation has turned the sixteenth-century villa and its formidable site into a study and conference center. Each month, a dozen or so scholars and their spouses take up a far from Spartan residence to write, paint, compose, or compile. This cadre is joined from time to time by platoons of conferees who arrive for two or three days of meetings on subjects as diverse as the future of weather, the politics of steel, or the teaching of American literature abroad. The scholar is offered gracious meals and warm hospitality, public rooms with fine tapestries, and a well-stocked library with Italian primitives glowing from the walls. On an easel in the breakfast room is a small, nearly perfect Cranach.

One is also given a studio with a desk, a chair, and a typewriter, and one rapidly begins to sympathize with the response of Red Smith to the question of whether he found it difficult to turn out his neatly phrased sports columns for the old *Herald Tribune:* "Not at all. I simply put a blank sheet of paper in my typewriter, turn the knob, and sit there until drops of blood appear on the page."

One month is a very long time indeed to sit at a typewriter without interrupting the vulgar self-assertion of work. It is not nearly long enough to explore all the byways of Bellagio and its lake in the course of procrastination. It was on such a morning ramble of delay that I stumbled across Comandante Adriano Pini and Leutnant Otto Haurowitz. They lie buried no more than a few yards apart in the cemetery of Bellagio. The burial ground is approached from the villa by way of the tiny fishing village of Pescallo, the central square of which has been cleverly disguised as the stage set of *The Pearl Fishers*. One walks past escarpments cluttered by beached dinghies, passes under trellised archways, climbs past a lakeside orchard to come to the iron gates of the cemetery.

Surrounded by snug walls, the cemetery—roughly the size of a tennis court—resembles nothing so much as an outdoor flower market. Tended daily, each grave is almost obliterated by crowds of chrysanthemums in white and rust, lavender and yellow. No browning petal disturbs the illusion of floral immortality. The well-carved marble headstones display not only the names of the dead but also their photographs, which look out at the visitor from weatherproof ovals. The final impression is that of an eternal family festival: all those Belgrados, Pollices, Venninis, and Scacchias preside cheerfully over the flowers of the season with Alps and olive groves as a backdrop.

Judging from the inscriptions, most Bellagians seem to have lived out full lives; here and there the photo of a youngster peeps out, elsewhere that of an occasional citizen dead by accident in the prime of his years. The grave of Comandante Pini is not graced by any such photograph. His stone identifies him simply as a *sommergibilista* (submariner) who was born in Bellagio in 1906 and who fell (*"caduto"*) at Pola in 1944. But where is, or was, Pola? My *Webster's* directs me to "Pula *or* Pulj *or* It. Pola, city & port NW Yugoslavia at tip of Istrian peninsula *pop* 45,000."

The histories of Pola and Comandante Pini are not unrelated. The seaport on the Adriatic and its larger sister port, Fiume, were until 1914 part of the Austro-Hungarian Empire. Italy joined the Allies against the Central Powers in 1915 thanks in no small part to the polemics of two nationalist writers, Gabriele D'Annunzio and Benito Mussolini, who demanded a full share for Italy of the weakening Hapsburg Empire. The peace settlement of 1919 did not yield enough of Istria to suit the Italians, and for the next few years Austria, Italy, and Yugoslavia squabbled over the area. D'Annunzio led an unauthorized expedition that managed to seize Fiume in 1919–20; the episode prefigured other rightwing shenanigans and—in the alliteration of historian Charles F. Dezell —"further fanned the flames of frustration and facilitated the growth of Fascism."

By 1944, Pola had been Italian for more than twenty years and served as a base for the Nazi armed forces. In the interior of the Istrian peninsula, control over the hills and passes was disputed by not only Italians, Germans, and Allied agents but also Yugoslav partisans of several rival bands. Italy itself was engaged in a kind of fratricidal war. In 1943, pressed by the American and English armies, Italy had signed her separate peace to become their "cobelligerent" in the war against Hitler. The Germans poured massive reserves into Italy and installed Mussolini as head of a new "Republican Fascist" regime in the north of Italy. The diplomatic corps accredited to the puppet regime (among them flunkies from Hungary, Japan, and Thailand) were quartered in Bellagio and entertained at the expropriated Villa Serbelloni. Most of the Italian navy, which for reasons of history and class had been the most anti-Fascist of services, had promptly steamed away to Malta to join the Allied fleet. Some, however, remained willing or unwilling adherents to the Fascist cause.

Looking at Pini's grave under a hazy November sun, I wondered whether he had died on "our" side or "theirs." I wondered what uniform he had worn, under what flag he had died. Was his death in the service of or in dissent from the Duce's 1932 "Doctrine of Fascism"?

> And above all, Fascism, the more it considers and observes
> the future and the development of humanity . . . believes
> in neither the possibility nor the utility of perpetual peace.
> It thus repudiates the doctrine of pacifism [which is] an
> act of cowardice in the face of sacrifice. War alone brings

up to its highest tension all human energy and puts the
stamp of nobility upon the people who have the courage
to meet it. Thus, a doctrine that is founded upon this
harmful postulate of peace is hostile to Fascism. This
antipacifist spirit is carried by Fascism even into the life
of the individual: the proud motto of the *squadrista*
[Blackshirt], *"Me ne frego!"* ["I don't give a damn!"],
written on the bandage of the wound, is an act of philosophy not only stoic [but] a new way of life for Italy.

Thoughts of Pini's uniform recalled to me the spring of 1938,
when as a small child I watched with alternating awe and fear the
daily parades of Mussolini's forces in the streets of Naples, to
which my parents had fled from Nazi Vienna. Through the partially shuttered windows of a fourth-floor *pensione*, one could see
rows of tall, graceful naval cadets in white standing out against the
darker, Alpine *bersaglieri* with their wildly plumed helmets. Everyone sported impeccably tailored uniforms: the *carabinieri* with
polished buckles, belts, and boots; the *squadristi*, black-shirted,
in jodhpurs and tasseled hats; the Guardia di Finanza with bright
stripes on cap and trousers. In retrospect, it seems that the whole
country had gone crazy over male military plumage, a kind of
dementia peacock.

It wasn't funny at the time. Ethiopia had fallen to the Duce,
Hitler was making noise about expanding to the east, and the
Western democracies were in disarray. Only the Spanish Republican armies were in the field against the Fascists, and by 1938 the
Republic had been split in two by Franco and his Italian supporters.
The Italian navy maintained a tight blockade of Spanish Republican ports. Comandante Pini was thirty-two; was it Valencia he
saw through the periscope? In Rome, D'Annunzio was declared
an "immortal" and Mussolini's scientists were aping the argot of
Hitler's Social Darwinism. On July 14, 1938, a curious "Manifesto
of Racist Scientists" was published in Rome in *Il Giornale d'Italia*
and other Italian newspapers:

> The concept of Racism in Italy must be essentially Italian,
> and its thrust is Aryan and Nordic. .... This means elevat-
> ing the Italians to an ideal plane so that they will have
> greater self-consciousness and responsibility. The Jews
> do not belong to the Italian race ... and that is because
> they are made up of non-European racial elements, entirely
> different from the elements that gave rise to the Italians. ...
> The purely European character of the Italians will become
> altered if crossed with any non-European race whatso-
> ever that serves as a transmitter of any civilization differing
> from the Aryan's millennary civilization.

Mussolini, in Trieste, commented on the reasons for this empha-
sis on Aryan brotherhood: "History teaches that empires are won
by arms but held by prestige. And prestige demands a clear-cut
racial consciousness which is based not only on difference but on
the most definite superiority." The cemetery at Bellagio does not
confirm the hypothesis of the Duce and his Racist Scientists. The
kind, avuncular faces that look out at one are neither "Aryan" nor
"Nordic"; they show the features of an older Italy, of a people
who responded to the drivel of Social Darwinism in a far more
humane fashion than did their neighbors to the north.

A smaller plot of land next to the main cemetery contains
the graves of those who were not Roman Catholics. Unlike the
native Bellagians, the population of this group is divided mainly
between those who died young of accident or disease and those
who had lived out their retirement years in nearby villas. Most
are English from the home counties, with a smattering of Dutch,
French, and Germans. A Russian count and a Hungarian youth
lie at opposite corners. Perhaps the most poignant description is
that of summer's end by the lakeside:

IN LOVING MEMORY

OF

SIDNEY HERBERT BRUNNER

OF WINNINGTON, CHESHIRE

AGED 23

WHO LOST HIS LIFE

IN SAVING HIS ELDER BROTHER

FROM DANGER OF DROWNING

ON THE EIGHTH DAY OF SEPTEMBER 1898

HIS BODY WAS RECOVERED

FROM THE LAKE ON THE TENTH

AND LAID HERE

ON THE FOLLOWING DAY

"THE WHITE FLOWER OF A BLAMELESS LIFE"

The flowers are not white on the foreigners' graves. A few per-
functory sprigs of holly or myrtle, or a faded rose lies about; a
browning chrysanthemum has been placed on the grave of Leutnant
Otto Haurowitz. Haurowitz, an artillery lieutenant (reserve) in
the Austrian army, was born in Prague in 1897 and died at
Bellagio on December 2, 1918, as a prisoner of war. The stone
was obviously placed there by his parents ("Here lies our beloved
son") who assure us that "he remains in the thoughts of all who
loved him."

I wondered about that date, December 2, 1918. The armi-
stice on the Western Front was observed on November 11, and
the battle front between Italy and Austria had pretty much evapo-
rated after the Italians and English had broken through at Vittorio
Veneto in October. Was Haurowitz sick? Did he die of wounds?
Was he being shipped home? The odds were low, I reckoned, that
he would have lived out a full life in his native city in the fashion
of the lucky Bellagians. Most likely he and his parents would have
perished at the concentration camp of Theresienstadt, where war
veterans named Haurowitz generally wound up.

I dropped a fresh flower on his stone and walked past
Comandante Pini back to Pescallo. It seemed to me that the two
warriors shared the misfortune of cultures whose poets require
bellicose heroes and whose scholars bend science to please their
regime. Without the Duce and his friend D'Annunzio that sad,

comic-opera war on the Italian front would never have erupted in 1915–18. And twenty years later, without the Rome-Berlin axis, Pola would not have become a site of contention. And if . . . and if my grandfather had wheels, as they say, he would have been a trolley car.

In the middle of these ruminations I looked at the harbor of Pescallo, where a small excursion boat now lay at anchor. She was painted white and sparkled in the morning mist; an Italian ensign trailed from her mast and the name *D'Annunzio* was painted on her stern. That poet's most famous work was written "In Praise of Sky, Earth, and Heroes"; he found his hero in Mussolini and his glory in Fiume. He was the laureate of *Me ne frego*.

An image floated into my mind, somewhat gentler than those of the warrior poet. I imagined that I saw the boat filled with tourists and young lovers in holiday clothing, as with flags flying the bark lifts anchor for Varenna on the opposite shore. The dashing Comandante Pini of Bellagio is at the helm and the seats are jammed with Belgrados, Pollices, and Scacchias off for a family picnic. Next to a Russian count is Sidney Herbert Brunner, age twenty-three, and next to the Hungarian at the stern is artillery lieutenant Otto Haurowitz. I imagine him off to Varenna as Frances Cornford saw Rupert Brooke off to the war in 1914:

> A young Apollo, golden-haired,
> Stands dreaming on the verge of strife,
> Magnificently unprepared
> For the long littleness of life.

The Cornford-Brooke connection with this image from Como is not entirely circuitous. Frances Cornford, granddaughter of Charles Darwin, became a great friend of Rupert Brooke at Cambridge, where they were fellow poets. After her marriage to the classicist Francis Cornford, their comfortable house off Madingley Road,

Conduit Head, became a center of donnish social life. On a wall of the playroom in Conduit Head is painted a mural that depicts no less than the apotheosis of Rupert Brooke, who died on an island in the Aegean en route to his war. The Cornfords' older son was named Rupert John, after the young poet whose meters suffused the mother's verse and whose presence charged the air at Conduit Head. It might be said that John Cornford had two hard acts to follow: father and demon. He lived his brief life as if in obedience to the classic Greek myths of family fate which preempted his father's attention. He became a skilled poet while still at school, acted out the turbulent script of adolescent revolt, threw in with the Communist Party, and went to Spain for a look-see in 1936. Perhaps for him, as for Orwell a few months later, "it seemed the only conceivable thing to do." He joined the International Brigades and was killed in the course of an ill-fated infantry attack on the Córdoba front the day after his twenty-first birthday. Frances Cornford's son was never to know the long littleness of life:

> Should spring bring remembrance, a raw wound smarting?
> Say rather for us fine weather for hurting,
> For there's no parting curse we fear.
> Here we break for good with the old way of living,
> For we're leaving only what wasn't worth having,
> And face turned forward, for there's no life here.
>
> (John Cornford, 1934, published posthumously)

The deaths of John Cornford and his fellow anti-Fascists who fell by the thousands in Spain were avenged by a veteran of the International Brigades on the persons of Benito Mussolini and his mistress, Clara Petacci. The last act of the Fascist tragicomedy was played out on April 28, 1945, by the western shore of Lake Como; the captain of the *D'Annunzio* will take you there today for a fee.

Geography, first. The city of Como, capital of the district, is at the southernmost end of the lake. North from the city winds a crooked road, a corniche, that provides access to either Switzerland or the Bavarian Alps. At the midpoint of the western shore, Menaggio, the road branches, leading west over the hills into Swiss Lugano or continuing north to Dongo before climbing to the Alps. The roughest stretch is between Menaggio and Dongo, where the road has been carved into the rock shoreline; signposts warn of sharp S turns, slippery grades, and fallen rocks. It was on this stretch of road that a detachment of partisans of the 52nd Garibaldi Brigade caught Benito Mussolini as he was fleeing Italy disguised as a drunken German noncom.

The story of the Duce's last days reads like a script in which Charlie Chaplin's *The Great Dictator* has been crossed with Ettore Scola's *La Nuit de Varenne*. It is difficult nowadays to believe that Mussolini, the aging dumpling, was as formidable a force in the Europe of the 1930s as was Hitler. But there is little doubt that the majority of Germans and Italians believed that:

> If every age has its characteristic doctrine, there are a thousand signs which point to Fascism as the characteristic doctrine of our time. . . . Fascism is opposed to all individualistic abstractions based on eighteenth-century materialism; and it is opposed to all Jacobinistic utopias and innovations. It does not believe in the possibility of "happiness" on earth as conceived by the economistic literature of the eighteenth century.
>
> (Mussolini, "Doctrine of Fascism")

By April 25, 1945, the test of arms had swung decisively in favor of nations that subscribed to the eighteenth-century notion of happiness on earth. After crossing the Po River, the Allied armies were in full advance over the north of Italy. The larger Italian cities had been freed of the Nazis thanks in no small measure to the active Italian resistance, which since 1943 had grown into a powerful coalition. The partisan brigades, coordinated by the Committee of National Liberation for Northern Italy, formed the de facto government of the newly liberated towns and demanded unconditional surrender of the Italian Fascists.

The hard core of Mussolini's men, the Black Brigades and the hierarchs of his fallen regime, fled north, first loading their vans with sufficient loot to pursue happiness if not on earth, then at least in Switzerland. Mussolini himself assembled a motley motorcade in which to flee Milan for Como. Escorted by his SS "protectors," he led the convoy in an open Alfa-Romeo. Behind him in another vehicle was his mistress, Clara Petacci, accompanied by her brother Marcello, a thieving lout even by standards of the puppet regime. In turn, Marcello was traveling with *his* mistress and their children. The caravanserai was completed by cars bearing a gaggle of ministers, high army and police officials, the Mussolinis' personal maid, and a considerable treasure of goods and documents. Accounts vary, but most agree that the treasure contained Clara Petacci's jewelry, the Duce's personal cash, diaries and correspondence, three sacks of gold medals and wedding rings given by Italians to finance the invasion of Ethiopia, and $90 million in gold bullion, which—to paraphrase Groucho Marx—was a lot of money in those days.

The party arrived in Como, which was filled to overflowing with members of the Black Brigades, German troops, and Fascist functionaries. Mussolini's wife, Rachele, and her daughter Anna, who had been stashed away at a villa above Como, made an unsuccessful try at crossing into Switzerland. Meanwhile, at the prefecture of Como, the Fascists debated whether to establish a defense line at the foot of the lake or to move to the foothills of the Alps, there to make a last stand with their German colleagues in the name of "Project Honor." It was eventually decided that Como could not hold. Therefore, early on the morning of April 26, Mussolini and his convoy moved to Menaggio, sans wife and sans mistress; the Petacci clan had also made a dash for the border. The bullion and cash brought up the rear.

One wonders whether the documents the Duce carried with him in his treasure van included the transcript of the speech he gave at the Royal Opera House in Rome on March 18, 1934: "But there is one danger that can threaten the regime, and this may be represented by what is commonly called the 'bourgeois' spirit— that is to say, a spirit of satisfaction and adjustment, a tendency toward skepticism, compromise, an easy life and advancement. . . . The creed of the Fascist is heroism, that of the bourgeois is egoism."

Twenty years of heroics were winding down in Italy: the Black Brigades at Como, the last organized forces loyal to the Fascist state, surrendered to the Committee of National Liberation on the same day, April 26. At Menaggio, the Duce had three hours of sleep before being woken with news that the Petacci clan had turned back without crossing the Swiss frontier. Briskly, Mussolini packed the caravan together, outpaced the SS, and drove his column left from Menaggio to a small resort hotel on the road to Lugano. It was the sort of hotel where, before the war, a trio would play the music of Porter, Coward, and Gershwin at meals and teatime. The entourage dismounted, thronged the lobby of the hotel, and debated the options. In the tumult, Mussolini and Clara made one last attempt to sneak away, only to be stopped at the rear entrance of the hotel by a German sentry whose orders were to keep the Italians together. That marked the end of Project Honor. Everyone returned to the hotel and its dining room: lunch was served.

To a man of appetite, the time between a good Italian lunch and a fine Italian dinner seems very long indeed. That April afternoon must have been interminable for the Duce, who found it filled with "more clouds of gray than any Russian play can guarantee." As in the song, love led the way. An irritable Clara and a dyspeptic Mussolini had a loud postprandial argument in their room, provoked by the presence nearby of a Signora Elena Curti Cucciati, another *objet d'amour* of the dictator. Clara screamed so loudly that Mussolini went to close the windows; he tripped over a rug in the process and received a great bruise on his cheek. More bad news: word came that Como had fallen to the Committee of National Liberation. Frantic debates and telephone calls filled the afternoon. Finally it was arranged for an airplane to fly the Duce and friends to Bavaria or the Austrian Alps. The nearest landing strip was at Chiavenna, less than twenty kilometers north of Dongo, and plans were made to set out the next day. At midnight, luck seemed to have changed in the Duce's favor, as a German column of trucks and armored cars arrived. The dictator would ride in one of the armored vehicles, and the entire column, Germans, Italians, Petaccis, et al., would head north on the corniche at dawn.

What had happened at the southern end of the lake had also taken place at its northern tip: the Black Brigades had exchanged Fascist heroism for self-interest and surrendered to the partisans. In Dongo, the leader of the Garibaldi Brigade was a Florentine lawyer with a name as euphonious as any in chivalric romance: Pier Luigi Bellini delle Stelle; his nom de guerre was Pedro. When at dawn on April 27 they heard that a German column was on its way, Pedro and his men set up a barricade. Felled trees blocked the trickiest curve of the tight corniche south of Dongo; excursion guides today point to the spot with glee. With mortars and automatic weapons at the ready, partisans assumed commanding positions on the heights above.

The German column ran into the roadblock just after daybreak, fired a few rounds, but could neither advance nor reverse its vehicles on the narrow road. Under a white flag, negotiations began. Whereas the Germans had greater firepower and more men, the partisans had the strategic advantage. To break the impasse, it was agreed that the Germans and their vehicles would be permitted to proceed to Austria, provided they left all civilian vehicles and Italian nationals behind to be dealt with by the partisans. In the course of the negotiations, Mussolini slipped away from the armored car, disguised himself in a German corporal's greatcoat and helmet; and dark glasses. Pretending drunken stupor, he huddled in a corner of a full troop carrier. But it is difficult to hide a face that has been on the coin of the realm. When the truck was searched, there was no mistaking that bulging face for a German noncom, drunk or sober.

The partisan who found him, Urbano Lazzaro, writes: "The man who made the world tremble, whom I revered when I was young and whom I had cursed when I was older, sits there huddled at my feet." Lazzaro arrested him "in the name of the Italian people" and—in a line from slapstick—assured the Duce that no one would touch a hair on his head while the dictator was in his charge. Cold comfort, that: Mussolini was completely bald. The Italian leader, his hierarchs, and the brawling Petaccis were all rounded up, brought to Dongo, and held in the town hall while their fate was discussed at various levels of an uncertain chain of command. Fearing that mob violence or unforeseen intervention might undo the day's work, Bellini delle Stelle removed Mussolini and a few of his top heelers to a small customs station in the hills above Dongo.

Orders came to transfer Mussolini and Clara Petacci down the lake, and the partisans brought them to a small farmhouse in the hamlet of Bonzanigo, high above the midway point of the western shore. The pair spent the night under guard, while the decision was made in Milan that they be prosecuted by a military tribunal of the Dongo region. The orders and authority for this action were carried from Milan to Dongo by Walter Aurizio, an engineer whose nom de guerre was Colonel Valerio.

Valerio hastily convened a tribunal in Dongo which sentenced the Fascist leader and his entourage to death for crimes against the Italian people. Valerio and a handful of men then collected the Duce and his mistress from the farmhouse. He drove with them toward the lake and asked them to dismount before the gate of the Villa Belmonte in the nearby town of Mezzegra. After their sentence was read, Valerio shot them on the spot. The hierarchs who had been held in Dongo were tried and also shot by automatic weapons in the main square, all, that is, except Marcello Petacci, who jumped frantically into the lake, where a fusillade of shots finished him off. All the bodies were shipped to Milan, and on the next day the corpses of Carla Petacci and Mussolini—he in Blackshirt uniform—were hung as in an abattoir by the heels. The place chosen was a service station on the Piazzale Loreto, where the preceding year the Germans had brutally executed fifteen partisans.

The treasure of Dongo disappeared without a trace. The tourist guides at Bellagio say they know which local matron wears Petacci's necklace, and which her tiaras; others swear that the hierarchs dumped gold bullion in the lake. Some say that a fisherman recovered a cache of the wedding rings and medals at a river mouth near the corniche where the roadblock had been. Other leads point to theft of *all* the treasure for personal or political gain by Communist officials at Como. The long postwar legal inquiries were inconclusive, and a series of unexplained disappearances, suicides, and murders of various suspects lends the appropriate touch of legend.

I hope the treasure is never found. I would be happy to know that it was all still down there, deep, at the bottom of the lake: all that gold brick, the drenched banknotes, the stubby rings, decorations, diamond necklaces, those waterlogged diaries. The treasure is a kind of talisman of peace; as long as it remains submerged, I fancy, the lake of Como will not know violence again.

> Understand the weapon, understand the wound:
> What shapeless past was hammered to action by his deeds,
> Only in constant action was his constant action found
> He will throw a longer shadow as time recedes.
> (John Cornford, ca. 1934, published posthumously)

It is not difficult to understand the weapon. The Duce's executioner, Colonel Valerio, was a veteran of the Garibaldi Battalion of the International Brigades in Spain, a comrade in arms of John

Cornford. The orders that Valerio carried were signed by Luigi Longo, the political commissar of the Second International Brigade. Although the Garibaldi Battalion had scored a major success over Mussolini's forces at Guadalajara in March 1937, the Fascist armies and German air power were too much for the anti-Fascists. For eight years they had been unable to realize their war cry of 1937: "Today in Spain, tomorrow in Italy"; what had begun in Guadalajara was not finished until Dongo.

The ferocity of Mussolini's execution needs as little excuse as that of Ceausescu's. The Fascist Party began in street violence—the *Me ne frego* Blackshirts were armed thugs—and came to power in the wake of assassinations. His opponents in jail and his critics in exile could learn the tactics of vengeance from the Duce's own writing. Of the thousand or so anti-Fascists penned in the prison of Ventotene, an island off Naples, more than a hundred were veterans of the Garibaldi Battalion and the Brigades, among them Longo and Valerio. They had ample time to consider Mussolini's order before his victorious march on Rome in the 1920s: "Discipline must be accepted, and when it is not accepted, it must be imposed.... Violence is not immoral. Violence is sometimes moral. When our violence is effective in a cancerous situation it is most moral, sacrosanct, and necessary. But O my Fascist friends, it is necessary that our violence have specifically Fascist characteristics."

We might say for John Cornford that the weapon that slew Mussolini was made of the stock of Fascist violence, had its barrel forged at Guadalajara and its action tuned at Ventotene; the bullets should have had *"Sic semper tyrannis"* on their jackets. One does, however, tend to pity the Petaccis; a gentler tribunal might have sentenced them to a year's cruise in the sole company of the then Duke and Duchess of Windsor.

The "wound" of which Cornford wrote is more difficult to understand. The name Valerio derives from the name of a Roman province; indeed, tincture of valerian comes from the root of the garden heliotrope of that region. Valerio included northern

Yugoslavia and its Istrian peninsula; the wars that claimed Comandante Pini and Leutnant Haurowitz can be traced to the ancient Roman thirst for the land of Valerio. But imperial ambition alone was not the only cause of the thirty-year-long European war of this century. Poets, politicians, and scholars of all political stripes and in each of the countries contributed to the myth of the hero, the Darwinian survivor, who embodied—in the Duce's phrase—contempt for the " 'bourgeois' spirit . . . of satisfaction and adjustment, a tendency toward skepticism, compromise, an easy life and advancement." D'Annunzio's quest for the hero is the Italian version of Frances Cornford's worship of the Golden Apollo on the "verge of strife." Perhaps the long littleness of life deserves less contempt on the part of poets.

The Duce's solution to the problem of the bourgeois spirit was the "principle of continued revolution" against the "political and economic liberal doctrines of the eighteenth century." It is perhaps ironic that the political and economic liberal doctrines of today were preserved by revolutionaries of the left. The present reign of the bourgeois spirit, which has for more than forty years brought calm and prosperity to Lake Como, was made possible in no small part by the heroism of "premature anti-Fascists" of the 1930s. Among those were the Communists John Cornford, Colonel Valerio, and Luigi Longo. Many of us owe our lives to their valor.

The splendid hydrofoils that zoom from Como to Bellagio to Dongo and back are filled with a generation that has been brought up according to the spirit of satisfaction, a tendency to skepticism, compromise, an easy life, and advancement. The seats are filled with schoolboys and schoolgirls of all classes; their Italian-made baseball hats and backpacks bear American logos; Japanese tourists and English cyclists snap photos of the pink villas that slide past their lens. Young couples hold hands in the autumn sun on the back deck; their baskets are loaded with Italian ham, Swiss chocolate, and Dutch beer. A slim, blond German woman plucks a Joan Baez song on her guitar. As the boat zooms along on its spray of air, no one on board wears a uniform more martial than jeans. Now, while the boat passes over the depths where the Treasure of Dongo is said to lie, I seem to hear the voices of Pini and Haurowitz telling me to forget it, to let it lie.

5

Losing a MASH

We were sitting around a library table on the sixteenth floor of Bellevue Hospital, discussing tactics in the teaching of medicine. Attending physicians, fellows, residents—products of a dozen medical schools over two generations—we had all undergone that intense period of ward training that has been a feature of American medicine since the 1910 report of Abraham Flexner, *Medical Education in the United States and Canada*. We were comparing our own experiences with those described in Melvin Konner's book *Becoming a Doctor*. Konner, an accomplished anthropologist and essayist, went to medical school at the age of thirty-six and proceeded to write an engaging account of his clinical years. His book not only sparked our discussion but earned our admiration. We concluded that what many call the best medical school in Boston must have added to its requirement for graduation the writing of a literate *Bildungsroman*, since no fewer than three other romances of medical education at Harvard in the 1980s have appeared (*Gentle Vengeance*, by Charles Le Baron; *A Not Entirely Benign Procedure*, by Perri Klass; and *Under the Ether Dome*, by Stephen Hoffman). We agreed that the Boston group had gotten the story of medical training just about right, plus or minus local folklore.

Controversy arose over whether clinical medicine couldn't be taught at a more humane pace. Surely, some argued, docs might be more compassionate if they had not been brutalized by the post-Flexnerian hazing ritual, that crunch of learning between the third year of medical school and the first two years on a hospital's house staff: four years without adequate sleep, security, or salary. Laity and medical educators alike have complained that the high-tech doctors who survive this rude ritual have lost touch with the pastoral aspects of medicine; that they lack patience, humanity, and compassion; that they don't listen to their patients.

One of us came to a conclusion remarkably like Konner's: "You put a bunch of bright, competitive people in white coats and scrub suits, assume they've memorized the human genome and the complement cascade, let them write orders on very sick people they've never met in street clothes, and then you wonder why they don't come on like Dr. Schweitzer."

"Nonsense," said another. "Nowhere else in the world is medicine done better. And it's done better here because we *do* teach science, and we *do* train house officers to stay up at night with sick patients who die if someone flubs an order."

I wondered if that attitude wasn't somewhat parochial. Other professions deal with life and death: pilots and politicians sometimes face crises that dwarf those of the clinic. The years of medical training are perhaps no more brutalizing than the apprenticeship undergone by young lawyers, venture capitalists, or brokers. The best of those professionals also work incredibly long hours, have to make equally touchy decisions, and play for very high stakes indeed.

A resident disagreed. "You can say what you like, but in big medical centers like this one, we deal with life and death all the time; we're not just driving an airplane. And when my intern and I drag out of the on-call room at three in the morning we're not doing it for a leveraged buyout or to beat a competitor."

"In fact," observed one of my older colleagues, "that's what we all remember best. Those early mornings in scrub suits with a senior resident yelling at us to put in a line."

"It's like boot camp," said one of the fellows. "You sweat like hell, but you come out a Marine."

An appalled woman resident objected: "That's what scares me, medical school shouldn't turn us into Marines! Soldiers are taught to kill: they're on the wrong side."

I mused out loud. "You know, we may not like it nowadays, but I suppose that house staff training *is* very much like basic training in the military. The Army or Marines may train you to crawl under machine-gun fire, but *we* train you to shock a real heart back to life. The soldier may spend his whole military career buying camshafts, and you might become a dean. But you'll never forget the day you first put on a white jacket, any more than I'll forget the day I put on an Army uniform. Besides, the Army seemed on the right side, then."

It is difficult to remember what turn the discussion next took, because I began to reconsider what I'd just said. *Was* it in fact necessary to train young doctors in the military mode? Wasn't it possible that we conflated martial with medical training in a puff of imperial pride?

On the office walls of doctors of my generation hang photographs of young men in white uniforms. There, in the front row, is the crew-cut "chief of service," the commanding officer. There, way in back of the fourth row, is that callow chap, the clean-shaven "house officer," who has yet to blunder into middle age. "We were on the house staff together, he was my chief resident," we tell each other. Rank, hierarchy, structure—is that what ought to dictate the teaching of medicine? Or is our military model based on the experience of our teachers? The men who taught us medicine and the men who taught *them* had been to war; many had been the most willing of warriors.

It cannot be said that my own two years in the service left me with undiluted respect for the military model. Not even nostalgia can erase memories of the unspeakable boredom that suffused the peacetime Army in the mid-1950s. During the diluted basic training we received as medical officers at Fort Sam Houston we complained that the Army ran on the principle that the incompetent must lead the unwilling to perform the unnecessary. But there were moments when the pageant got to us, when bugles blew retreat and the colors were furled in a mauve San Antonio sunset that caught the heart. And even the dreary stalemate of the Korean War had not yet diminished some of the Second World

War glory of those who trained us. One learned that the ribbons sported by our drillmasters—fellows only a few years older—had been won for chasing the Germans out of Sicily, assaulting the beaches of Normandy, or opening the gates of Dachau. Feelings of gratitude were mingled with constant wonder that this drawling crew of layabouts had beaten the Wehrmacht and kept me from being turned into kitchen soap.

Many of my Army colleagues, snatched from training programs at elite hospitals, muttered their own paraphrases of Proudhon's quip, "I would die for the common man rather than have to live with him for a week." For others of us the service was an eye-opener, a crash course in American diversity, an outdoor seminar in experimental sociology. We were also permitted to lay mines and to fire carbines.

Crawling along the infiltration course at Camp Bullis, or wilting through lectures on the layout of latrines, one hoped eventually to be stationed at the periphery of the new American empire: perhaps near the temples of Kyoto or the forest of Fontainebleau. In the event, I became a turnpike warrior, posted to Fort Dix, New Jersey, so that I could help—in the words of the large Texan who sent us off—"to defend our way of life against the forces of Atheistic Communism that threaten to engulf the Free World."

The charge was easily fulfilled in the pine barrens near Bordentown, where the only Communist I met was a potter from New Hope. I defended democracy for the better part of a year by examining the backsides of recruits and playing pinball in the officers' club. During a rainy fall and dreary winter I volunteered for any assignment that would remove me and my family to more congenial surroundings. It was no small delight, therefore, when I drew by chance temporary duty described by our commanding colonel as "a soft deal on the shores of Lake Ontario." For there, at Oswego, New York, the First Army ran a summer training camp for its antiaircraft artillery units and reserves. The artillery people shot with 90-millimeter cannons at small drone planes,

and Army regulations decree that where cannons are fired, a doc
is required. I would become the post surgeon of this artillery
camp and could move with wife and baby to lovely Oswego on the
lake; my duties would be nine to five with weekends free, because
the firing range was open only while the technicians from the
Cadillac motor division of GM were around to manipulate the
radio-controlled target planes.

There was one small complication before we could make
what appeared a welcome summer retreat from the heat of
southern New Jersey. At the end of May, I would have to move
some enlisted men and equipment from Fort Dix to the Oswego
range—a few hundred miles to the north—and deliver a mobile
army surgical hospital to Camp Drum, which was somewhat
farther northeast along the lake, at Watertown, New York. This
transfer was routine, the colonel assured me, and would be
handled by my executive officer, a Medical Service Corps lieutenant named Hooper. Once Hooper and I had the MASH safely
into Watertown, we could take a week off, find homes in the
town of Oswego for our families, and bring them up to the
cool lake for a summer of fun. I immediately liked Hooper,
who hailed from Syracuse. He was in his mid-thirties and had
become an optometrist after his infantry days in Europe, only
to be recalled during the Korean War, in the course of which
he had learned to manage field hospitals. It was left unclear
why this amiable man had not risen above the rank of first
lieutenant.

Soon enough, I found myself seated next to Hooper in the
backseat of a command jeep. We were rolling north at the head of
a convoy of eighteen trucks—mainly old Dodge deuce-and-a-halfs—
and assorted ambulances. On my lap was a clipboard with a
listing of all that the convoy contained, everything from "sterilizer,
chrome, portable, twelve gallon vol" to "crutch, wooden, rubber
arm support, laminated," all these in quantities that might have
seemed excessive for the French retreat from Moscow. In accord
with Army custom, I had signed for the whole lot; two carbon

copies of my debenture remained at the base. As commanding officer de jure, I was now responsible for millions of dollars of medical and automotive hardware, not to speak of the welfare of the seventy or so enlisted men riding behind us. All seemed in hand, however, since Hooper had exercised his de facto role and gotten the convoy assembled in crackerjack form.

On that fine spring day the sun shone and blossoms of fruit trees dropped like snow on the hood of our jeep. Hooper and I wore dress khaki with spiffy combat boots; the men wore green fatigues with shiny brass. On their arms, many sported red crosses on white bands to distinguish medics from the drivers; small pennants of red and white fluttered from flagstaffs on our fenders. The scene was very martial and perhaps for that reason its captain led this unit of the First Army through New Jersey whistling the refrain from "Red River Valley." In my ears the lyrics were those of the Abraham Lincoln Brigade: "There's a valley in Spain called Jarama . . . "

We left Fort Dix at seven on a Saturday morning and were not due in Watertown—Camp Drum—until Monday morning at eight. Plans were to make it to Oswego in one long trek and to drop a few men and supplies for the artillery range there. After two nights at Oswego, we would move the MASH to Camp Drum bright and early on Monday morning. Two disasters interrupted this plan. In the first instance, several of the trucks developed mechanical failure, and we were very slow at getting them going again. We were in consequence behind schedule when we arrived in Glens Falls late on Saturday afternoon, to telephone ahead to Oswego. The second foul-up was not our fault. The artillery range, commanded at the time by a colonel whose interest in 90-millimeter guns was subordinate to that in 90-proof gin, had made arrangements for two officers, but not for a MASH. It became clear that no tents were ready for the men and no victuals were available; the training season was not to begin for another three weeks. We ourselves were not yet under Oswego orders and were in any case not supposed to reappear there until after we had signed over the MASH to Watertown. We were on our own. It was clearly impossible to make it to Camp Drum that day, so Hooper and I were left with the problem of providing housing and food for three-and-a-half score men and the not simple problem of over-night parking for a MASH.

Hooper made what I considered a brilliant suggestion. "Look, Captain, all the enlisted men are from the First Army area, most of them are reservists, from the Troy-Utica area. They all come from New York, or at farthest from western Massachusetts. Tell them you'll give them the rest of the weekend off. They'll go home, eat, sleep, and get to Camp Drum on their own by Monday. That way we don't have to feed or house them. All they have to do is fill up their trucks with gas."

I wondered about the logistics of this for a bit, but then Hooper turned the tide of doubt. He had learned that many a young doctor's sense of duty could be diverted by an appeal to the table. "Not only can the men get a good night's sleep, but I know the Finger Lakes region well. There's this fabulous restaurant in Skaneateles—Krebs', it's called—and they have some rooms. They've got this unbelievable New York white wine you won't find any-where else in the world, and then they serve blue trout in pure butter."

What was good enough for Faust was good enough for me. Mephisto Hooper bought my soul for the price of blue trout and white wine. I decided forthwith not to check with the CO at Watertown but to take action on my own. I spelled out the bargain to the men of our MASH: we would all assemble at the gates of Camp Drum at eight on Monday morning, they were free to head for the sacks at home on condition they gave us their word to return promptly, with full gas tanks. They seemed grateful and happy, and dispersed within minutes to drive ambulances and deuce-and-a-halfs over the highways to Troy, Utica, and points east.

With Hooper now at the wheel, we sped on to Krebs'. I wish that I could report that the two dinners we had there were worth all that followed, but if truth be told, I remember chiefly the wine. The menu was ample but plain; the fare was distinguished with respect to its ingredients but not its preparation, which merely provided a substrate for the delicate flavor of the then undervalued wines of the Finger Lakes. But while perhaps not then worthy of a Michelin star, the inn was more than adequate for two off-duty officers; we spent the time between meals playing cards. Our *grande bouffe* ended, we were able to arrive at Watertown at seven on Monday morning by dint of driving through much of New York State in the middle of the night. We parked our jeep about two hundred feet from the gates of the camp and made our morning ablutions with the aid of helmet liners and water from a canteen. Spit-and-polish clean, Hooper and I waited for the troops to arrive.

By five minutes before eight, I had become worried and impatient; by eight I was in agony. None of our vehicles had arrived. We watched as car after car filled with troops from the camp rolled through the gates. Inside, the place was a bedlam of truck noise, troop echoes, bugle calls. Outside the gate, not an army truck was to be seen. Eight-fifteen. I was wet with angst. I was going to be court-martialed for having lost all those trucks, all those millions of dollars; I would be in debt the rest of my life. I looked at the clipboard and could not believe that I had ever signed my name to such a manifold. A "scissor, chrome, surgical, 3½ inches" cost $14.75—and there were ten gross of those!

I could not bear to speak with Hooper. He reassured me that the boys would be along any minute and that no one expected a convoy to be exactly on time. I worried some more. It was now nine and we were still alone in our jeep. I told Hooper to wait by the gate and took the jeep into camp. The sentry responded with a salute; I identified myself and gave him a copy of our orders. He asked where the rest of my unit was, and I stammered that they were "forming up down the road"; he directed me to post headquarters.

They were expecting me at the colonel's office, and I was shown in immediately. It was now nine-fifteen. The colonel, whom I'll call Cooper, because he looked like Gary, was an infantryman. His chest displayed battle ribbons of two wars and featured purple hearts and bronze stars sufficient for the whole cast of *Sergeant York*.

"Captain Weissmann, reporting, sir!" I gave him my best copy of a Hollywood salute.

"Y'all bring that rollin' hospital in heah?" he asked me in an accent I will not attempt any further to reproduce.

"Well, sir, not exactly. I mean, I am here, and my exec is here. We are, actually, ah, er, waiting for the men to form up."

He rose from behind his desk, went to the window, and saw only my now empty jeep on the empty roadway. He picked up a copy of my orders, accepted the clipboard from my hand, looked them both over for half a year, and finally gave me a hard stare.

"Weissmann, that's a New York name, isn't it?"

I had a hunch what he meant by that. "Yes, sir."

"You were due in at eight o'clock in the morning with eighteen deuce-and-a-halfs, some ambulances, and seventy-odd men. A whole effing United effing States effing Mobile effing Army . . . Where in hell are they?"

Since I had neither gasoline nor match at hand I was unable to commit the first act of suicide that sprang to mind. American reserve Medical Corps officers are not issued swords; that ruled out the second. I ventured the third by opening my mouth. I told him about the bargain I had struck with the men.

"You're supposed to be their commander, not their camp buddy! I don't care if you are some smart-ass New York doctor, you can't just let a bunch of men go off in government property all over the state. You'll be in hock right up to your Park Avenue ears! If I don't hear those trucks rolling in soon, you're liable to be in the stockade mighty quick and mighty poor. Before you scatter a bunch of men and trucks all over the map, boy, you ask someone!"

It was now closer to ten and the only sound I could hear was the firing squad in the next room checking their carbines. I wondered who would clean up the puddle of sweat I was leaving on the varnished floor.

The colonel took one look over the empty street, then he sat down facing me. "You really screwed up, didn't you? Well, there's only one thing for me to do now." He reached into his desk drawer.

He's going to kill me right now with his service revolver! I thought. He brought out a fairly full bottle of Jack Daniel's, followed by two bar glasses. "Doctor, why don't you and I just sip some whiskey while we wait for the boys to come in off their holiday?"

And so, for the next hour and a half, my petrified, younger self and the tall man from Tennessee sat there as slowly, very slowly, the street outside filled up with trucks and ambulances and the men of our MASH were hustled into rank by a very sheepish Hooper.

I thought about that morning at Camp Drum as our discussion at Bellevue came back into focus. It had covered the map of clinical learning and we wound up by defining its limits as "drill" and "problem solving." We decided that the discomfort we feel nowadays in the presence of the military ritual extends to the military aspect of a doctor's house staff and student drill, the rite of passage we had all experienced. But we also agreed that university teaching differs from military teaching in one important way; whereas in the absence of drill battles may be lost, without problem solving, the war is over.

Questions remained. To what extent should doctors train by rote, to what extent by trial and error? When the stakes are as high as life and death, is it appropriate to work by the old rule of "See one, do one, teach one"? Are we acting responsibly when we permit the chance of error by a doctor in training? Who pays for each goof? Is there a contradiction between good medical care and learning by doing?

From Thomas Arnold at Rugby to John Dewey at Columbia, educators have spelled out the dialectic between the *form* of drill and the *function* of problem solving. We might argue that, as in the canon of architecture, medicine is best taught when form follows function.

No one was hurt by my loss of the MASH. There was no battle missed or opportunity wasted. No one died and no one suffered. Except for my small embarrassment, no sentiments were greatly bruised. Hooper and I emerged as more dutiful soldiers in consequence of the colonel's largesse. We learned the strength of the rules by having been forgiven their violation. We had been caught by that oldest of tricks by which the young are taught: a pardon. It is a difficult lesson for a prospective teacher to ignore.

When the convoy finally formed up and drove down the parade strip to our bivouac area, it made quite a fine sight in the cool northern spring sun. Our jeep in the lead, we passed between ranks of new 90-millimeter guns waiting on their beds to be tracked to the range. Their crews gave us a wave. I was reminded of a passage by George Orwell in *Homage to Catalonia:*

> As our train drew into the station a troop-train full of men from the International Column was drawing out, and a knot of people on the bridge were waving to them. It was a very long train, packed to bursting-point with men, with field-guns lashed on the open trucks and more men clustering round the guns. . . . It was like an allegorical picture of war; the trainload of fresh men gliding proudly up the line, the maimed men sliding slowly down, and all the while the guns on the open trucks making one's heart leap as guns always do, and reviving that pernicious feeling, so difficult to get rid of, that war *is* glorious after all.

Difficult, said Orwell, meaning not impossible.

6

Gertrude Stein on the Beach

The photograph shows a score of students in the summer dress of a century ago collecting specimens at low tide from a harbor near Woods Hole in Massachusetts. The harbor is Quisset, and its waters today remain rich in marine life; its heights are still dominated by a Yankee cottage called Petrel's Rest; the house is still surrounded on four sides by a veranda and fronted by a flagpole. The young people are on a collecting trip for the course in invertebrate zoology at the Marine Biological Laboratory; its students still collect specimens from the inlets of Buzzards Bay. The photo was taken on July 31, 1897, and the young woman in the middle is Gertrude Stein. She has turned, smiling, to her brother Leo, who holds up a specimen jar. "Look what I've found!" he gestures to the photographer. Many in the group are smiling—it is the height of summer, they are young and have disembarked at a marine Cythera where lush creatures drift on the tide. Leo Stein has snared a ctenophore, a solitary free swimmer that resembles a jellyfish.

For a century now, images of the Marine Biological Laboratory have been kept like wallet snapshots in the memories of scientists who return there yearly, and of their students who do not. Those summer snapshots do not evoke memories of a routine, workaday research institute. They conjure up spirits of a blithe community that springs to life each year—like Brigadoon—for experiments by a northern sea warmed by Gulf Stream currents. Not all students of the MBL become scientists, some may not even learn much science, but few will forget those

Gertrude Stein and Her Brother Finding Ctenophores on Quisset Beach, 1897.
Marine Biological Laboratory Library Archives, Woods Hole.

moments at the bench or on the beach when the cry goes up: "Look what I've found!"

At Woods Hole in 1897, Gertrude Stein was twenty-three years old; she had just finished Radcliffe and was to enter the Johns Hopkins Medical School in the fall. That summer she enrolled in the embryology course of the MBL and often accompanied Leo and the invertebrate zoologists on collecting trips. W. C. Curtis, who is shown in the photograph in white cap and knee boots just to the right of Stein, remembered in the Falmouth *Enterprise:* "For us that summer she was just a big fat girl waddling around the laboratory and hoisting herself in and out of the row-boats on collecting trips." Adding incest to injury, he might have added that she was in thrall to her fast-talking brother; some might read the photo as a record of the intense bond. Stein has written that as children she and Leo tramped alone in the woods of northern California; her adoring gaze in the Quisset photo suggests an American future for both of them: from the redwood forests to the Gulf Stream waters, this land was made for you and me.

The photo suggests motifs other than those of a family romance, for the image is a stunning icon of natural science. The anonymous photographer has snapped a tableau of figures in a landscape so arranged that all the compositional lines—from hillside on the upper left to beach grass at the lower right—converge on Leo, who holds high the collecting jar with his discovery. The creature from the ocean has been plonked into a glass pot to become a specimen for science. The composition has elements of Joseph Wright's neoclassical *Experiments with the Air Pump*, in that the figures are so disposed as to lead us to the apex of a visual

J. WRIGHT, *Experiments with the Air Pump*. National Gallery, London.

Class Photo of the Marine Biological Laboratory Embryology Course, 1897.
Marine Biological Laboratory Library Archives, Woods Hole.

pyramid at which life has been caught in a jug. The photo leads
our eye, via the sight-lines of Gertrude and another young woman,
straight to Leo, who looks to the lens with his prize held high.
Viewing the photo almost a century later, we know that the scales
of discovery tipped toward the sister, and therefore we tend
to read the picture as an action shot of the artist as a young
woman. Caught there on the beach at Quisset, she is forever happy
by the summer sea from which smiling students fetch treasures
for the lab.

No other picture of Stein shows her quite so perky as on that
day at Quisset. The group photo of her embryology class, taken
later in the summer, shows her preoccupied and unsmiling. Indeed,
nothing about science or medicine seems to have given her much
joy after her tussle with ctenophores. After indifferent attention

to laboratory and clinic, she failed to graduate from the Johns Hopkins Medical School with her class of 1901. Although she had completed the bulk of her work, she seemed to have floundered over obstetrics—she who had gotten all that marine embryology right. She tells us that it was in the course of her obstetrical work that she became "aware of the Negroes" in the Baltimore clinics serviced by Johns Hopkins; from that experience emerged the story of Melanctha in *Three Lives*, the mulatto who abandons a humdrum doctor in favor of more louche companionship.

Gertrude Stein and Johns Hopkins separated as if by mutual consent. In *The Autobiography of Alice B. Toklas* Stein tells us:

> The Professor who has flunked her asked her to come to see him. She did. He said, of course, Miss Stein all you have to do is to take a summer course here and in the fall naturally you will take your degree. But not at all, said Gertrude Stein, you have no idea how grateful I am to you. I have so much inertia and so little initiative that very possibly if you had not kept me from taking my degree I would have, well, not taken to the practice of medicine, but at any rate to pathological psychology and you don't know how little I like pathological psychology, and how all medicine bores me. The professor was completely taken aback and that was the end of the medical education of Gertrude Stein.

Whether from boredom with medicine or deeper battles of the self, no joy shows in her picture with the class of 1901 at Hopkins. She stands glumly half hidden in the back row behind other women and the shorter, swarthier of the men. She left for Europe and, after aimless wanderings with her brother, settled in Paris to find her own vocation. Gertrude Stein soon outdistanced Leo, who had stopped dabbling in biology; she discovered new art and new friends on the banks of the Seine. The Iberian portrait of her painted by Picasso in 1906 shows a confident young writer

Johns Hopkins Medical School, Class of 1901. Johns Hopkins Library, Baltimore.

who was crafting *Three Lives* and in the course of it changing forever the way we hear words.

Those who look to details of biography for "explanations" of literary or artistic styles can usually extract as much material as needed to convince. In the case of Gertrude Stein, the most convincing "explanation" of her unique style was offered by B. F. Skinner, writing in *The Atlantic Monthly* of April 1935. In an article entitled "Has Gertrude Stein a Secret?" the Harvard professor of psychology traced Stein's literary technique to her undergraduate research work on automatic writing with William James, Skinner's predecessor at Harvard in experimental psychology. The case is persuasive, even if Skinner's aesthetic judgments are not. But on a July day at Woods Hole, with ctenophores and jellyfish awash on the tide, another set of influences on Stein seems just as likely. My hunch is that Gertrude Stein was an old-fashioned Woods Hole mechanist, a reductionist of the school of Jacques Loeb. Her revolution of words owed as much to Loeb's *The Mechanistic Conception of Life* as to her study "Normal Motor Automatism," which she had written for William James, or to "Les Demoiselles d'Avignon" of her Picasso years (the first versions of which showed a medical student as spectator).

In the summer of 1988 the Marine Biological Laboratory celebrated its centenary and the Dedication Day lecture was given in honor of Jacques Loeb (1859–1924). Loeb was the leader of the new, mechanistic school of American biology, the adherents of which tried to explain the phenomena of biology by the equations of physics and not the quirky logic of vitalism. In 1897, Loeb was teaching the physiology course at Woods Hole, and the implications of his biophysical approach were the talk of the MBL. He had demonstrated that the chemical nature of salts in the environment of a cell controlled its irritability, movement, and reproduction in predictable ways. He was on his way to creating life in a dish, to forming fatherless sea urchins by chemical means. Parthenogenesis was announced two years later, but Loeb's work on tropisms and salt solutions had already paved the way for what he considered the fundamental task of physiology: "to determine whether or not we shall be able to produce living matter artificially."

Loeb and his school of mechanists believed they were the legitimate heirs of the eighteenth-century *philosophes*, and Loeb's book *The Organism as a Whole* (1916) is dedicated to Denis Diderot in the words of John Morley's tribute to the *philosophe:* "He was one of those simple, disinterested, and intellectually sterling workers to whom their personality is as nothing in the presence of the vast subjects that engage the thoughts of their lives."

The mechanist's credo, with its belief that it is possible to frame disinterested, value-free thoughts unshaped by "personality," has since been dismissed as shallow reductionism by three generations of philosophers, poets, and divines. Value-free science, those folks argue, is an illusion. But, to paraphrase John Sayles, just because they argue sweeter doesn't mean they're right. Doctors of my generation would reply that reductionist principles in science have permitted us to conquer tuberculosis, syphilis, polio, and scarlet fever. Using mechanistic models, we have uncoiled the human genome and scanned the living brain; we've soothed mad minds with lithium and patched sick hearts with Teflon. We have fulfilled Loeb's prophecy of "producing mutations by physico-chemical means and nuclear material which acts as a ferment for its own synthesis and thus reproduces itself."

But Loeb claimed more territory for science than that of the body. He extended its empire to the mind. Replying to William James's request for his views of brain function, Loeb responded in 1888: "Whatever appear to us as innervations, sensations, psychic phenomena, as they are called, I seek to conceive through reducing them—in the sense of modern physics—to the molecular or atomic structure of the protoplasm, which acts in a way that is similar to (for example) the molecular structure of the parts of an optically active crystal."

Loeb detailed this reductionist proposal to the one man perhaps least likely to be persuaded. William James, physician, professor of anatomy before he became a professor of psychology, had argued eloquently the opposite and more generally held view before an audience of Unitarian ministers at Princeton in a lecture entitled "Theism and the Reflex Arc." In a ringing defense of theism against the reductionists of the reflex arc, he told the liberal clergy:

> Certain of our positivists keep chiming to us, that, amid the wreck of every other god and idol, one divinity still stands upright,—that his name is Scientific Truth. . . . But they are deluded. They have simply chosen from the entire set of propensities at their command those that were certain to construct, out of the materials given, the leanest, lowest, aridest result,—namely the bare molecu-

lar world,—and they have sacrificed all the rest. . . . The
scientific conception of the world as an army of molecules
gratifies this appetite [for parsimony] after its fashion
most exquisitely.

The dialogue between those who lean toward Loeb and those
who tend to agree with James has been carried on for a century
by the waters of Vineyard Sound and Buzzards Bay. Mechanists
maintain that the control of living things must precede our understanding of them; holists contend that when we understand them
we may not hanker after control. Woods Hole has always had
room for both parties in this dialogue, as it has for those who
come to verbal blows over the conflict between nature and nurture,
structure and function, Red Sox and Yankees.

Stein got a whiff of both sides in the course of her research
career. She heard the siren song of vital forces from the voice of
gentle James; she worked with one of Loeb's closest colleagues,
Franklin Pierce Mall, not only in the embryology course at Woods
Hole but also at Johns Hopkins. Yet by the time she wrote *Three
Lives*, her critics got it just right: she was on the side of the
mechanists. Wyndham Lewis—no great friend of poor folk—argued
in his review that Stein's book put demotic speech into the "metre
of an obsessing time" and, although "undoubtably intended as an
epic contribution to the present mass-democracy," gave "to the
life it patronizes the mechanical bias of its creator."

My hunch that Gertrude Stein's revolution in words is based
on Loeb's mechanistic conception of life derives not only from a
reexamination of B. F. Skinner's hypothesis but also from trends
in our culture that have become more prominent after his critique.
The best biography of Stein (*The Third Rose*, by John Malcolm
Brinnin), contains no reference to Loeb or to the Marine Biological Laboratory. The best biography of Loeb (*Controlling Life:
Jacques Loeb and the Engineering Ideal in Biology*, by Philip J.
Pauly), does not mention Stein. Both books discuss with varying
degrees of insight the interaction of their principals with William

James, Franklin Pierce Mall, and B. F. Skinner; both books tell stories that contain substantial parallels.

Stein and Loeb were both orphaned as adolescents and brought up by well-off relatives as secular Jews, Stein in Oakland and Baltimore, Loeb in the Rhineland and Berlin. Both emigrated as young adults, both spoke their adopted languages with awkward accents. Both performed experiments on brain function early in their careers, attracting the attention of William James; indeed Loeb wrote to James fishing for a job in the New World. When Stein entered Johns Hopkins, she worked on mechanical models of spinal tracts with Mall, Loeb's colleague from Woods Hole and the University of Chicago. Finally, both engaged the far from casual interest of B. F. Skinner.

Pauly describes how Skinner was persuaded by Loeb's argument, as spelled out in *The Organism as a Whole*, that mechanist principles could be applied to the study and control of behavior. Skinner was also captivated by *Arrowsmith*, in which Sinclair Lewis depicts Loeb—as Martin Arrowsmith's mentor Dr. Gottlieb—as a secular saint of science. Pauly correctly identifies Skinner and the other behaviorists of T-maze and pigeon-box as the rightful heirs to Loeb's mechanistic conception of life. Although the founder of experimental psychology at Harvard, William James, had championed the cause of vitalism against the raiders of the reflex arc, his successor was quite prepared to work for the opposition. Skinner found support for his views in the work of James's best-known student: he was the first to draw attention to Gertrude Stein's undergraduate work on automatic writing. He pointed out the origins of her verbal experiments by unearthing the paper "Normal Motor Automatism," by Leon M. Solomons and Gertrude Stein from the Harvard Psychological Laboratory, published in *Psychological Review* of September 1896. (What a pride of lions and Leos! Loeb's not undistinguished brother, a pioneer in studies of inflammation, was also named Leo.)

Solomons and Stein reported on experiments designed to test whether a second personality—as displayed in cases of hysteria—

could be called forth deliberately from a normal subject. The authors undertook to see how far they could "split" their personalities by eliciting automatic writing under a variety of test conditions. They concluded that hysteria is a *"disease* of the *attention"* (italics theirs), basing their argument on the finding that when distracted or inattentive, normal subjects show the abnormal motor behavior of hysterics. It may be no coincidence that Solomons and Stein performed laboratory work on hysteria in the very year that Sigmund Freud and Josef Breuer published their *Studies in Hysteria.* The subject was much in the air on both sides of the Atlantic, not least because—as William J. McGrath has pointed out—the study of hysteria offered science an opportunity to strike at the foundations of religion. Explain away divine madness by the reflex arc and you explain away divinity. James as a theist was persuaded that experimental psychology would validate all varieties of religious experience. His students, on the other hand, came to a behavioral conclusion that favored the reflex arc: Solomons and Stein wrote that "an hysterical anesthesia or paralysis is simply an inability to attend to sensations from this part."

Skinner showed little interest in Solomons and Stein's discussion of hysteria, however congenial to the mechanistic conception it might have been. He was more concerned with tracing Stein's literary style to her experiences of automatic writing. Using themselves as test subjects, Solomons and Stein were able to show that with a little practice they could regularly produce automatic writing as they took dictation while reading another text: "The word is written or half-written before the subject knows anything about it, or perhaps he never knows anything about it. For overcoming this habit of attention we found constant repetition of one word of great value."

After they had succeeded in training themselves by this sort of cognitive drill, and after sessions with Ouija boards to call up their alter egos, automatic writing became easy. Stein found it convenient to read what her arm wrote, but following it three or four words behind her pencil. In this fashion, "a phrase would seem to get into the head and keep repeating itself at every opportunity, and hang over from day to day even. The stuff written was grammatical, and the words and phrases fitted together all right, but there was not much connected thought."

Skinner—a traditionalist with respect to the arts—argued that these experiments explained why there appeared to be two Gertrude Steins. The first Stein was accessible, and had written such serious works as *Three Lives* and *The Autobiography of Alice B. Toklas;* the other Stein was dense, and wrote stuff that was grammatical, with words and phrases fitting together all right, but without connected thought. The second Stein had written *Tender Buttons*, her portraits, and *The Making of Americans.* (*Four Saints in Three Acts* was yet to come!) Skinner gave mild positive reinforcement to the first Stein, but strong negative reinforcement to the second, chiding her that "the mere generation of the effects of repetition and surprise is not in itself a literary achievement." He complained that the second Stein gave no clue as to the personal history or cultural background of the author, and dismissed her most adventurous book with a phrase from their common master, William James: "*Tender Buttons* is the stream of consciousness of a woman without a past."

On the surface, Skinner seems to have scored a point. It is easy to pick up resonances between the samples of automatic writing that Solomons and Stein had presented and the stuff of Stein's later work. Thus the first two passages below, examples of automatic writing from the 1896 article, *sound* like the third and fourth passages, which came from later Stein. But a closer look will show all the difference:

> This long time when he did this best time, and he could thus have been bound, and in this long time, when he could be this to first use of this long time ...

> When he could not be the longest and thus to be, and thus to be, the strongest ...

One does not like to feel different and if one does not like
to feel different then one hopes that things will not look
different. It is alright for them to seem different but not to
be different.

> (from "Meditations on Being About to Visit
> My Native Land," 1934)

What a day is today that is what a day it was day before
yesterday, what a day!

> ("Broadcast on the Liberation," 1944)

Skinner's theory of the two Steins permitted him to "dismiss
one part of Gertrude Stein's writing as a probably ill-advised
experiment and to enjoy the other and very great part without
puzzlement." The irony seems to have been lost on our leading
reductionist that he was reducing Stein's new style to its leanest,
lowest, most arid origin: the knack of automatic writing she had
acquired in the course of her undergraduate experiments. Other
interpretations might occur to those who believe that behavior—
not to speak of literature—might be described in more complex,
dynamic ways.

William James never got to read the copy of *Three Lives* that
his student sent him; he died of a heart attack with the book
unopened. He had written to Stein his acknowledgment of her gift:

> I promise you that it shall be read *some* time! You see
> what a swine I am to have pearls cast before him! As a
> rule reading fiction is as hard to me as trying to hit a
> target by hurling feathers at it. I need *resistance*, to
> cerebrate!

What a challenge to fiction by the brother of Henry James!
Hurling feathers, indeed! But of course, Gertrude Stein had not
written simply one more work of fiction. She had fabricated a
new language, which encountered enough resistance and caused

enough cerebration for a gaggle of Jameses. It could be argued that Stein spent the best part of her professional life opposing the vitalism of James with the mechanistic conception of Loeb. She was proud that Marcel Brion had praised her for "exactitude, austerity, absence of light and shade, by refusal of the use of the subconscious."

Not only is her ode to joy on the Liberation—"What a day is today that is what a day it was day before yesterday, what a day!"—pure Stein, but it is couched in the language of our century: short repetitive sequences. Short repetitive sequences run through modern literature from Morgenstern to Vonnegut, from Beckett to Pinter; they charge the beat of modern music from rock to Philip Glass. Short repetitive sequences also constitute the language of our genes; when we talk DNA or RNA we speak pure Stein. I am not surprised when I hear a molecular biologist explaining a stretch of DNA in the four-letter code of nucleic acids: What a TAA is ATAA that is ATA what a TAA it was, what a TATAA, what a TAA, what a TATAA!

Gertrude Stein worked in the manner Loeb attributed to Diderot: she wrote disinterested sentences whose sound no false note of personality was permitted to disturb. Her champions praise her as the last daughter of the eighteenth century and the herald of the twentieth. Like the cubists, she broke the common plane of thought to make compositions from its basic verbal elements. As Loeb reduced the structure of living things to the "bare molecular world," so Stein reduced language to its bare molecular level, where phonemes throb to their own rhythm. Stein's new language expanded the technology of prose as cubism expanded that of painting. Her language was to the painting of her day as a digital display is to the analogue graphic of ours: signs of the present with an eye to the future.

Gertrude Stein tells us that she had learned from William James that "science is continuously busy with the complete description of something, with ultimately the complete description of everything" (*Lectures in America*). But words, sounds, *things* were not descriptions: "A daffodil is different from a description, a jonquil is different from a description. A narrative is different from a description. . . . A narrative is at present not necessary" (*How to Write*).

Neither modern writing nor modern art was going to *describe* things; that was the job of science. Nor should the moderns write narrative; the last century had smothered words with stories. No, the task of writers in the twentieth century was to free words and images from the baggage of sentiment. Free from myth, meaning, and station, each jonquil or daffodil, each magpie or pigeon could stand fresh on the page. A rose is a rose is a rose—and with that line, said Stein, a rose was red for the first time in English poetry for a hundred years. She had reinvented the rose and was free to create an army of roses at will, each red for the first time.

Stein's reduction of language to its basic elements would not have pleased William James. As if in obedience to the rule of parsimony, she had pared from words their moral and aesthetic associations. Did she remember that her Cambridge master had preached to the Unitarians a summa against Occam:

> But if the religion of exclusive scientificism should ever succeed in suffocating all other appetites out of a nation's mind . . . that nation, that race will just as surely go to ruin, and fall a prey to their more richly constituted neighbors, as the beasts of the field, on the whole, have fallen a prey to man.
>
> I myself have little fear for our Anglo-Saxon race. Its moral, aesthetic, and practical wants form too dense a stubble to be mown down by any scientific Occam's razor that has yet been forged. The knights of the razor will never form among us more than a sect.

Gertrude Stein was rather richly constituted, herself. Separated from any of her classmates at Radcliffe and Johns Hopkins by barriers of religion, sex, and appetite, she proceeded to outshine them all from an ocean away. With the inner pluck of her Melanctha or black Teresa, she found new ways to clear the dense stubble of Victorian piety.

Over the main entrance to the Lillie Auditorium of the Marine Biological Laboratory today hangs an enlarged photograph of "the big fat girl" on her collecting trip to Quisset. In the centennial year of 1988 she shared the place of honor with the founders of the MBL and with Jacques Loeb. The men are still remembered by official bronze tablets describing their achievements; Gertrude Stein's picture is that of the student looking around. If Loeb's tablet reminds us what it is that scientists discover, Stein's picture reminds us that our students frequently discover themselves.

Loeb and the mechanists were no less revolutionary than Stein and the cubists; both movements changed the rules of reason in the name of the twentieth century. In the years before 1914, mechanist and cubist alike marched under the banners of secular humanism to anthems of the machine. Both groups set out to control life, to re-create it, content no longer to remain in tune with its laws. The mechanistic conception of life meant that in the new century science would be in the business of forming life in the dish. Writing to Ernst Mach in 1890, Loeb announced the mechanist's program: "The idea is now hovering before me that man himself can act as creator even in living nature, forming it eventually according to his will." We would call that enterprise biotechnology. A century later, products of our biological revolution— the army of molecules that James feared—flow in growing numbers from lab bench to bedside. Each molecule is like every other, each made according to will, each dictated by the language of the genes and written in short, repetitive sequences: TAA, now TATAA, now now TAAATAAT, now TAAT!

Stein had chimed in half a century ago: "The characteristic thing of the twentieth century was the idea of production in a series, that one thing should be like every other thing, and that it should be alike and quantities of them" (*Paris, France*).

From drugs to genes, from soup to nuts, our century has

made things like every other thing and quantities of them. The writer to whom a rose is a rose is a rose would have appreciated a machine to which DNA is DNA is DNA or, for that matter, a painter who tells us that a can is a can is a can. Wendy Steiner has called attention to an interview with Andy Warhol in which he told his interviewer, "I think everybody should be a machine. I think everybody should be like everybody . . . because you do the same thing every time. You do it over and over again."

As Stein and Loeb foresaw, the twentieth century has made it possible to create living things at will, each cell like every other cell and quantities of them. We can do it over and over again; we call the process "tissue culture" and its study "cell biology." The students who collect creatures at Quisset today are cell biologists who can read from ctenophore and human cells the same short palindromes of DNA.

The victories of mechanist and cubist might be considered a mixed blessing. In science, our mastery of animate nature has given us tools with which to solve the cipher of genes, the floor plan of cells, and the wiring of our nerves. We have just begun to treat cancer, to stop heart attacks, to cool terrors of the mind. As for the arts, we have lived in the century of Picasso, Stravinsky, and Brecht. But those of the reductionist persuasion cannot escape the nastier fallout of our revolution. Our culture cannot be said to have grown uniformly richer after the coming of Stein and the cubists; we now have Mamet instead of Ibsen and soup cans instead of Renoir. Our writers have so pared serious literature that it is read by very few; our serious composers have so trimmed their measures that a generation is deaf from the tribal chants of rock music; we are so used to having machines tell us stories that our most popular tales are told by comic-strip heroes. God may be dead, but Batman lives.

Our reductionist science is in the dock for less trivial reasons; we have undergone what William James called "the great initiation" into the game of guilt. We cannot escape blame for the fouling of our environment, the anomie of our cities, the commercialization of research, and the pedantry of learning. More darkly still, we remember each August on Hiroshima day the most destructive outcome of a mechanistic physics. Adherents of a mechanistic biology have yet to devise a morality that can protect us from that sort of mischief.

But remembering Stein the student and Loeb the teacher of the MBL ten decades ago, one is struck by the generous impulses that energized their work. The aims of that mechanistic conception were the control of life in order to understand it and cure its ills, the reduction of life's blooming, buzzing confusion to the manageable laws of chemistry and physics, and the divorce of biology from the doctrines of vitalism or theism that had been used to justify rank and bigotry. Indeed, the tribute Stein paid to Picasso could be paid her and Loeb as well:

> A creator is contemporary, he understands what is contemporary when the contemporaries do not yet know it, but he is contemporary and as the twentieth century is a century which sees the earth as no one has ever seen it, the earth has a splendor that it never had, and as everything destroys itself in the twentieth century and nothing continues, so then the twentieth century has a splendor which is its own and [they are] of this century, [they have] that strange quality of an earth that one has never seen and of things destroyed as they have never been destroyed as they have never been destroyed. (*Picasso*)

7

Inflammation:
From Khartoum to Casablanca

Redness and swelling with heat and pain—*rubor et tumor cum calore et dolore*—have been recognized as the four cardinal signs of inflammation since the writings of Cornelius Celsus in the first century of the common era (30 B.C.–A.D. 38). Celsus—who is sometimes mistaken for the Celsius of thermometry— was describing not disease but the normal response of wounded flesh. For most of history, wounds tended to get infected, and therefore it is not surprising that our ancestors handed down defenses not only against cuts but also against microbes. The drab Darwinism of biology suggests that whereas inflammation may help the individual cope with cuts and bruises, most of the redness and swelling with heat and pain is there to make sure that our species is not wiped out by microbial epidemics. Cuts and bruises hurt the one, pandemics kill the many. Our lavish arsenal of host defenses cannot have been stocked against such recent threats as ionizing radiation, Saturday-night specials, overturned tractor-trailers, or freebased cocaine. From Celsus to complement, the more we learn about inflammation, the simpler its message becomes: our cells and humors defend the self against invisible armies of the other. We call our losses infection and our victories immunity. It has occurred to me that the language we use to describe this conflict owes less to biology than to the rhetoric of our times, more to politics than to pathology.

That inflammation is a kind of warfare between men and bacteria was not appreciated until the "microbe hunters" of the nineteenth century recognized the opposing forces and order of battle. By 1908, when the Nobel Prize was given to Paul Ehrlich for his work on humoral immunity (antibodies) and to Élie Metchnikoff for his work on cellular immunity (phagocytosis), it had become clear that we mammals use antibodies and cells in concert to identify and destroy invaders. Metchnikoff's phagocytes were able to run and eat (we call these functions chemotaxis and phagocytosis) because Ehrlich's antibodies told receptor molecules on the cell that there were strangers at the gate. The language that announced the discovery was that of Darwinian survival:

> When the aggressor in this struggle is much smaller than its adversary the result is that the former introduces itself into the body of the latter and destroys it by means of infection. . . . But infection also has its counter. The attacked organism defends itself against the little aggressor. It protects itself by interposing a resistant membrane, or it uses all the means at its disposal to destroy the invader.
>
> (*Immunity in Infective Diseases*)

The tendency to couch descriptions of inflammation in terms of nineteenth-century battle has proved irresistible. Indeed, the assumptions of the microbe hunters were based not only on models of Darwinian zoology but also on the military legends of the nation-state. Here the distinguished pathologist Joseph McFarland sums up the field of inflammation from Rudolf Virchow to Vali Menkin:

> To many, the situation here encountered resembles a battlefield on which the leukocytes meet the invading bacteria and contest their further increase and invasion until they triumph, and, the infection overcome, the inflammation subsides.
>
> (*Cyclopedia of Medicine, Surgery and Specialties*)

The microbe hunters drew their images of battle from romantic accounts of set battles waged more often than not by British

troops against lesser breeds. Those imperial campaigns were
directed by generals who viewed the destruction of foreigners
through the lenses of binoculars. One catches the whiff of inflammation in this account, by John Bowle, of Kitchener's revenge
for the uprising in the Sudan that killed the noble Gordon in
1896:

> The campaign culminated in the battle of Omdurman . . .
> when some 60,000 of the Khalifa's horde flung them-
> selves with superb courage against Kitchener's line, to be
> mowed down by machine guns, rifles and artillery. . . . By
> 11:30 a.m. Kitchener handed his binoculars to an *aide
> de camp*, remarked that the enemy had had a "thorough
> dusting" and ordered the advance on Omdurman and
> Khartoum. The victory had cost 48 killed, including
> 3 British officers and 25 other ranks, and 434 wounded,
> as against over 11,000 "dervish" dead and about 16,000
> wounded and prisoners. Gordon had been more than
> avenged; the British and Egyptian flags again floated
> over Khartoum, and when, at the service of thanksgiving
> the troops sang "Abide with Me," Gordon's favorite
> hymn, even Kitchener was seen to weep.
>
> (*The Imperial Achievement*)

Substitute "endothelium" for "line," replace "machine guns,
rifles and artillery" with "macrophages, leukocytes, and fixatives
(antibodies)," and we can appreciate that the language in which
the nineteenth century learned how white corpuscles deal with
microbes is the language that described how white troops disposed of dervishes. Metchnikoff, Ehrlich, Cohnheim, and Adami
peered through microscope lenses to watch battalions of white
cells avenge the revolt of microbes. Caught in the Victorian
structures of hierarchy, the gentle scholar Metchnikoff taught the
lesson of Darwinian phylogeny from the evidence of phagocytosis
in this way:

The diapedesis of the white corpuscles, their migration though the vessel wall . . . is one of the principal means of defense possessed by an animal. As soon as the infective agents have penetrated into the body, a whole army of white corpuscles proceeds towards the menaced spot, there entering into a struggle with the micro-organisms. The leukocytes, having arrived at the spot where the intruders are found, seize them after the manner of the Amoeba and within their bodies subject them to intracellular digestion.

Metchnikoff was not the only champion of white corpuscles; we owe their classification as basophils, eosinophils, and neutrophils to Ehrlich's doctoral thesis on aniline dyes. Blue, red, and white colors on the microscope slide depended on the way in which positive or negative charges on molecules lined up in the granules of the white cell; aniline dyes marked the combatants as clearly as red or blue tunics identified cavalry units in the Franco-Prussian War of 1870. Indeed, aniline dyes were the response of German synthetic chemistry to French control of the colonies that supplied natural dyestuffs. Ehrlich's studies with dyes—which introduced to hematology the language of colors and fixation—helped Germany become the arsenal of chemotherapy and had the happy side effect of launching immunochemistry. Ehrlich's dictum, *"Corpora non agunt nisi fixata"* ("Bodies that do not attach do not act"), was the basis not only for the first treatment of syphilis—Salvarsan—but also for modern ligand-receptor theory. That theory explains, for example, how the AIDS virus attaches to discrete receptors on the cells of immunity. It might be argued that Ehrlich's doctrine also applies directly to the means whereby cells of the bloodstream—white cells and platelets—stick to vessel walls and to each other in the course of inflammation.

Central to the humoral theories of Ehrlich and the cellular ones of Metchnikoff was the late-Victorian conviction that the body would not injure itself wittingly. The nation-states of Europe placed their faith in the social doctrine of Darwinian survival, convinced that the self-interest of each nation coincided with the welfare of each citizen; in like fashion, the microbe hunters were sure that the body had a *horror autotoxicus*—an incapacity to turn the tools of defense into weapons of self-destruction. Time and events have reversed that nineteenth-century conviction. The bad news of the twentieth century—from Flanders fields to the fall of Paris, from the Siege of Madrid to Tiananmen Square, from the Battle of Algiers to the mess in Beirut—has added anxiety to the orderly prose of biology. Nowadays, when we speak of inflammation, we speak of unplanned mischief, as Lewis Thomas does here:

> I suspect that the host is caught up in mistaken, inappropriate, and unquestionably self-destructive mechanisms by the very multiplicity of defenses available to him, defenses which do not seem to have been designed to operate in net coordination with each other. The end result is not defense, it is an agitated, committee-directed, harum-scarum effort to make war, with results that are remarkably like those sometimes observed in human affairs when war-making institutions pretend to be engaged in defense. If, to push the analogy, there were no limit to the number of people who could set off for northern Minnesota at the season of the great fly-over of geese and no limit on the type and power of the weapons to be used by each, we would undoubtedly observe . . . with M-16s, howitzers, SAM missiles, lasers, and perhaps tactical nuclear rockets, considerably more destruction of people than geese, of host than invader.
>
> *("Adaptive Aspects of Inflammation")*

One might trace the sea change in our opinion of all that redness and swelling with heat and pain, the change in our belief that inflammation is benign, to the first Great War of this century. It may not be a complete coincidence that the terms "allergy," "anaphylaxis," and "serum sickness" began to crowd the clinical literature while the medical profession was preparing the national armies of Europe for slaughter in the trenches of 1914. The immunologists of Europe had come to understand that cells could respond to inflammation as readily by revolt as by enlistment. Soon, the grinding offensives of the First World War had succeeded not only in trimming the rhetoric of battle of operatic glamour but also in striking the set of nationalism. Class struggle began to dissolve the ties of patriotism as the effects of that war of attrition spread over Europe. By 1918, it was apparent that the war had dismantled the ceremonies of class on which the Victorian nation-state had relied. The captains and the kings had killed each other off, leaving corporals to rule a diminished world. Ford Madox Ford recognized the changing of the guard in *Parade's End* (1922):

> He was devising the ceremonial for the disbanding of a Kitchener battalion. . . . Well the end of the show was to be; the adjutant would stand the battalion at ease; the band would play Land of Hope and Glory, and then the adjutant would say: There will be no more parades. . . . For there won't. . . . No more Hope, no more Glory, no more parades for you and me any more. Not for the country . . . nor for the world, I dare say. . . . None . . . Gone . . . No . . . More . . . parades!

Carrying forward the analogy that I have drawn between the language of politics and that of biology, I might observe that science in the 1920s and 1930s learned about histamine, serotonin, enzymes, and peptides—widely diffused mediators of inflammation —as the nations learned about other rapidly spreading mediators of inflammation: Fascism, National Socialism, and Stalinism. Biologists were taught by Sir Henry Dale and Sir Thomas Lewis that our very own cells can synthesize and release chemicals as disabling to the organism as any toxin released by microbes. That unpleasant lesson coincided with one of the few points of doctrine agreed on by parties of both right and left: that the body politic of bourgeois democracy carried the seeds of its own destruction. No longer were differences among people drawn by national borders alone; to the separations of class were added the divisions of ideology. Again, it may be no accident that we learned about shock lung and the crush syndrome (now attributed at least in part to activation of anaphylatoxins in the circulation) from Loyalist surgeons in the Spanish Civil War. That rehearsal for the world war against Fascism reached a stalemate at the medical school in Madrid in November 1936:

> Hours of artillery and aerial bombardment, in which neither side gave way, were succeeded by hand-to-hand battles for single rooms or floors of buildings. In the Clinical Hospital, the Thaelmann Battalion [of the International Brigades] placed bombs in the lifts to be sent up to explode in the faces of the Moroccans [of the Franco forces] on the next floor. And, in the next building, the Moroccans suffered losses by eating inoculated animals kept for experimental purposes.
>
> (Hugh Thomas, *The Spanish Civil War*)

Nevertheless, until the civil warfare in Madrid, it had been clear on which side of the battle line each soldier stood. But in Madrid the Fascists boasted of a "fifth column"—secret right-wing partisans who would join with the four regular columns of Franco troops to conquer the republic. "Right" and "left," "Communist" and "Fascist," these terms had a generally accepted meaning of sorts. Yet when the Second World War came and the Germans occupied most of Europe, even those boundaries became blurred. Distinctions among classes, ideologies, nationalities, religions, and genders became most confused, and especially so in the colonies of France occupied by the Germans. A model of this confused state was the mind of André Gide in the Tunis of 1943.

Gide—the gay ex-Communist litterateur, friend of de Gaulle and Malraux on the one hand and of cultivated Germans on the other—here records in his journal the advance of American troops on the German-occupied town:

> Several trustworthy farmers confirm the lamentable, absurd retreat of the American forces before the semblance of German opposition. The sudden appearance of a handful of resolute men forced the withdrawal of those who, very superior in numbers and equipment, would have had only to continue their advance to become masters of their objective . . . Tunis.
>
> Germans everywhere. Well turned-out, in becoming uniforms, young, vigorous, strapping, jolly, clean-shaven, with pink cheeks . . . Can there be a more wretched humanity than the one I see here? One wonders what God could ever possibly come forth from these sordid creatures, bent over toward the most immediate satisfactions, tattered, dusty, abject, and forsaken by the future. Walking among them in the heart of the Arab town, I looked in vain for a likable face on which to pin some hope: Jews, Moslems, south Italians, Sicilians, or Maltese, accumulated scum as if it were thrown up along the current of clear water.
>
> (*Journals*, IV)

From a similar matrix of "accumulated scum" and "jolly" Germans, Hollywood distilled *Casablanca*. That tough tearjerker set the measure of language for my generation. Listen to any line of its crisp dialogue, and beneath the brusque patter you can pick out the anthems of the fervent Old Left. The Popular Front, having been defeated in France, sputtered to life on a Warner Bros. back lot. *Casablanca* made sense; since then, wars have been muddled. Redness and swelling with heat and pain seemed to be the cardinal emotions of *Casablanca*, and since Bogey was the last hero we could trust, we were sure that its passions were worthwhile. But in the dreary half-century since the film, we have learned to distrust our leaders, our heroes, and our wars. We have gotten very good only at rounding up the usual suspects.

The muddle extends to science. We have isolated and defined more potent substances of inflammation: the components of complement, the kinins, and the prostaglandins. But we have been disappointed to find that our own cells and fluids collaborate with hostile invaders to release these. Sometimes such Quislings and Lavals turn on us in the absence of an enemy. In exposing the treasons of lymphocytes, we have come to view them as a cast of Levantine characters. In our film-derived discourse, Peter Lorre supports the "contrasuppressor" cell, and Sydney Greenstreet draws a check on the bursa of Fabricius. Controlled by a network of codes—could we call the signals of genetics anything else?—the alliance of inflammatory cells shifts, their affinities wane; wounds heal but scars remain.

The new synthesis makes only superficial sense. Unlike "La Marseillaise" in *Casablanca*, the humors of immunity fail to raise our spirits. Our psyches are depressed by the products of inflammation; we have learned that the battle cries of injury (interleukins, interferons, tumor necrosis factor) make us febrile, debilitated, sleepy, and cross even as they arouse battalions of lymphocytes. Related molecules activate the troops of defense: phagocytes, which wear receptors on their sleeves as if they were the armbands of local resistance. Paul Henreid leads the forces of the immune interior, where they are annihilated by a retrovirus.

But in this postbacterial world, the phagocytes fail, white cells do damage, our antibodies form complexes (the very coin of neuroses) and plug vessels to our vital organs. In the course of these confused responses, much harm is done and resolution is not invariably achieved. Every few years we add a new felon to the list of usual suspects: substance P, anti-idiotypes, leukotrienes, lipoxins, and the appropriately named free radicals.

Since the beginning of the cold war we speak the language of neither war nor peace; we can no longer decide if our tissues are entirely inflamed or partially immune. In the discourse of politics and of science, we have replaced defined suspects with uncertain suspicions. In that sense, the high sentiment of *Casablanca* has yielded to the flat affect of the spy story, such as Elliot West's *The Night Is a Time for Listening:*

> A courier gets hit on the head—not by the opposition, but by some cheap crook who never saw him before and is just after his wallet. The goods you've waited for never get there and a whole mission is scratched. . . .
>
> "You want it to work don't you? What could be better than if she's part of the cover? That's one they'll really never dream of."
>
> "To be an agent," Disa said to herself sadly. "On the other side this time," Darsos said, turning to her. "Bear that in mind."

The affect of our new molecular biology is—like Norfolk—very flat. We have just learned that the hierarchy of genes is controlled by runs of DNA (called homeoboxes), which do not set us apart from fruit flies. Rejecting Darwin's notion that we are at the pinnacle of earlier forms of life, we now believe that we are nothing more glamorous than mute vectors of selfish genes. All the signals of chromosomes seem to be able to work "on the other side this time." Every codon has an anticodon; every strand of DNA can be read for sense in one direction and perhaps even greater sense in the other. We have been assured (by Smith, Bost, and Blacock in the *Journal of Immunology*) that

> assuming each individual has a proteinaceous receptor for all ligands (both peptide and nonpeptide), then the complementarity of nucleic acids and the aforementioned pattern in the genetic code dictates the potential for an endogenous peptide recognition unit. These peptide rec-ognition units in turn may be thought of as endogenous

homologues of all ligands of antigens. Individuals, then, are a composite and a reflection of all universal shapes represented in the ligand or antigen repertoire to which they respond.

In other words, we recognize the invader—call him antigen, ligand, or Ishmael—and recognize him because we have his template in our genes, but "on the other side this time." We are told that we have seen the enemy, and he is coded on the cassettes of our genes in language a fruit fly can understand. Structures of language, structures of nucleic acids—capable of transcription, and betrayal. On either side, in any direction.

But stop! I'm not quite ready for that kind of diminished script just yet. No, I'm ready for that proud lump in my throat when I see that last shot of Bogart and Rains strolling off to Brazzaville to join the Free French. I want to hear the swelling music that plays at what could be the start of a beautiful friendship. I want to believe that all the redness and swelling with heat and pain is up to some good. Ingrid Bergman will be there, waiting to heal the wound. And still on the same side, our side, this time.

8

Hay on the Vineyard:
The American Revolution in Art

Then there is the story of a great shipping magnate who is close to death on his own Mediterranean island. He calls his three sons to the bedside as he is about to dictate his last will and testament. He turns to the eldest and asks: "Is there anything in particular that you wish me to leave to you from among my many possessions?"

"Well, Father, we are all very well taken care of. We already have lots of money and our shares in the business. But since you're good enough to ask, I *would* like some of the extra houses: the villa at Antibes, the hunting lodge in Wyoming, the flat in Mayfair."

"Very well, my boy, you shall have them," says the father, and calls the next older son, of whom he asks the same question.

The son replies: "As my brother said, you have been generous enough; but I would like something a bit more personal to remember you by. I'd like the cars we all love so well: the Rolls, the Caddies, the Bugatti."

"Very well, my son, you shall enjoy them," says the father, and calls the youngest son, who responds:

"Dad, you've been terrific. I have enough money to buy all the cars and houses and everything. You don't have to leave me anything special."

"But son, isn't there anything that you've ever wanted, that I failed to give you?"

"No, Pop, I've got everything."

"Wasn't there anything that I never gave you when you were a little boy—anything at all?"

The youngest son scratches his head for a minute and then smiles. "Well, Dad, you never bought me a Mickey Mouse outfit!"

The tycoon turns to his lawyer: "Buy him the Veterans Administration."

The Veterans Administration may indeed qualify as a Mickey Mouse outfit with respect to red tape, but it runs a hospital system of remarkably high quality. As a result of enlightened postwar policy, most VA hospitals are closely affiliated with medical schools. With minor exceptions, therefore, the medicine that is practiced and the research that is carried on at VA hospitals is clearly at university level. At the Manhattan VA hospital, where I consult in rheumatology, good clinical medicine is enhanced by a cadre of scientists whose work is up to the minute in fields that range from genetic polymorphism to arachidonic-acid oxidation. What is really Mickey Mouse about the Manhattan VA hospital is what you see, not what you get: the place is a Disneyland of decor, a junkheap of government art.

Built during the Eisenhower years, the hospital is a drab high-rise set diagonally on an urban plot. Its highest floors seem to have developed a brick hernia of balconies, while its lower floors have grown tumors of the wing. The inside of the building is worse in aspect than the outside; the interior decor—so to speak—follows modern practice in hospital design by disguising the public areas as a bus terminal in Havana. In the hospital, crackpot decorators take yearly swipes at the walls with supergraphics or pastel stripes. These have all but effaced the staid corridors of the 1950s, whose walls were tiled and olive drab and hung with examples of WPA art of the 1930s and 1940s.

New Art has displaced the old. There seems to be room in the VA budget for bright, once trendy prints: right now the decorators are high on Peter Max. By and large I miss the old WPA-like prints, the scenes of rural America by John Steuart Curry or Grant Wood, the cityscapes of Edward Hopper or Armin Landeck. Over the years, I had become quite fond of a reproduction of Thomas Hart Benton's *July Hay* of 1943, which hung in one of

T. H. BENTON, *July Hay*. Metropolitan Museum of Art, New York.

J. POLLOCK, *Autumn Rhythm*. Metropolitan Museum of Art, New York.

the corridors of the medical wards I visit each week. Aside from its formal values—the painting is an icon of the American regionalist movement—it promised summer and sunshine on February days when dirty snow hit the New York streets. But a short while ago this fading print was replaced by Jackson Pollock's *Autumn Rhythm* of 1950. To my eye both are stunning pictures. The two figures in the Benton canvas, as much an action painting as the Pollock, are in the middle of a palpable swirl of form and pigment: Benton's farmers and Pollock's drips of paint engage our interest equally. Once we recognize it as a regionalist painting of the New York School, the Pollock may be seen to be as much an advertisement for America as the Benton. But a stranger to these pictures, on first seeing the Pollock on the VA wall where the Benton had hung, might well conclude that the abstraction had been painted on another planet. And in one sense it *was* painted on another planet: America after the Second World War, after the Holocaust, after Hiroshima. Separated by less than a decade in time, the two paintings are also separated by the American revolution in art.

As I looked at the abstraction on the VA wall, it occurred to me that whereas Benton is probably unknown outside the United States, nowadays educated folks from Kyoto to Marseilles would be able to spot *Autumn Rhythm* as a Pollock. What irony! Benton and the regionalists wanted to put American art on the world map by reverting to native scenes, whereas Pollock and the abstract expressionists turned their backs on subject matter and established an international style. Art since 1950 has been born in America. Most of the paintings—European as well as American—that hang on the walls of the VA hospital are by now familiar products of the American revolution in art. How appropriate it all seemed, for it is thanks to a similar revolution in American biomedical research that in routine fashion nearby labs at the VA hospital were measuring enzymes in blood and mapping human genes. Both revolutions took place between 1940 and 1960.

After rounds, I began to leaf through the biographical chapters in *Annual Review of Biochemistry* and *Transactions of the Association of American Physicians*. These led to the kinds of hypotheses that only a cultural historian might venture or a brash amateur propose. At any rate, from my box seat at the biological revolution and the bleachers of the one in art, it looks as if they share at least three features in common.

In the first place, both American biomedical science and American painting are based on strong native traditions that have generally valued empiric results over the claims of theory. In painting, our history has been written by the Hudson River School (George Inness, Asher Durand), the luminists (Fitz Hugh Lane, Martin Johnson Heade), the Philadelphia realists (Thomas Eakins, Samuel Murray), and the American impressionists (Mary Cassatt, Childe Hassam); in biology, one thinks of the geneticists (Thomas Hunt Morgan, Hermann Muller, George Beadle, Edward Tatum), of the chemists (Robert Woodward, Linus Pauling), or the renal physiologists (Alfred Newton Richards, Homer Smith). Each tradition set the stage for what in another context the historian

Crane Brinton has called a "revolution of rising expectations," a revolution that transformed our national motifs into a worldwide movement.

Second, our art and our science were each supported by an enlightened act of government. The cadres who went on to found abstract expressionism were supported by Roosevelt's WPA and its Federal Art Project; the fledglings of molecular biology were trained by intra- and extramural support from the National Institutes of Health during the Eisenhower years. Students of art *and* of science were supported by the GI Bill; after the war I shared laboratory space with ex-paratroopers and studio space with former Marines. Nowadays, when even our presidents teach us to distrust the acts of central government, we ought not to ignore those old success stories of social democracy.

The final ingredient was added from Europe. As a result of Hitler's crimes, the United States gained some of the Continent's more inventive painters and scientists. Artists with unique outlooks from many countries found a place to work and to teach; New York accommodated newcomers with styles as divergent as those of Piet Mondrian and Salvador Dalí, Amédée Ozenfant and Max Ernst. The sciences were enriched in all branches; in biochemistry alone, America gained—among others—Rudolf Schoenheimer, Konrad Bloch, Fritz Lipmann, Carl and Gerty Cori, and Severo Ochoa. The removal to America of this innovative group shifted the center of creative gravity to the New World. Before Hitler, it was customary for Americans of scientific bent to do a tour in one of the great research universities of Germany or Austria. Before Pétain, American art students served time in the ateliers of Paris. In the postwar period, the traffic was reversed; our laboratories and studios have schooled a new generation of Europe's best artists and scientists.

The switch from Benton to Pollock on the VA hospital wall had other overtones. Although *July Hay* looks as if it might be the quintessential painting of the American Midwest, it was actually painted on Martha's Vineyard, where Benton spent his summers.

The vegetation in the foreground is the wild grape and rose of New England, not of Missouri. And it was on Martha's Vineyard in the mid-thirties that Jackson Pollock himself served as a model in many of the best-known of Benton's regionalist paintings. Pollock was a student of Benton's in New York and spent five summers working as a kind of handyman in a shack on Benton's Vineyard property. He made no secret of coveting Benton's wife, Rita, and both Bentons remained in his thoughts. Looking back on those days in the course of a 1950s interview, Pollock said, "I'm damn grateful to Tom. He drove his kind of realism at me so hard I bounced into non-objective painting." But the story is not so simple; the revolution of the abstract expressionists had other roots.

In 1950, when the new movement had not yet swept the field, Meyer Schapiro complained that America had produced no artist comparable to the great French modernists (Picasso, Braque, Matisse), nor for that matter comparable to our native men of letters: "There is no Melville or Whitman or James among our painters. . . . In the generation of modernists born since 1900, the leading Americans stand on the same plane as the best of the Europeans: a less gifted group than their revolutionary elders." Schapiro rendered his verdict a generation after modern art crossed the Atlantic for the first time. In the great Armory Show of 1913, Americans had encountered the new postimpressionism of Cézanne, the cubism of Braque and Picasso, the fauvism of Matisse, the futurism of Picabia. Schapiro describes that show and its message for Americans:

> The plan of the show contained then a lesson and a program of modernity. It was also a lesson of internationalism, although the emblem of the show was the native pine, a reminder of the American Revolution as well as of the eternal greenness of the tree of art. Since the awareness of modernity as the advancing historical present was forced upon the spectator by the art of Spaniards, Frenchmen,

Russians, Germans, Englishmen and Americans, of whom
many were working in Paris, away from their native lands,
this moment belonged to the whole world; Europe and
America were now united in a common cultural destiny,
and people here and abroad were experiencing the same
modern art that surmounted local traditions.

That upbeat, cosmopolitan spirit was soon dissolved in the passions of the First World War; American modernism survived by
and large in the enclaves of Greenwich Village and among the
associates of that remarkable dealer, photographer, and publicist
Alfred Stieglitz. His sparkling group included Charles Demuth,
Marsden Hartley, John Marin, and Georgia O'Keeffe—Stieglitz's
wife. The cold eye of modern criticism shows that paintings of
the Stieglitz group in the twenties were really only slighter versions of cubist and futurist originals. Marin painted Manhattan
skyscrapers in the planes of Robert Delaunay's Eiffel Tower and
New England seascapes as enlargements of Cézanne still lifes.
But before the attention of the Stieglitz group was drawn to other
parts of the country, these New York artists had opened American
eyes to the new industrial scene: a manmade landscape that
included smokestack and skyscraper, Third Avenue El and Brooklyn Bridge. On the one hand, their vision of the busy city was later
fused with the cool modernism of the precisionists (Charles Sheeler,
Niles Spencer, Louis Lozowick). On the other, the cityscapes of
Marin and O'Keeffe influenced a generation of "proletarian"
artists in the thirties. Each of these urban strains—carrying with
it the whiff of the immigrant—was at odds with a major thrust of
American culture in the twenties and thirties.

The modernism of the Stieglitz group and of the precisionists
ran afoul of a growing nativist trend. America, having rejected the
League of Nations as it had rejected Woodrow Wilson, turned
inward to its own concern. Hemmed in by Prohibition and behind
high tariff walls (does anyone still remember the names Smoot
and Hawley?), the land of Edgar Guest and Booth Tarkington

cultivated its splendid garden. In this environment Thomas Hart Benton stopped dabbling with the modernism of Paris and assumed the task of "returning American painting to its people."

Benton painted the first regionalist picture in 1926. It shows a craggy couple at a table on which a skimpy meal has been placed, which they ignore; behind them a sampler assures us that "The Lord Is My Shepherd." Perhaps to declare his withdrawal from the Babel of European modernism, Benton used two deaf-mutes as his models. George and Sabrina West, neighbors of Benton's, were members of a remarkable group of the heritably deaf whose ancestors had migrated to Martha's Vineyard in colonial times. (The genetics and medical anthropology of

T. H. BENTON, *The Lord Is My Shepherd.*
Whitney Museum of American Art, New York.

this island group—and its tolerant acceptance by the unimpaired—
has been well described in Nora Ellen Groce's recent book *Everyone
Here Spoke Sign Language.*)

The sign language of Benton and the regionalists was not
hard to read. It spelled out the nativist rejection of modernism, a
call for a return to American rural values, an appeal to the silence
of self and soil. Personal restraint—the containment of glance and
gesture—has been a major theme in Protestant art since Lucas
Cranach. By the time Grant Wood came to paint *American Gothic*
in 1930, it had become clear to the art world that everyone here
spoke the sign language of nativism. Encouraged by critics, American regionalists took up the battle with Paris. Lloyd Goodrich
argued in *The New York Times* in 1929: "As a corrective to the
indiscriminate worship of the judgement of Paris there is no
harm in reminding ourselves occasionally that there is such a
thing as native quality in art and that the way of artistic growth
may very well lie in the development of this quality rather than
the pursuit of the latest word."

But painters of the nativist stripe were not content with
the simple celebration of the midwestern sky at noon or the
coasts of Maine in summer; they also went on to document the
alienating effects of the city. Edward Hopper's coffee shops and
street corners cannot be said to constitute a hymn to the buzzing
city of tomorrow. But perhaps the most explicit critique of the
life of the city can be found in murals that Benton painted for
the Whitney Museum and the New School for Social Research.
In these, the city is seen as through the eyes of Gilgamesh, to
whom the town is a great foreign whore. The man of nature is
at risk in this polyglot city. Patterning his style as much on the
expansive Mexican muralists as on his usual mannerist models,
Benton drew rude caricatures of city types: bearded intellectuals,
"pansy critics," Communists, stockbrokers with beaked noses,
and drunken women at bars with pimps. Benton's longtime
friend and associate Thomas Craven joined the attack on modernism in his 1934 *Modern Art.* Craven's point of view would not
have been out of place in the Berlin or Rome of the thirties:

Stieglitz, a Hoboken Jew without knowledge of, or interest in, the historical American background, was, quite apart
from the purified art he had swallowed—hardly equipped
for the leadership of a genuine American expression; and
it is a matter of record that none of the artists whose
names and work he has exploited have been notably
American in flavor. All have had talent; some like Marin
or O'Keeffe a touch of genius; but their abilities, for the
most part have performed in a vacuum.... But of late
years, Stieglitz's prestige has steadily declined. In spirit,
his present gallery, An American Place, is ... alien to the
current drive for an explicitly native art. The new trend in
painting, following Benton's pioneering example, is toward
strong representation and clear meanings which may be
shared and verified by large groups of people and in this
movement the elusive apparitions of the Stieglitz group
have no function.

With Benton of *July Hay* dominating the American scene in the
country, and an attenuated modernism on view in the city, what
brought Jackson Pollock of Wyoming to the revolution? Two
major influences of European origin seem to have precipitated
the break: the automatism of the surrealists and the abstractions
of Hans Hofmann.

Gertrude Stein had investigated automatism as a clue to
hysteria. Pollock was drawn to it possibly because of his own
volatile temperament (a euphemism for a mood disorder and
violent alcoholism). He may have been attracted to other aspects
of the irrational for similar reasons; he simultaneously became
an automatist and a theosophist and Rosicrucian. André Breton,
author of the surrealist manifesto of 1924, defined automatism
as intending to "express, verbally, in writing, or by other means,
the real process of thought. Thought's dictation, in the absence
of all control exercised by reason and outside all aesthetic or
moral preoccupation." It should not surprise us that a school of
painting grounded on "the absence of all control exercised by

reason" and formulated in response to the First World War had powerful appeal for an agitated Jackson Pollock in the midst of the Second.

By 1941, the surrealists had arrived en masse to enliven the New York scene: Breton himself, André Masson, Matta, Dalí, and Ernst. Ernst's wife, Peggy Guggenheim, opened an influential gallery where many of the surrealists and early abstract expressionists met and where many were given their first shows. The earliest convert in New York to the surrealist side was Arshile Gorky, whose abstractions form a link between the automatism of the surrealists and the conscious daubs of action painting. Gorky was ravished by those aspects of the surrealist process which permitted him to react to "thought's dictation" by a kind of reflex calligraphy. Perhaps his finest work—painted in response to his own cancer and before his suicide—is appropriately entitled *Agony*.

Schapiro said of Gorky: "Here in New York, the surrealists of the Old World found their last original disciple." But Gorky was not their last disciple; that title belongs to Hans Hofmann. In the New World, the surrealists had already acquired that grand veteran of the European art wars. Hofmann had worked with the Delaunays in Paris and become a master teacher of abstraction in Munich. In his sixties during the 1940s, he had been painting and teaching in the United States since the mid-1930s. Indeed, Benton and Hofmann were teachers and Pollock was a student at the Art Students League of New York in the 1930s; few institutions in Europe were that eclectic. Each of the three was a hero to one or another of my classmates when as an adolescent I studied painting there a decade later.

Hofmann, as he had in Munich, soon established himself as a formidable teacher, opening schools in New York and Provincetown. One of his students was the talented Lee Krasner, who was to become Pollock's wife. Pollock and Krasner persuaded Peggy Guggenheim to visit Hofmann's studio and to give him his long-overdue first solo show. By March 1944, then, there were in place all the ingredients of the American revolution

A. GORKY, *Agony*. Museum of Modern Art, New York.

in art. Its first patron was both an heiress of American enterprise and the wife of a European surrealist. Pollock was from Wyoming and had married a New Yorker. Lee Krasner had studied with Hofmann in Provincetown while Pollock had studied with Benton on the Vineyard. Pollock had come to surrealism by way of Gorky the Armenian, and both had been employed by the Federal Art Project of the WPA. Meanwhile, in the world that was not "outside all moral preoccupation" American armies were preparing for the June invasion of France. D-day, June 6 of 1944, one might suggest, was the moment when the hegemony of France in art was ended.

The relationship of European masters and spirited American disciples reminds me of similar relationships in biomedical

research. As a young postdoctoral fellow in the 1950s, I listened to brilliant debates at the Enzyme Club in New York. Distinguished émigrés were dispersed among equally distinguished
American-born scientists from Columbia, New York University,
the Rockefeller Institute, and Cornell. One listened to discussions that featured Efraim Racker and Severo Ochoa, William
H. Stein and Stanford Moore, Fritz Lipmann and Erwin Chargaff,
Bernard Horecker and Vincent du Vigneau. It was a heady
time, because discoveries made by those men and their students
were about to transform not only the science of biochemistry
but also the practice of medicine. Thanks to that biological revolution launched after the war, thanks to the success of the
NIH concept, medicine is no longer engaged in the agelong, empiric
exchange of drugs for symptoms, but has become an effective
young science of its own. The debates of Danton and Marat at
the Cordeliers had no greater impact on who lived and who died.

The transactions of the Enzyme Club were not simply an
example of lettered Europeans giving the law to a lesser breed.
The young Americans were heir to their own strong tradition of
quantitative science; the Lineweaver-Burke plots of enzymology
and the Henderson-Hasselbach equations of physiology are native
products. Moreover, the American style of give-and-take changed
the way in which the émigré professors responded to new ideas.
Trained in laboratories for which the law of science was the word
of the professor, the émigrés adapted to the ready democracy of
the bull session while keeping the sense of *Ordnung* in which
they had been raised.

I am reminded of arguments over the citric-acid cycle of
metabolism when I read the exchange between Hofmann and
Pollock in 1942 (related by Cynthia Goodman in *Hans Hofmann:*

> Hofmann to Pollock: "You don't work from Nature. You
> work from the heart. This is no good. You will always
> repeat yourself."
> Pollock to Hofmann: "I *am* Nature."

H. HOFMANN, *Self-Portrait* (1942). André Emmerich Gallery, New York.

The reason I am reminded of biochemistry is that it was Hofmann—not Pollock—whose style changed most radically between 1942 and 1944: it was Hofmann who loosened up his abstractions by automatism and brush drippings. His encounters with the surrealists and with Pollock brought forth his finest work. So too did the European masters of biochemistry change their direction when they encountered the young Americans. Severo Ochoa, chairman of biochemistry for many years at NYU, won the Nobel

H. HOFMANN, *The Resurrection* (1948). André Emmerich Gallery, New York.

Prize not for the careful, traditional work on enzymes of the citric-acid cycle that he had begun in Europe, but for his innovative work on the assembly of RNA, an enterprise that flourished in the less hieratic laboratories of New York.

By 1950, there appeared a letter to Roland Redmont, president of the Metropolitan Museum of Art, to protest "provincialism" in his selection of contemporary American art. The artists picked by the museum represented the two main streams of the older tradition: rural regionalism and urban modernism. The protesters against the traditional included almost all of those who were at the time creating the American revolution in art: William Baziotes, Willem de Kooning, Adolph Gottlieb, Hans Hofmann, Robert Motherwell, Barnett Newman, Jackson Pollock, Richard Pousette-Dart, Ad Reinhardt, Mark Rothko, Clyfford Still, and Bradley Walker Tomlin. Baziotes, Pollock, Reinhardt, and Rothko had been supported by the WPA. In like fashion, the generation of biochemists and physicians whose work of the 1940s and 1950s earned for them the glittering prizes of Stockholm in the 1960s were trained either by the NIH itself or by its extramural programs.

Neither revolution has been entirely without its costs. I'm afraid that revolutions as successful as those of postwar painting and biochemistry tend to breed equally successful reactions. Abstract expressionism destroyed for a while a vital, representational tradition of American art that in modern times has produced talents as great as Mary Cassatt, Maurice Prendergast, James Whistler, and Louis Lozowick—and paintings as pleasure-giving as *July Hay*. Modern biochemical medicine has for too long persuaded its practitioners that patients are simply the sum of abnormal laboratory values. Too many of us now believe that when we understand the gene, we know the person.

But listen to a young Japanese biochemist in Rome or an Italian postdoc in Tokyo speaking the meliorist language of our genes in fluent American English, and you may not be displeased that two benign revolutions were made in America. Walk into any great museum from Houston to Minneapolis, from

L. LOZOWICK, *High Voltage*. Hirschl & Adler Gallery, New York.

Paris to Düsseldorf, and look at the shattering pink of a Rothko, the blue of a Motherwell, or the black of a Reinhardt; and you may come to believe that Meyer Schapiro was talking not only about the abstract revolution in painting when he assured us that:

> Looking back to the past, one may regret that painting now is not broader and fails to touch enough in our lives. The same may be said of representation, which, on the whole, lags behind abstract art in inventiveness and conviction; today it is abstract painting that stimulates artists to a freer approach to visible nature

and man. It has enlarged the means of the artist who represents and has opened to him regions of feeling and perception unknown before. Abstraction by its audacities also confirms and makes more evident to us the most daring and still unassimilated discoveries of older art.

9

Haussmann on Missiles

The scene is a caucus room of the House Office Building, where the Armed Services Committee is holding a hearing on the administration's seventeenth plan for deployment of the MX missile. The chairman, Harold ("Harry") Covair (D–Neb.), and the ranking minority member, Patrick ("Pat") A. N. Kroot (R–N.J.), are questioning a stocky man dressed in the heavy black of mid-nineteenth-century fashion.

REPRESENTATIVE COVAIR: For the record, would you state your name and position?

HAUSSMANN: Baron Georges Eugène Haussmann, prefect of the Seine from 1853 to 1870. At present, I am the chief advisor to Secretary Cheney on the important matter of urban redeployment.

COVAIR: And your professional qualifications for your role in the redeployment program are . . . ?

HAUSSMANN: I presided over the complete transformation of the face of Paris in the short period of a decade and a half. We destroyed over 20,000 old buildings and erected 40,000 new ones. We created new boulevards that traversed Paris east and west, north and south. These include much of the rue de Rivoli; the boulevards now called Sebastopol, St.-Michel, and Opéra; and those that radiate from the Étoile. We built the great pavilions of Les Halles, created such parks as the Bois de Boulogne and Bois de Vincennes, reconstructed the hideous sewers, and paved the streets with macadam, a

material named after John Loudon McAdam (1756–1836).
Without Mr. McAdam's discovery, we would be back in the
squalid Paris of Louis XVI! In the event, we relocated tens of
thousands of the poor of Paris from the center of the city to
newly annexed suburbs, where this rabble no longer posed
threats to health or public order. No other great city—not
London, Berlin, or Rome—ever underwent such a complete
change of face and population. In short, I founded the principle of urban redeployment.

REPRESENTATIVE KROOT: What were your reasons for carv-
ing those broad streets from the ancient neighborhoods of
your city? You didn't even have automobiles; it cannot have
been due to pressure of traffic.

HAUSSMANN: I began with the stated aim to disencumber the
large buildings, palaces, and barracks in such a way as to
make them more pleasing to the eye and to afford easier
access on days of celebration and a simplified defense on
days of riot. As I stated in my memoirs, I wanted "to assure
public peace by the creation of large boulevards that will
permit the circulation not only of light and air but also for
troops. Thus, by an ingenious combination the lot of the
people will be improved, and they will be rendered less
disposed to revolt."

Indeed, that is why, as Queen Victoria remarked on
her visit to our town, we covered the streets with macadam
"to prevent the people from taking up the pavement as
hitherto." An astute military observer will immediately appreciate how the boulevards provided straight fields of fire, and
we placed them strategically so that government forces could
easily turn the flank of a barricade. You must remember
that in 1830, in 1848, in 1851, and again in 1852, our
proletariat and rabblerousers threw up barricades of cobblestone against the government. We used urban redeployment
to protect us against the greatest threat to our security:
revolution from within.

KROOT: Thank you. We appreciate that you are qualified by your experience to help us with urban redeployment. Secretary Cheney has told the members of this committee that you are here with a new plan that will follow logically on the old report of former President Reagan's Commission on Strategic Forces, headed by Brent Scowcroft. General Scowcroft has brought it up again; he wants to move missiles around on trolleys. Would you tell us about *your* plan? What is it called, by the way?

HAUSSMANN: The Urban Redeployment Defense Union—URDU, for short.

COVAIR: I take it you quarrel with the recommendations that for economy's sake we should either plant the new MX missiles in existing Minuteman silos or move them about on trucks?

HAUSSMANN: I realize that these may be the only possible *political* solutions for your country. I personally would have preferred the old Scowcroft plan, which was more expensive and innovative. He proposed building a series of real and decoy missiles designed to roll on tracks that cover the territories of four of your states. That is the sort of grand, far-reaching plan of which a Haussmann would be proud!

COVAIR: But you must realize that public opinion wants more attention paid to the environment, to crime, to drugs, to the desecration of our flag.

HAUSSMANN: Let me assure you that URDU will attend to all these needs. Let me outline my plan for you. To begin with, it is clear to me that whereas the area of the United States is much larger than that of Paris in 1853, you have innumerable resources available to you that we lacked. You have automobiles, electronics, dynamite, lasers, computers, and so forth. Your have greater manpower and technical expertise; we relied entirely on simple mechanical devices. So the magnitude of the problem does not worry me, nor do its social consequences.

Now, as I've said, I agree entirely that the economically sound solution is *to keep the missiles stationary*. But since the ultimate aim of your missile program is to safeguard your urban centers, I propose that you should redeploy your cities. *Render your cities mobile!* If you do that, any aggressor missiles would be uncertain as to where their targets are located. At the moment, I'm sure the Russians have ICBMs aimed at Washington, New York, Los Angeles, or Omaha. But if tomorrow New York were suddenly, and randomly, translocated to a site near Wichita, or Los Angeles to Wyoming—why, there would be no conceivable way for an enemy to predict a target site! You would be well advised to shuttle cities, not missiles.

COVAIR: But that's fantastic! You cannot expect us to launch such an impossible feat of engineering within the next decade.

HAUSSMANN: It is certainly no more fantastic to me than the idea of landing a man on the moon. Indeed, my plan seems much more practical than your recent commitment to a "foolproof" laser defense of outer space!

COVAIR: But how would you propose to move these cities?

HAUSSMANN: Along several giant systems of railroad tracks disposed over your country after the fashion of my famous boulevards. We would simply put your forty largest cities— Boston, say, or New Orleans—on rolling stock. We would, of course, also be building railbeds broad enough to carry these cities. The tracks would crisscross the country. Moreover, your major areas are already prepared for this concept. Have I not heard talk of the "Boston–New York–Washington corridor"?

COVAIR: Now, while this may seem a small problem to you, I'm worried that large parts of this beautiful country would be ruined by this major network.

HAUSSMANN: Well, I admit that you'll have to break up a few conurbations. You will probably have to raze such warrens as Dayton, Providence, Evansville, and Sacramento. But in

Paris we had to clear a proportionally greater area. We cleaned up such festering slums as the Buttes Chaumont and created a good, middle-class park.

COVAIR: Even if you had the technology, Baron, wouldn't this scheme be prohibitively expensive?

HAUSSMANN: I've faced that problem before. You see, between 1853 and 1869 we spent 2.5 billion francs—about forty times what had been spent under the previous regime of Louis Philippe. But we worked that one out easily. Indeed, we anticipated Reaganomics by over a century. I formulated a *théorie des dépenses productives*—of productive expenditure, that is. And—read my lips—we levied no new taxes! I pointed out that certain expenditures that may not *seem* necessary can be justified as leading to "a general increase in revenues." The URDU program will eliminate not only Bridgeport and Gary but unemployment as well!

KROOT: I'm beginning to see the advantage of this defense system. Can this type of solution be brought to bear on other problem areas of American life?

HAUSSMANN: I hesitate to make suggestions outside my field of expertise. But it had occurred to me that your deployment of doctors might benefit from some such a plan as URDU. I hear that there are many parts of your country—rural areas and the slums of the cities—that suffer from a lack of doctors. Nonsense! You have a maldistribution of patients! Simply move all the inhabitants of the underdoctored areas to cities and towns in which a doctor would *want* to live; that will take care of the problem. Remember that in Paris I found it reasonable to achieve "the amelioration of the state of health of the town through the systematic destruction of infested alleyways and the centers of epidemics." Let's return to the missile solution.

KROOT: How on earth did you ever conceive of such an imaginative proposal?

HAUSSMANN: Well, if truth be told, I was wandering around my Paris last month. And exactly on the site where my great favorites used to stand—those confections of steel and glass known as Les Halles—I saw that there had been placed, as from another planet, a four-tiered shopping center that looks exactly like one in Kalamazoo. And the view of my Étoile is ruined by the skyscrapers of La Défense, a vision of Houston. In front of the Louvre, someone has deposited a pyramidal birdcage! To think that the brothers Goncourt accused *me* of building an "American Babylon"!

I reasoned that if the forms of transatlantic architecture are so powerful as to disfigure Paris, then surely U.S. engineers can revise their own landscape in the service of national defense. As a rabid antisocialist, I felt compelled to offer my plan to Secretary Cheney. He assured me that the financial requirements of URDU were well within the imperial budget requested by the Pentagon for what your press had called "Star Wars."

COVAIR: But haven't you forgotten one thing? If you move Cleveland to the Mojave, or New York to the Green Mountains, what will happen to their suburbs, to Shaker Heights or Englewood?

HAUSSMANN: Well, although a detailed analysis has not yet been worked out, I have drafted a few early schedules. I would propose, for example, that we move another, expendable city into the void. I've targeted Richmond, Virginia, to rotate with Cleveland on odd Thursdays and Hanover, New Hampshire, to exchange with Manhattan on even Mondays. On my visits to your suburbs, I've failed to notice significant social differences between Shaker Heights and the suburbs of Richmond. No, the inhabitants of the *banlieue* will not notice the shuttle; perhaps the Ohio people will have to learn to drink coffee before their meals on odd Thursdays. But that seems a small price to pay for a shifting defense.

COVAIR: But won't this enormous redeployment cause major social change? Won't massive spending on defense cut down on other social programs?

HAUSSMANN: It did, to a degree, in Paris. For example, although my programs increased workers' wages, these did not keep up with the cost of living. By 1870, rents doubled, and while wages rose by 30 percent, the cost of living rose over 45 percent. In 1862, I noted that over half the population of Paris lived in "poverty bordering on destitution" and that the average worker had to work eleven hours for a day's pay. But my faith in the "trickle-down" theory was justified. While the wages of coal miners in the Anzin colliery rose 30 percent between 1852 and 1870, the company's dividends tripled. Only wage earners were inconvenienced: I consider this a small price to pay for the Paris of the Second Empire!

KROOT: With all this success, Baron, why were you forced to retire before your chief of state?

HAUSSMANN: That was a messy business! It seems that I had a little "slush fund" known as *la caisse des travaux de Paris*. I was caught in a historical predicament similar to one that almost tripped your President Nixon in his early career. But, *hélas*, we lacked radio or television, and I owned no dog called Checkers. I was undone by the snooping rabble of the Chamber of Deputies. In the United States of the 1990s, my small difficulties would ruffle no feathers. *La caisse des travaux* was no HUD!

KROOT: Returning to URDU, don't you think that this is a provocative plan? Won't the Russians retaliate?

HAUSSMANN: Never! A country that runs out of windshield wipers in the rain cannot begin to think of moving Leningrad to the Urals. No, when I advised Mr. Gorbachev last week, I told him to keep their cities stationary and to move the missiles.

10

Gulliver in Nature

Like beach plums, new journals appear in crops overnight. They arrive in the periodical room of the library at Woods Hole from Bethesda and Beijing, Stockholm and Haifa, Johannesburg and Leeds. There are too many of them, they are published too often, they stare from their racks to reproach us for sloth. It would be comforting to dismiss their contents as trivial or redundant, but that would be unfair. No, sad to say, the bulk of what appears in the biomedical literature is not only sound but new. We are condemned to keep up, to pay the piper for living in the golden age of biologic science. Probably we *ought* to feel guilty for not holding our own at this feast of fact.

A generation ago, Aldous Huxley complained about the saturating effect of instant information; he grumped that in the final analysis we may have to choose between being well educated and being well informed. And he was talking only about printed words! In Huxley's day, scientific journals wore covers of dismal gray or taupe and displayed nothing more eye-catching than a discreet table of contents. Our culture fed on words alone. But nowadays the gloss and hype of the visual seem to have taken over. These days our periodical rooms resemble newsstands or supermarkets, emporia where print has been replaced by pictures to give us the choice between being half amused and half titillated.

These days the journals *Nature* and *Science* sport lurid prints of erupting volcanoes or Aztec masks. *Cell* presents its high-tech display of neon genes. Greeting-card art appears on the cover of *Cancer Research* and a bland Chagall decorates the

Journal of the American Medical Association. The clinical journals of Europe feature ads for rejuvenation in sans-serif type
while the *Journal of Shellfish Research* recalls Julia Child's program on bouillabaisse. *Biochemistry* and *Prostaglandins* sport
graceless monochromes of molecules and *Development* raises
eyebrows with its snapshot of a fluorescent fetus. The various
Proceedings, Transactions and *Comptes Rendus* of the learned
societies still remain clothed in the classy typography of yesteryear,
but by and large today's journals reflect the aesthetics of a Sia-
mese *clong.*

The merchandise goes quickly; we devour the material for
content rather than design. Fortunately, the goods have not become
as sleazy as their wrappers. By midafternoon the journals are
scattered: some lie opened and well-thumbed on the reading
tables, some have wandered off to the Xerox machine, others
remain piled in heaps. They have been scanned, noted, and used.
Browsers outnumber diggers, but it is always a pleasure to watch
an occasional gasp of "Aha!" interrupt the more common shrugs
of "So what?" Perhaps the most poignant response is that of the
scholar who has just been scooped: he stares at the page as if
grieving a casualty list that contained the name of his child.

It is hard to ignore the debt that scientific prose owes to
battle dispatches, a genre we acknowledge by calling our hottest
tidbits "brief communications," "short reports," or "brief definitive
reports." A romantic might regard these short missives as letters
home from our long campaign against unruly nature. A cynic
might argue that they contribute to the unsatisfactory signal-to-
noise ratio of our literature. I suppose I ought to be more impressed
by signals of major publications, but my own prejudice is in favor
of letters and communications; the noise they make is the honest
buzz of bees at work.

Long and short aside, one is forced to admit that we are
knee-deep in other people's data, awash in a tide of the real. So
much has been written by so many that we are as likely to do an
experiment as to dig through the library to find out if someone

else has done it before. As usual, this behavior was predicted by a *philosophe*. Here is Diderot, grouching in 1755 over the surfeit of print:

> The number of books will grow continually, and one can predict that a time will come when it will be almost as difficult to learn anything from books as from the direct study of the whole universe. It will be almost as convenient to search for some bit of truth concealed in nature as it will be to find it hidden away in an immense multitude of bound volumes.

Our cynic will point to Diderot and argue that the time is already here when the study of books is no longer "convenient." He would argue that the sort of general-interest communiqués printed in *Nature* and *Science* ought to be replaced by electronic information systems that will alert each of us to limited quanta of information in our subspecialties. But I tend to the opposite view and therefore rarely miss an issue of *Nature* or *Science*, preferring the brief letter or report to almost any other form of scientific writing. The form is not confining: Loeb and Beutner put membrane potentials on the map in a 1914 letter to *Science*, and Watson and Crick got the double helix just right in a 1953 letter to *Nature*. More recently, Montagnier and Gallo pinned down the AIDS virus in the columns of *Science*.

The trendy new layouts of those journals no more dissuade me from picking over most of their contents than full-page ads for the books of clairvoyants prevent me from reading *The New York Times Book Review*. No, each week I scan *Nature* and *Science* as gladly for news of black holes and superconduction as for tidbits from my own field of research. Over the years I've been entertained by the wide range of our science, which scans with equal rigor anthill and sky. It's not getting any easier, though, for the casual reader. If the universal language of science is broken English, we seem to write it in the dialects of our separate disciplines. Indeed,

the jargon of shop slang has made reports on avian mating pat-
terns as tough to decipher as the riddle of genes.

What a relief, therefore, to come across work in *Nature* that
speaks the language of Jonathan Swift. On June 4, 1987, I opened
the pages of the magazine to find two full-color pictures of four
pats of cow dung plopped on a green pasture. I was reminded of
the first time I had ever encountered the discipline of dung
studies. It was in that part of *Gulliver's Travels* wherein Swift
describes his hero's visit to the "projectors" of the Academy of
Lagado. The wacky projectors constitute a group caricature of the
members of the Royal Society, and their most outrageous experiments are not too far from actual projects discussed at the Society.
Swift describes the most ancient member of the Academy:

> His face and beard were of a pale yellow; his hands and
> clothes daubed over with filth. When I was presented to
> him, he gave me a very close embrace (a compliment I
> could well have excused). His employment from first
> coming into the Academy was an operation to reduce
> human excrement to its original food. . . . He had a weekly
> allowance from the society of a vessel filled with human
> ordure, about the bigness of a Bristol barrel.

The subject matter of the June letter to *Nature* was nothing less
than an account of what happens when excrement is *not* reduced
to "its original food." The article is by Richard Wall and Les
Strong of the Department of Zoology of Bristol University, and it
has the unpromising title of "Environmental Consequences of
Treating Cattle with the Antiparasitic Drug Ivermectin." The
pictures of what the authors call "pats" on grass illustrate their
chief finding, which is that the feces of cows given ivermectin
become undegradable by dung beetles. This observation has major
environmental consequences for pastureland.

As I have learned from Malcolm Roe's comment in the
same issue of *Nature*, there are no fewer than 14,000 species of

dung beetles which set up shop in and around the droppings of mammals. The beetles, which range in size from 4 milligrams to 19 grams (!), belong to the scarab family; recent visitors to Egypt will readily appreciate the connection. The beetles seem to specialize in the dung of mammals that share their habitat. Roe recounts a misadventure of animal husbandry in Australia: cattle introduced from elsewhere dropped their pats on ground colonized by beetles that had become so adapted to the droppings of kangaroos that they could not cope with the dung of cows. "This dung in consequence persisted on the ground for long periods, suppressing grass production and providing breeding foci for flies." African dung beetles had to be imported to do the job, in an effort launched in 1964 by the Commonwealth Scientific and Industrial Research Organisation and given the Swiftian name "Dung Beetle Project."

Marine recruits and interns excepted, the beetles bow to none with respect to efficient coprophagy: "In the Tsavo national park of eastern Kenya, up to 48,000 beetles have been recorded visiting a 3 kg pile of elephant dung in 2 h, during which time all the soft edible material had either been eaten in situ, rolled up to 22 m away from the deposit or buried below it." Roe has an appetite, so to speak, for this sort of quantification. He points out that up to four kilograms of soil are elevated to the surface for every kilogram of elephant dung deposited in East Africa! Thus the beetles not only remove dung and decrease the number of flies, but also aerate the soil and enhance the percolation of ground water.

Wall and Strong worried that the drug ivermectin, which is now "routinely administered to cattle, horses, sheep and pigs in many countries" might also kill the useful coprophages. And sure enough, they were correct. Their experiments were performed in a fashion that Dean Swift would have relished. Circular formers of corrugated cardboard were filled with two kilos of cow dung, "weighted out on a hand-held spring balance," obtained from animals given the drug and from controls. The pats were placed on a closely cropped pasture and examined for up to 100 days. The soil beneath them was removed and both pats and soil were examined for their flora of dung beetles.

The pair of colored photographs in *Nature* showed the results of this study, which is as convincing a bit of experimental science as any I have ever read. The first pair of pictures shows that whereas forty days after dung from control calves had been deposited the pat was mostly digested, dung from ivermectin-treated calves was undegraded. The second set of pictures, taken ninety-four days after deposition, showed that the experimental pats remained undigested, serving the function of long-acting mulch. Counts of invertebrates in pats and soil confirmed these sprightly pictures: whereas 780 of the busy dung beetles were found in control pats, only 17 were recovered from pats from drug-treated calves. Conclusion: Whereas ivermectin clearly promotes the health of livestock by killing their parasites, the drug may well spoil the ground on which they graze.

Swift, the doubting cleric, would have been delighted not only by the pungent prose in which Wall and Strong described their adventures in pat-agonia, but also by their conclusions. Lemuel Gulliver was speaking not of Lagado but of the Royal Society when he complained that the levers of science had unhinged the ancient order:

> The professors contrive new rules and methods of agriculture and building . . . whereby, as they undertake, one man shall do the work of ten; a palace may be built in a week, of materials so durable as to last for ever without repairing. All the fruits of the earth shall come to maturity at whatever season we think fit to choose, and increase an hundred fold more than they do at present, with innumerable other happy proposals. The only inconvenience is, that none of these projects are yet brought to perfection; and in the mean time the whole country lies miserably in waste, the houses in ruins, and the people without food or clothes.

Swift speaks to us in the voice of Gulliver, the ship's surgeon who recounts the clumsy projects of the Academy in deadpan fashion. Gulliver describes a land in which natural law has been subverted by the Age of Newton. Newtonian math and science have turned the feudal system into cloud-cuckoo-land. Powered by magnets, an absentee court rules from a floating island in the sky: law is literally over the heads of the citizenry. The lords of Laputa are distracted while the laboring classes are idle. Ill-fitting clothes are designed by rule and compass according to erroneous computation. Tasteless food is served in the form of precut squares, circles, and cones. The houses are built "without one right angle in any apartment"; the streets are filthy and the gutters plugged; each Laputan is so self-absorbed—or diverted by private music—that no conversation is possible without mechanical aid. The overall scene should not want elaboration for readers of *The Bonfire of the Vanities*.

Swift held the new science responsible for this state of affairs. His academicians occupied themselves not only with analyzing dung but also with extracting energy from vegetables, bending the path of flames, making silk without silkworms, and writing books by means of machines. Gulliver chiefly admired and found unaccountable the strong disposition in them "towards news and politics, perpetually enquiring into public affairs, giving their judgement in matters of state, and passionately disputing every inch of a party opinion. . . . I rather take this quality to spring from a very common infirmity of human nature, inclining us to be more curious and conceited in matters where we have least concern, and for which we are least adapted either by study or by nature."

Neither the professional nor the lay activities of professors should seem completely unfamiliar to readers of today's *Nature* or *Science:* their pages deal with dung beetles, oxidative phosphorylation, lasers, synthetic polymers, and computers. All those fancies of 1726! One need not add that the political exertions of molecular biologists follow in the grand traditions of Laputa.

It has been argued that satire is the natural tool of the social conservative. From Aristophanes to Evelyn Waugh, Molière to Tom Wolfe, more fun has been poked at new schemes than at old gods. Swift has been used as a text by opponents of science from the political right and left; in the Laputan episode he's in there with the Bible-thumpers. But Swift was not only troubled by the threats to social arrangements that the new science posed. Like Orwell two centuries later, he was perhaps even more concerned with the garbling of sense that comes from befouling our language.

Swift began his attack by spoofing the rhetoric of the Royal Society, the discussions of which were conducted in simple, declarative sentences; Newtonian science was based on a study of things, not words. In Laputa, Gulliver found a land where excess attention to science and enterprise had led not only to neglect of the arts but to debasement of grammar. Gulliver was introduced to the school of languages where "the first project was to shorten discourse by cutting polysyllables into one, and leaving out verbs and participles, because in reality all things imaginable are but nouns." Readers of Wittgenstein's *Tractatus*—if that influential work may be said to have readers—will recognize the sentiment.

This fancy was carried to epistemological conclusion in the second project of the language school. Since words stood for things, the sages considered that

it would be more convenient for all men to carry about them such *things* as were necessary to express the particular business they are to discourse on. . . . However, many of the most learned and wise adhere to the new scheme of expressing themselves by *things*, which hath only this inconvenience attending it, that if a man's business be very great, and of various kinds, he must be obliged in proportion to carry a greater bundle of *things* upon his back, unless he can afford one or two strong servants to attend him. I have often beheld two of those sages almost sinking under the weight of their packs.

In this brave Newtonian world of things, where sages carried backpacks as if at a perpetual Gordon conference, Gulliver found only one kindred soul. This elderly noble "being not of an enterprising spirit . . . was content to go on in the old forms, to live in the houses his ancestors had built, and act as they did in every part of life without innovation." There, of course, is the rub: no *things*, no innovation.

Here, indeed, we come to the confluence of Gulliver and the glossy new visual aspect of *Nature*. It is easy for those of us still entangled in the older, comfortable order of words to make fun of our postliterate time, in which the medium is said to be the message. But how stuffy to ignore the signals of the present! It might be said that I received the message of Wall and Strong with respect to ivermectin by the medium of those glossy pictures of dung in *Nature*. Indeed, I realize that photographs are simply a convenient twentieth-century version of Laputan *things*. All those cover photos in the Woods Hole periodical room—they too are *things*, the nouns of science: the gene, the protein, the anemone. How often have I watched scientists corner each other at meetings to bring out their collection of *things:* photos of cells, snapshots of skulls, maps of the genome. When we speak of science and discovery, the medium is a part of the message: the cancer gene is a blot on a piece of filter paper, the enzyme is a blip on a graph. We carry those messages—the *things* we have discovered—around in our backpacks as our teachers lugged nouns about in sentences.

To one mired in the tradition of Gulliver, those who live in the postliterate world of today seem like mutants, analphabetic aborigines who have lost adjectives, adverbs, and clauses, who cannot read newspapers in black and white or print without pictures. The members of that generation seem to have been born with stereo implants in their ears and television nystagmus of their eyeballs.

But a more tolerant observer might suggest that although Newtonian science may have turned the world topsy-turvy in 1726, its revolution has made it unnecessary to keep a journal of the plague year ever again, and in our century it landed men on the moon. The study of dung has helped "the earth . . . come to maturity at whatever season we think fit to choose and increase an hundred fold." Perhaps the old culture of words has indeed been replaced by the *things* of photography and film, but I am persuaded that the placement of *things* in Charlie Chaplin's *Great Dictator* or Terry Gilliam's *Brazil* scores artistic points that Swift might have envied.

Like it or not, innovation comes to us these days disguised as a video disc. But that shouldn't trouble us. When we open our new journals to trace the coilings of genes as unraveled by 3-D images on computer screens, or see photos in which garish dyes track the AIDS virus, the pictures of our time speak the language of the kingdom of nouns. Those *things* are new and they produce the sensation of the new. Just so might the monks of Reims have sensed the coming of a new age as they looked up from their manuscripts to see illiterate craftsmen beginning the great rose window of the cathedral.

11

The Age of Miracles
Hadn't Passed

Native of Pesaro in the Marches of Ancona, Michelina Metelli
was married at the age of twelve to Lord Malatesta of the
dukes of Rimini. She became a widow at twenty, and shortly
afterwards her only child died. She distributed her goods to
the poor and, after St. Francis' example, begged her bread
and sought humiliations. . . . She also devoted herself to the
care of lepers, tending and kissing their leprous sores, and
sometimes, they say, miraculously restoring them to health.

OMER ENGLEBERT, *The Lives of the Saints*

Eighteen hours after she was rushed to Bellevue Hospital, Dyanne
Watrous was miraculously restored to health. She had been admitted in shock, half comatose, and with open sores over much of
her body. Her mother told medical residents that Dyanne, now
thirty-one, had suffered from "lupus disease" since her late teens
in a Harlem high school. The condition had responded to cortisonelike drugs over the years; despite it, Dyanne had been able to
do well in high school and secretarial college, to bear a son and
hold a job in a Wall Street brokerage house. With pluck, she had
survived two miscarriages, an abortion, and bouts of cocaine
addiction.

Then, some three months before Dyanne was brought to the
hospital, things fell apart. She stopped taking cortisone on the
advice of an herbal therapist and soon grew listless; fatigue forced
her to give up work. She became progressively more depressed,

lethargic, and bedridden; her weight dropped from 120 pounds to 87. On the morning of admission, Dyanne had been suffering from prolonged, shaking chills and could not be roused by her mother.

At Bellevue, an astute medical team quickly sized up the problem. They decided that in addition to her underlying disease—which had affected mainly her skin, joints, and platelets—Ms. Watrous had an acute infection of the bloodstream. She also showed signs of that relative exhaustion of the adrenal glands which follows prolonged treatment with cortisonelike drugs. Many patients with lupus require treatment with these powerful drugs as diabetics require insulin, to make years of normal existence possible. When as a young medical student I saw at first hand the miraculous response of patients with lupus to cortisone, I became an instant convert to rheumatology. The secular orders offer their own epiphanies.

By the time we saw Ms. Watrous in consultation, she had been restored to the land of the living by antibiotics, which fought the bloodstream infection, and by intravenous hydrocortisone, which overcame adrenal insufficiency. Our patient was alert, but understandably tired. She seemed pleased to see a flock of rheumatologists; since high school she had known that her condition fell into our bailiwick. Unwrapping her dressings, we found that her skin bore not only the chronic lesions of lupus but also new scarlet blotches over her shins and the tips of her fingers. These resulted most likely from an unusual reaction (toxic epidermal necrosis) to her bloodstream infection. After we had finished our examination, she sat up primly in bed to face our row of white-coated doctors. Her ebony head was wrapped in a white cotton turban that covered her marred scalp, her chest heaved under a blue hospital gown, red blotches speckled what could be seen of her skin. After we had listened to more of her story, I held her hand and asked her to describe how she felt, overall, in comparison to a few weeks ago.

"Doc," she replied, "never mind weeks. Compared to what was it, Tuesday? It's like a miracle happened!"

Sure enough, I thought. In fact, on that bright spring morning, as sun shone through the windows of 16-East at Bellevue, the entire scene—the primary colors, the spare furnishings, the blotched invalid upright in bed—reminded me of those fourteenth-century predella panels that illustrate a miracle of healing wrought by one or another of the company of saints. Later, away from the bedside, when we discussed the management of Ms. Watrous, the predella image persisted. I wondered out loud whether a panel illustrating her miraculous recovery might be more appropriately dedicated to Alexander Fleming (1881–1955), the discoverer of penicillin, or to Philip Hench (1896–1972), who first treated rheumatic diseases with cortisone. The choice would be a toss-up: certainly both qualify as "heroes without halos"—to borrow a phrase of Phyllis McGinley's. Both were canonized, but at Stockholm rather than Rome, the more common practice nowadays.

A young colleague pointed out how outdated my quandary was: "Simple. It all depends on the DRG that you pick: 416 it's Fleming, 240 it's Hench. Let HCFA decide!"

A briefing is required, lest you think that DRG is a new sports car or that HCFA (pronounced "hickfah") is a ritual bath in the Ozarks. For the last several years, American hospitals have been reimbursed not for what it costs to take care of patients, but according to a complex book of schedules that divides all human maladies into twenty-three major "diagnosis-related groups." These spell out not only who pays how much to whom when and if, but also for how long and for what. As might be expected from a program based on a compound adjective, it is monitored by an agency based on the gerund, the Health Care Financing Administration. Its two aims are noble: the cutting of cost without the cutting of corners. Most would agree that the first has been achieved.

Be that as it may, my choices for Ms. Watrous's patron saint were not made easy by the DRG handbook. Had her primary diagnosis been that of an infection of the bloodstream #416 (*septicemia age > 17*), she would have had 7.4 days in hospital and merit $7,093 reimbursement. On the other hand, a DRG for lupus #240 (*connective tissue disorders with complications*) would have also permitted a stay of 7.3 days but netted a mere $4,262 to the hospital. Since she ran into trouble from adrenal insufficiency, the appropriate DRG might also be #300 (*endocrine disorder with complications*), with only 6.0 days, and $4,848. An unfriendly QA inspector might accuse us of prolonging her stay had we tagged her with #416 or #240. "QA," by the way, stands for "quality assurance" and means its exact opposite.

All this categorical confusion had diverted the discussion from sainthood, but an item in *The New York Times* (via AP, April 17, 1988) pulled me back to *The Lives of the Saints*. It seems that the inspector general's office of the Department of Health and Human Services had accused American hospitals of overbilling the Feds by "$2 billion a year." On the basis of a review of old records rather than fresh interviews with either docs or patients, this QA task force concluded that many of the "unnecessary admissions were 'social admissions' such as providing a bed for an elderly person without any other place to stay; admitting someone who really belonged in a nursing home; and in a few cases admitting someone who simply did not need acute medical care.

"The report found the unnecessary admissions tended to be concentrated in five diagnostic groups: back problems, diabetes, bone cancer, digestive disorders and upper respiratory infections."

I stopped worrying over the choice between Fleming and Hench and, in outrage, began to compare my DRG handbook with *The Lives of the Saints*. Both volumes provide detailed schedules of miraculous cures, but the company of saints was not expected to deliver these on demand or anticipate their cost; miracles are priceless in the eyes of God. Surely the saints would have bedded those "without any other place to stay" and admitted those with diabetes or bone cancer!

One wonders what rebuke would have met the Blessed Guy of Cortona (d. 1245) who housed and fed St. Francis of Assisi, then without any other place to stay. After washing St. Francis's feet, Guy said, "When you again need tunics and cloaks, do not hesitate to purchase them; I will pay for them." Would HCFA authorize the payment? Would its accountants refer to St. Audrey (d. 679) if considering patients whose admission for upper respiratory infection is considered "inappropriate"? This saint "wore inconvenient and clumsy clothing; after matins she remained at prayer in the choir until morning. An abscess of the throat from which she died towards the end of her life has made her the patron of those who suffer similar ills." The QA team would certainly reproach a modern administrator who followed the example of Abbot Hugh of Grenoble (1053–1131), by refusing orders to report on the comportment of his Carthusians with the gentle "Why set down faults?" St. Peter himself might be in for reprimand. St. Petronilla (first century) was his particular favorite, yet, "there came the day when, afflicted with paralysis, she was incapable of any work. 'Why don't you cure her?' Titus asked St. Peter. St. Peter answered: 'It is good for her to remain like that.' " The Feds might read it as DRG #17 (*nonspecific cerebrovascular disorder without complication*), or 4.7 days and $2,837. Since "God, however, restored her health," I would interpret St. Peter's admonition as a lesson in patience and faith.

It is depressing to think what guidance medical bureaucrats would draw from these exemplary lives. Englebert's book describes as many of the ills that befell the saints as those they were able to cure. As in the inspector general's report, the major ills of saints are concentrated in a few DRGs. Since many of the blessed were also martyrs, DRGs #444 and #445 are the most common (*multiple trauma, age > 17*), with and without complications. Yielding a hospital stay, short of martyrdom, of 5.3 or 3.7 days and expenses of $3,663 or $2,313, these DRGs describe the deaths of, among others, Sts. Catherine of Alexandria (dates unknown), Barbara (d. 235), Placidus (d. 540), John of God (1495–1550), and Sebastian (d. 288). St. Sebastian miraculously survived multiple wounds from Diocletian's archers (DRG #444), only to be cudgeled to death and thrown in a sewer (DRG #27, *traumatic stupor and coma > 1 hour;* 4.3 days, $6,584). DRG #457 (*extensive burns without operating-room procedures*) would cover Sts. John Before the Latin Gate (d. 95), Justina and Cyprian (d. 304), and Joan of Arc (1412–31). They each would be permitted 4.1 days and $11,299.

DRG #148 (*major small and large bowel procedure, with complications*) is the most generous with respect to length of stay and reimbursement: 14.5 days and $14,449. Into this category fall St. Erasmus (d. 303?), who was eviscerated by means of a windlass, and St. Ernest (d. 1148), whose insides were twined about a stake by his persecutors.

This sort of clinical detail is missing from the DRG handbook: its pages lack the touch of purpose. Better to have stories of devotion and martyrdom written by someone as eloquent and witty as the patron saint of writers, St. Francis de Sales (1567–1622) who might be considered the moral equivalent of Waugh.

Not all saints died as martyrs, nor are all martyrs saints; Dr. William Ober has reminded us that nowadays a martyr is defined as someone who has to live with a saint. Martyr or not, the saints were effective healers. Their cures also cluster in a small number of DRGs. Leprosy and plague were most susceptible: DRG #423 (*other infectious and parasitic diseases diagnoses* [*sic*]) permits 8.0 days in bed and $6,843. St. Peter (d. 64) healed lepers with his shadow, Sts. Romanus (d. 463) and Michelina (1300–56) by kissing the lesions, St. Francis of Assisi (1182–1226) with prayer. Plague shares the same DRG with leprosy; its conquerors include St. Roch (d. 1327), Avertanus (d. 1370), Emiliani (d. 1537), and St. Charles Borromeo (d. 1548).

Other DRGs well handled by the saints were #419 (*fever of unknown origin, age > 17;* 5.9 days, $4,364) and #47, blindness (*other disorders of the eye, without complications;* 2.6 days, only $1,612). My favorite saint of this DRG is St. Macarius the Younger (d. 408) who brought back sight to the blind cub of a hyena and who was rewarded the next day by the hyena with the gift of "a magnificent sheepskin." This story touches all but university presidents.

Although *The Lives of the Saints* makes better reading than the DRG handbook, there are miracles in our new schedules that the saints might envy. I would love to read about St. Christiaan of Barnard or St. Michael De Bakey, who have revived more failing hearts, DRG #103 (*heart transplant*; 25.8 days, $53,209) or DRG #104 (*cardiac valve procedure with pump and with cardiac catheterization*; 17.4 days, $32,768), than all the saints in Englebert. Where are Sts. Selman of Waksman (tuberculosis), Max of Theiler (yellow fever), Jonas of Salk (poliomyelitis)? So great are their miracles that the diseases they conquered have all been reduced to DRG #423, alongside plague and leprosy.

The Lives of the Saints treats cures as unique events that testify to the glory of God; the DRG handbook publishes schedules of medical miracles that have become as routine as the Pan Am shuttle. The DRG schedules deprive us of words, of narrative, of secular devotion, of that flutter of delight when a miracle passes. I doubt that anyone is likely to find the healing vocation in the DRG handbook: what we have gained in power, we have lost in glory. Those dreary DRG numbers tell us that social justice makes poor reading.

Making rounds at Bellevue, checking in to see that Ms. Watrous remains improved, I watched a preppie woman resident wrapping her patient's shin. I was reminded of St. Christina the Astonishing (1150–1224), a holy woman who served the poor and sick with extreme devotion, despite her anguish at the stench of unwashed human flesh. "After contact with it, some time was necessary before she could stand her fellow man." She misbehaved at her own funeral: so many of her unwashed devotees crowded about her coffin, that the coffin—with fastidious Christina kicking inside—bounded away to the rafters of the church to escape the smell of humankind. But the saint returned, to mark a sanctuary for the sick. In such a sanctuary, there are no "unnecessary admissions."

12

A Slap of the Tail:
Reading Medical Humanities

Those of us who were in tune with the greening of American colleges in the 1960s have become displeased by some of the fruits of that gentle rebellion. One such crop—to continue the metaphor—was the gradual abolition over the last two decades of cultural literacy as a requirement for admission to professional graduate schools. But times change, and general culture is getting a better press again. Indeed, *lack* of exposure to liberal arts is now blamed for the skewed morals of lawyers, the flawed ethics of MBAs, and the loss of "humanistic" values on the part of doctors. Although no one has spelled out how a close encounter with *The Decameron* will preserve young docs from sins of indifference at the bedside, remedial courses in "medical humanities" have nuzzled their way into the crowded curriculum of our best medical schools.

However well intentioned these offerings may be, they strike me as missing the mark. Although there are exceptions—programs at Galveston, Rochester, and East Lansing come to mind—the usual course in medical humanities does not mandate the rigorous study of history, philosophy, or the arts, nor is it generally taught by the most creative scholars of the university. The subject matter tends to run to diluted lit-crit, psychological group support, and large doses of what Alfred North Whitehead called the cross-sterilization of the social sciences. At one school I know, the sessions are dismissed by students as "that touchy-feely hour." It is difficult not to be persuaded that medical humanities are to the humanities what military music is to music.

How did *medical* schools get into the business of teaching

literature, ethics, and philosophy? It has been argued that putting medical humanities in the curriculum is the natural response of educators to the charge that doctors are overspecialized, semi-literate, and deaf to their patients. My own hunch is that these courses are a belated attempt to compensate for the medical schools' narrow admissions policies. From the mid-1960s to the mid-1980s our prospective students were required to spend their college years boning up on chemistry, biochemistry, and molecu-lar biology. Students with pastoral rather than scientific ambi-tions were discouraged and the quick learners were favored over the learned. The admission policies were based only in part on the notion of *relevancy* as students demanded it then; they were based also on the complementary notion of *complexity*, much favored by medical deans. Medical educators feared that our bright new science—medicine after the biological revolution—had become so complicated that the sooner undergraduates discovered inositol trisphosphate or topoisomerase, the better they would perform in the clinic.

There is just so much more to know these days, we are told. But that notion has always been pure twaddle: in my father's youth it was obvious to *his* professors that the new medicine of the Microbe Hunters could not be applied without intimate knowl-edge of systematic botany, comparative entomology, and bacterial fermentation. Those collections of facts, those disciplines are as relevant to clinical medicine in 1990 as they were in 1928. When doctors nowadays think of two-stage carcinogenesis, Lyme arthritis, or the consequences of *Yersinia* infections (postinfectious dis-eases of the spine), they require facts from the study of plants, deer ticks, and obscure microbes. But we no longer make room for such matters in our curricula. Now, as then, we have not been slow to fill the student's day with *other* collections of fact.

We deceive not only our students but ourselves when we teach that science is fact rather than process. An admissions policy based on factual science rather than cultural process has eroded the traditional view that medicine is a learned profession, the essence of which, as Abraham Flexner assured us in 1910, "resides in the application of free, resourceful, unhampered intelligence to the comprehension of problems—the problems of disease, the problems of social life—bequeathed to us by history and complicated by evolution." Flexner was convinced that ours was a learned profession by virtue of its roots in "cultural and idealistic soil."

If our students haven't dug about in the cultural and idealistic soil by the time they hit medical school, we're in trouble too deep for salvage by remedial courses in medical humanities. Thanks in no small part to Flexner's crusade against the shoddy educational practices of his day, two generations of American doctors were expected to enter medical school able to distinguish between John Quincy and Henry Adams, John and Thomas Dewey, or Isaiah and Irving Berlin. But those expectations went the way of the tailfin, and nowadays we have been reduced to presenting the stuff of *Masterpiece Theater* to students deprived of experience in the broader culture. We would be better advised to teach medicine to cultivated students rather than culture to medical students.

By the time they arrive in medical school, students ought to be left alone to chew on the meat of our tough new science. They should be expected to spot the misplaced gene, the blocked receptor, the hidden epitope, with the cultural confidence of Pasternak's Dr. Zhivago: "Though he was greatly drawn to art and history, he scarcely hesitated over the choice of a career. He thought that art was no more a vocation than innate cheerfulness or melancholy was a profession. He was interested in physics and natural science, and believed that a man should do something socially useful in his practical life. He settled on medicine."

I doubt that our students who are drawn to art and history but who want to do something socially useful are well served by our efforts in the medical humanities. In fact, I wish we would stop teaching these courses altogether. Now, immediately. Cease and desist, once and for all, now and forever!

This wish derives not from any misgivings on my part over the liberal arts, but from the deep admiration that comes only from a true amateur, a fan. The amateur's enthusiasm for the arts was spelled out by William James, sometime professor of anatomy at Harvard, in a fan letter to his brother, Henry: "I envy ye the world of art. Away from it, as we live, we sink into a flatter, blanker kind of consciousness, and indulge in ostrich-like forgetfulness of all our richest potentialities, and they startle us now and then when by accident some rich human product, pictorial, literary, or architectural, slaps us with its tail."

It is in that spirit I want to describe some of the books that have slapped me with their tail. This rummage among golden oldies is a reading list for an imaginary course in medical humanities *which must under no circumstances be taught.* Perhaps it will evoke fond memories among my fellow autodidacts; perhaps it will introduce them to "some rich human product" they do not yet know. These volumes sit together on the top shelf of my library at Woods Hole; I've read a few on assignment, most for pleasure. In one or another fashion, each deals with the real subject matter of medical humanities: "Man learns wisdom by affliction school'd," but not in his lifetime. Some among this score of books qualify as literature, some are simple potboilers; all have been talked about by doctors, fewer by patients, fewer still by writers. They may be said to have provided part of the "cultural and idealistic soil" of my profession. The list, in which I've included only works in English, contains no more than one book per author and excludes some of the best doctor-writers, of whom I've written about elsewhere (Lewis Thomas, William Carlos Williams).

I'll begin with the three authors I've already mentioned. Abraham Flexner's 1910 volume *Medical Education in the United States and Canada* changed the American way of teaching and learning medicine. Indeed, the primitive world of premodern scholarship he describes is today almost unimaginable to young doctors unless one remembers that television evangelists are now permitted to hand out graduate degrees and that Kentucky Fried medical offices have been opened in shopping malls. The Flexner report is required reading in our noncourse.

Boris Pasternak's *Dr. Zhivago* is a traditional Russian novel by an untraditional, modernist poet. The picaresque adventures of his hero remind us of what we have lost in the revolutions of this century—the traditional culture—and of what we have gained—equality, of a sort. Reading *Dr. Zhivago*, one realizes that many of our best doctor-writers—Anton Chekhov, Arthur Schnitzler, Somerset Maugham, Walker Percy—tend to work within very traditional forms. What they add to conventional genres is that note of complacent irony which follows a correct and gloomy diagnosis: the doctor is secretly pleased that he knows what is about to happen and pities those who know not.

Many will agree with the proposition that William James was the most splendid of Americans ever to have been awarded the degree of doctor of medicine. James founded not only our first laboratory of experimental psychology at Harvard but also our leading school of philosophy, pragmatism. Student of our most eminent nineteenth-century biologist, Louis Agassiz, he became teacher of our most innovative twentieth-century writer, Gertrude Stein. His correspondence with his brother can be read as a dialogue between the Two Cultures; William's prose does not suffer from comparison with Henry's. William's defining phrases ("the stream of consciousness," "blooming, buzzing confusion," "the moral equivalent of war") have passed into our language. He was also a preeminent humanist who defined the subject matter of what we will not be teaching in our course. The humanities, William James insisted, are

the study of masterpieces in almost any field of human endeavor. . . . You can give humanistic value to almost anything by teaching it historically. Geology, economics, mechanics are humanistic when taught with reference to the successive achievements of the geniuses to which these sciences owe their being. Not taught thus, literature remains grammar, art a catalogue, history a list of dates, and natural science a sheet of formulas and weights and

measures. The sifting of human creations—nothing less
than this is what we ought to mean by the humanities.

The most agreeable approach to William James is by way of a
one-volume sampling by Jacques Barzun (*A Stroll with William
James*). On Barzun's elite turf, James looks at the life of the mind
as if it were lit by a New England dawn in which objects seem
sharper and clearer than they really are. Barzun is a fit cicerone
to James: I've pressed his *Teacher in America* so often on others
that it has disappeared from my shelf. Barzun prepares one for
the massive, two-volume *Principles of Psychology*, which James
brings to the pragmatic conclusion that

> the popular notion that 'Science' is forced on the mind *ad
> extra*, and that our interests have nothing to do with its
> constructions, is utterly absurd. The craving to believe
> that the things of the world belong to kinds which are
> related by inward rationality together, is the parent of
> Science as well as that of sentimental philosophy; and the
> original investigator always preserves a healthy sense of
> how plastic the materials are in his hands.

If the humanities are the "sifting of human creations," we sift one
of the more recent successes. General readers seem to agree that
if Lewis Thomas is our best writer on scientific medicine, Oliver
Sacks matches him on the clinical side. His book *Awakenings* has
been reissued, no mean achievement these days!

When Ludwig Wittgenstein had completed the defense of
his doctoral thesis, one of his examiners was so impressed that he
concluded, "It is my personal opinion that Mr. Wittgenstein's
thesis is a work of genius; be that as it may, it is certainly well up
to the standard required for the Cambridge degree of Doctor of
Philosophy." It is my personal opinion that *Awakenings*, written
in 1973, is a work of genius; be that as it may, it is certainly well
up to the standards required for republication. Amplified and

brought up to date, it is Sacks's account of the dramatic—and wrenching—reversion to normal behavior of twenty patients suffering from far-advanced Parkinson's disease to whom he gave the "miracle drug" L-dopa. But the book is not only a collection of astonishing case histories but also a memoir, a moral essay, and a romance.

Those who learned from Sacks's best-selling *The Man Who Mistook His Wife for a Hat* will find this earlier book equally engaging. Both succeed in expressing the joy he derives from "the fusion of scientific and 'romantic' penetrations, finding [h i s] mind and [h i s] heart equally exercised and involved, and knowing that anything different would be a dereliction of both." In *Awakenings* we experience what happens to patients when the spell of long-standing disease is broken by the magic of powerful drugs. These patients with Parkinson's disease, due to the sleeping sickness of 1916–27, awake in 1969 as if touched by a sorcerer's wand. But the drug turns out to be a mixed blessing: as described by Sacks, "awakening" is only the first act of a romantic melodrama. For some patients, time has stood still, while others "retained the power to remember, to compare, to dissect, and to testify."

In the second act, which Sacks calls "tribulations," the patients' moods, gaits, and utterances rise and fall, swoop and flutter as the action veers between the turgor of too much and the stupor of too little medication. These travails are "expressed in dramatic histrionic terms; the person shows forth in all his reactions, in a continual disclosure or epiphany of himself; he is always enacting himself in the theatre of his self." Not only must the patient accommodate to the jagged performance of a new persona, but the physician also has to reach another level of knowing. Sacks describes that process on the part of the physician, of crawling beneath the skin of the hurt other.

The art of Sacks is based on his unsentimental refusal to use illness as metaphor and to regard it instead as an unfortunate, random act of nature that none can escape and some can transcend. If, as Joyce has remarked, sentimentality is unearned emotion,

Awakenings earns its cumulative emotional impact by giving us not twenty case histories but twenty stories, separate narratives of "physiology as it is embedded in people, and people as they are embedded and living in history."

Awakenings draws strength from its narrative drive, but it also rests on the pillars of clinical science. In the epilogue Sacks reaches his apogee:

> It is the function of medication, or surgery, or appropriate physiological procedures, to rectify the mechanisms which are so deranged in these patients. It is the function of scientific medicine to rectify the "It." It is the function of art, of living contact, of existential medicine, to call upon the latent will, the agent, the "I," to call out its command- ing and coordinating powers, so that it may regain its hegemony and rule once again—for the final rule, the ruler, is not a measuring rod or clock, but the rule and measure of a personal "I." These two forms of medicine must be joined, must co-inhere, as body and soul.

We sift back half a century to come up with two books that planted the Flexnerian model of the doctor-as-scientist deep in the soil of this century's imagination. One is almost a masterpiece. *Arrowsmith*, by Sinclair Lewis, and its lesser cousin *Microbe Hunters*, by Paul de Kruif, were responsible for sending more students of my generation to medical school than the GI Bill of Rights. Both books shine with a brash, naive American enthusiasm. They are not new literature but literature about the new: Their heroes are the masters of a bacteriology that was on the verge of discovering antibiotics. *Arrowsmith* is based on the scientific if not the romantic life of Paul de Kruif. Sinclair Lewis had taken on de Kruif, formerly of the Rockefeller Institute, as his full collabora- tor on a novel about "a modern doctor." After aimless voyages and a crescendo of angry rows, "Red" Lewis and de Kruif had one final falling-out. Red had dangled the carrot of coauthorship before his younger assistant; he withdrew it in a fit of temper provoked by a trivial dispute over a weekend invitation. My reading is alcoholism, from which both suffered. De Kruif recounts the quarrel in his autobiography, *The Sweeping Wind:*

> "Paul," he said, "you are not a fit man to work with me on Martin Arrowsmith."
>
> "Red," I replied, "you can take the book and shove it."
>
> "All right," said Red, "I can get a Berlitz bacteriologist to help me finish it."
>
> "Good-by, Red," I said. . . .
>
> Just after our knock-down-and-dragout, in the glow of our reconciliation, Red showed me what was to be a letter to our publisher. *"And in all this there's a question as to whether he (de Kruif) won't have contributed more than I have."* . . .
>
> But as he went on at the dialoguing of our scenario, he corrected his opinion; and as he sweated through two complete drafts of the novel, Red's memory dimmed. And so when *Arrowsmith* reached the page-proof stage in 1925, on the page after the title page there was a little acknowledgement that left not much more for me but thanks for technical assistance.

All that de Kruifian fury—that angry temper which had gotten him dismissed from Rockefeller in the first place—was now diverted into the production of a lively volume of scientific biography. De Kruif's energy paid off: *Microbe Hunters* hit the best-seller list shortly after *Arrowsmith.*

In 1962 de Kruif rendered belated judgment on his collaboration with Sinclair Lewis. He pointed out that although all the science in Lewis's book *might* have happened, none of it actually did. De Kruif found that the character of Max Gottlieb, Lewis's prototype of the serious scientist, was more than improbable. He was a muddy mélange of my revered chief, Professor Novy [of Michigan] and of Jacques Loeb, who was my master in a philosophy of the mechanistic conception of life, of God a mathematician, of God a Univac, of God a superstition, of God a childish concept, of God nonexistent. Jacques Loeb went one better than his adored Voltaire. Loeb thought Voltaire was wrong when he said that if God did not exist it would be necessary to invent him. According to good old Jacques Loeb, it was enough to say that God did not exist.

This sort of pedestrian prose (good old Jacques Loeb, indeed!) contrasts with the words that Red Lewis put into the mouth of Martin Arrowsmith:

Suddenly he loved humanity as he loved the decent, clean rows of test-tubes, and he prayed then the prayer of the scientist:

"God give me unclouded eyes and freedom from haste. God give me a quiet and relentless anger against all pretense and all pretentious work and all work left slack and unfinished. God give me a relentlessness whereby I may neither sleep nor accept praise till my observed results equal my calculated results or in pious glee I discover and assault my error. God give me strength not to trust to God."

From stylistic evidence alone, we might judge that de Kruif did indeed provide only technical assistance to Lewis. The two blasphemous passages might be said not only to illustrate the difference between literature and feature journalism but also to sum up Jacques Loeb's *The Mechanistic Conception of Life,* another book missing from my shelf these days.

But if de Kruif had a close brush with literary immortality, he came even closer to scientific laurels. At Michigan, de Kruif had worked with F. G. Novy on anaphylatoxins, those substances generated from the complement system in plasma that cause man and animals to go into shock in the course of immune reactions. And when de Kruif went to work at the Rockefeller Institute, he continued other studies he had begun with Novy, working out how bacterial colonies were transformed from "rough" to "smooth." The extension of this work at Rockefeller in the two decades that followed—the discovery of the transforming principle and its identification as DNA by Oswald Avery, Colin McLeod, and Maclyn McCarty—laid the foundation for our new era of molecular biology. De Kruif was convinced that had he stuck with serious science, rather than dabble with popular journalism (he ended his days writing pious pieces for *Reader's Digest*) he might have been in line for a glittering prize or two.

But the chance of Paul de Kruif's ever receiving a Nobel Prize for his science seems to me as preposterous as James McNeill Whistler's claim to command in the U.S. Army. Whistler is said to have been walking along the Thames embankment with Oscar Wilde when he confided to Wilde that he, Whistler, had been dismissed from West Point because of his failing grade in a required chemistry course. His professor had asked him to describe silicon. Cadet Whistler explained that silicon was a gas. "So you see, Oscar, had silicon been a gas, I would have been a general by now!" Wilde thought for a moment, and replied, "The chances, sir, of silicon being a gas, even today, seem far greater than those of Whistler ever having been declared general!"

De Kruif's temper, his sentimentality, his short-lived enthusiasms would seem to have disqualified him for any success in rigorous science. His later literary output never matched the flair of *Microbe Hunters*, in which Pasteur, Metchnikoff, and Ehrlich came to life in the popular imagination and against which we need to set the popular deconstructions of our own time. A far better nonfiction account of the bacteriological battlefront is that by Hans Zinsser in *Rats, Lice and History*. Zinsser was a professor of bacteriology at Harvard and attained before the Second

World War a deserved reputation as our leading man of medical letters; he was not only a distinguished scientist but also a noble intellect. *Rats, Lice and History* is written in overt homage to the structure and typography of Henry Fielding and Tobias Smollett (M.D.). The book is only in part the history of typhus and its vectors; it also recites in magisterial prose the epic of contagion. Although it ought to be pertinent to the study of our present-day plague, the book is unremembered.

Lewis's hero Arrowsmith made a unique scientific discovery, that of bacteriophage, in which he was scooped by a Frenchman, Felix d'Herelle. In *Shannon's Way*, a book far more persuasively written than *Arrowsmith*, Dr. A. J. Cronin tells the story of a poor British scientist who winds up unraveling the etiology of brucellosis, only to be scooped by an American. *Shannon's Way* is a spare, tightly crafted romance of discovery. It is difficult to know why—on merit alone—*Arrowsmith* and *Microbe Hunters* are still on bookstore shelves whereas the books by Cronin and Zinsser have not survived. They deserve resurrection in our noncourse.

Science and medicine are nonfictional material, and perhaps for that reason the familiar essay may be the genre most suitable to their public exposition. The collection of essays by the late Sir Peter Medawar, *Pluto's Republic*, is probably the most engaging prose ever to issue from the pen of a Nobel laureate. Medawar was a formidable advocate of the cause of astronomy against astrology, of the conscious against the unconscious, and of ameliorative biology against the dreary dons of the selfish gene.

A fine intellectual feast would begin with the *menu de dégustation* of Medawar's *nouvelle* essays followed by the fresh sorbet of Robert K. Merton's *On the Shoulders of Giants*. Merton offers a book-length analysis of the roots and fate of the title phrase, usually attributed to Newton. The volume can also be read as a celebration of the joys of pure inquiry, of the community of scholars, and of the Jamesian notion that "you can give humanistic value to almost anything by teaching it historically." Professor Merton is a sociologist of science, Medawar was a fine medical scientist; their books reassure us that the spirit of James—generous, tolerant, civilized—still informs practitioners of science.

Either of two more recent books might serve as a syllabus for the course we are not about to offer. If we want the traditional mix of ethics, psychology, and lit-crit, we might use Howard Brody's *Stories of Sickness*. Dr. Brody's eloquent book presents a formidable challenge to those of us who would like to drop programs in medical humanities. He shows us how the languages of literary criticism and social science can be applied to the tales of illness that doctors and patients tell each other. Dr. Brody, who teaches at Michigan State University, persuades us that healing is best accomplished when the patient/narrator and the physician/auditor agree on the meaning of a text to reach a joint explanation of the "illness experience." Using appropriate materials from medical ethics, sociology, and the wider culture (the writings of John Donne, Virginia Woolf, Thomas Mann, and Susan Sontag, among others), Brody argues that "the story plays a therapeutic role, for better or worse, in every physician-patient encounter in which the patient is capable of symbolic communication." He convinces us that the patient masters his experience of illness "either by feeling personally powerful enough to affect the course of events" or by feeling that his individual powerlessness can be compensated for "by the power of a healer—or healing group—with whom he has shared his story." The physician is not passive in his role as auditor, for unlike magicians, cultists, and divines, he must "bring all available scientific knowledge to bear upon that story."

For Brody, the great power of modern biomedical science derives from its capacity to give explanations of the text that are at once satisfactory and testable. "The physician's words to the patient—the revised, medicalized and professionalized version of the story of the illness—are part of the healing process as well." The patient tells a story, the doctor deciphers a plot. E. M. Forster has pointed out that when we are told that "the King died and then the Queen died," we are offered a story, but when a writer explains that "the King died and then the Queen died of grief," we are given a plot. We might say that medical science provides the plot for all those stories of illness in language that makes sense in two cultures.

Brody recognizes that the impetus to courses in medical humanities came from "a conviction that medical care has become too technologically focused, and that if proper attention were paid to its human and interpersonal dimensions, it could regain a level of care and compassion that it was judged (correctly or incorrectly) to have had in the past." But he is unaware of any evidence that the teaching of humanities will breed more compassion: "It is not generally felt to be the case, for example, that philosophers who study and teach ethical theory are more compassionate or kindly as a group compared to their colleagues who teach formal logic." But Dr. Brody, compassionate and kind, has made even medical humanities a pleasure to read.

W. H. Auden observed that "pleasure is by no means an infallible critical guide, but it is the least fallible." William Ober's *Bottoms Up!* also gives pleasure and does so by displaying its own erudition as it contributes to ours. Once we forgive this charming author his outrageous choice of book title we discover a bravura selection of essays that shows what a first-rate intelligence can do with the tools of scholarship and a sense of play. Ober is at home in musicology, iconography, and poetics; nothing in the traditional humanities is alien to his pen. His attention and prose range widely over the ground of our common culture, from Egyptian papyri to the illustrations of *Fanny Hill*, from Ibn al-Khabib's fourteenth-century monograph on bubonic plague in Granada to Robert Musil's fin-de-siècle agonies in Vienna.

The wide scope of these essays does not fragment the book, since as in any successful collection, the real subject of each essay is the mind of the author. The Ober who emerges from the rich assembly of facts and judgments is a congenial, cosmopolitan gentleman. He proves to be as fit a guide to Rimbaud's verse as to the poet's fatal illness, as engaged by Johnsonian rhetoric as by the doctor's melancholy. From the very first sentence—"The story of man's inhumanity to man is older than recorded history"—we find ourselves instructed by a skeptical and tolerant observer.

Gentle humor abounds. Here we find Carlo Gesualdo, a sixteenth-century madrigalist, avenging his honor by slaying his wife, Donna Maria, and her ducal lover: "Duke Fabrizio had been shot through the head with an arquebus and was also wounded in the head, face, neck, chest, stomach, arms, hands, shoulders, and flank by multiple sword thrusts which passed through his body from front to back." The details of the execution might suffice for the routine forensic pathologist. Ober, however, adds that a "somewhat discordant note is struck by the unexplained statement that Duke Fabrizio, when slain, was wearing one of Donna Maria's night dresses. This might pose a problem for the costume designer of this opera, but not the librettist." Then Ober shifts gears; he manages to use this bizarre act as a clue to unraveling the emotional tangle of Gesualdo's madrigals. He connects the composer's music and private demons to our "later age with its own martyrdom and pain, for which his music is singularly fitting."

Ober's interest in the mental pathology of saint and sinner leads him to accounts of the history of spanking (hence the book's title), to a discussion of the contributions made by hashish and absinthe to French symbolist poetry, and to an analysis of Margery Kempe's fourteenth-century visions. These concert-grade performances in the art of the essay constitute a reminder of what the world of books was like before the major publishers fought for space on the shelves of supermarkets to sell the memoirs of bimbos and scalawags. Civilization rears her lovely head in its pages, and William Ober has caught her features.

13

Daumier and the Deer Tick

Daumier had rented a modest apartment in the Île St.-Louis,
on the quai d'Anjou. Over the top of it extended an enormous attic which in the eyes of the landlord was quite
valueless. For in this once noble but now deserted neighborhood, space at that time counted for nothing. All the artist
had to do to make himself a vast and splendid studio was to
have this attic plastered and open up large windows on the
roof where there had been a skylight. This attic he had
connected with his rooms by means of a frail and elegant
spiral staircase.

THÉODORE DE BANVILLE, *Petites études: Mes souvenirs*

Nowadays, the frail and elegant staircase has long been boarded
over and Daumier's old studio—still a rental property—is reached
by way of the main stairwell. One night last winter, my wife and I
found ourselves climbing those ancient stairs to attend a song
recital by Tobé Malawista. The concert was in the nature of a
farewell party given by Tobé and Stephen Malawista for their
colleagues and friends at the end of a sabbatical year in Paris; the
Malawistas had the good fortune to live in Daumier's studio.
Steve is an old colleague of mine. A fellow rheumatologist, he is
best known for having headed the group at Yale that first described
Lyme disease and went on to identify its cause and cure. Last year
he had been studying molecular biology at the Institut Pasteur,
and Tobé had worked hard at her voice lessons.

After the dark of the wind-swept *quai* and the gloom of those five flights of wooden stairs, we were glad to arrive at the brightly lit studio. A chatty crowd of sixty or more faced a temporary platform that had been constructed at one end of the loft for the soprano and her accompanist. We barely had time to find two unoccupied places in the rear before friendly waves and bilingual salutes gave way to an opening round of applause. The soprano and pianist made their entrance.

The first piece was a fluttering aria by Scarlatti, "O cessate di piagarmi" ("Oh, stop tormenting me"), sung by Tobé in a far from amateur voice that sparkled in the middle registers. The audience beamed in approval as their hostess showed not only charm but command. Italian gave way to a stately air of Handel: "Oh, had I Jubal's lyre"; the extensive repeats of the Baroque master gave me time to look around the crowded studio.

Daumier's attic, as high but somewhat longer than a squash court, had been altered since Banville's visit by additions of a kitchen and bedroom. The axis of the studio was defined by two great skylights, north and south; at one end of the room a metal staircase gave access to the roof. The plaster walls were hung with several recent oils of the fauvist persuasion. Much of the present-day furniture had been cleared to accommodate the audience, seated on rows of rented chairs. There was no trace of the square, black enameled stove that was the chief item of fixed furniture in Daumier's time and around which his visitors and assistant would sit, each with a "liter or so in hand" as the brothers Goncourt describe.

Scanning the audience assembled in their paisley, suede, silk, loden, denim, and tweed, I spotted some of Steve's *équipe* from the Pasteur, molecular biologists from suburban Villejuif, hematologists from New York Hospital, rheumatologists from Brooklyn; later I met lawyers, doctors, musicians, art dealers, and philosophers. We were an assembly of both sexes, several nations, and many cultures. How appropriate it all seemed: Were we not in spirit the very subjects of Daumier's art? Were we not, in Henry James's words, our century's version of the "absolute bourgeois" to whom Daumier held up the "big cracked mirror" of caricature?

Daumier moved to the Île St.-Louis in 1846 after his late marriage to a young seamstress. He was thirty-eight and prepared to settle down; he had already known both fame and misfortune as a popular caricaturist. In the 1830s Daumier's lithographs of King Louis Philippe as Gargantua or a fat pear had cost the cartoonist six months in the political prison of Ste.-Pélagie. But now, in the waning days of the July Monarchy—the regime that Tocqueville called the least cruel and most corrupt in French history—Daumier was firmly married and gainfully employed. He was commissioned by *Charivari*, an independent four-page daily, to produce several full-page lithographs each week, sharing the third-page slot with Grandville's menagerie and the kinder, gentler spoofs of Gavarni.

The Île St.-Louis had much to recommend it to Daumier. In the first place, rents were cheap. The old houses on the *quais*, which dated from the age of Louis XIII, were by and large in disrepair. Tenements less grand than these were overcrowded by workers, artisans, and small shopkeepers who had been displaced from the new constructions around the Hôtel de Ville and the Cité. Ancient neighborhoods were toppled in the name of progress and sanitation, while the building speculators of the July Monarchy followed the regime's advice of *"Enrichissez-vous!"* The gentrification of Paris moved ever westward, a trend not reversed until the 1970s. The Île St.-Louis had settled into the picturesque squalor of a fringe neighborhood.

Daumier was attracted to the Île not only for its raffish life, but also for its spectacular views. No painter of rural scenes, Daumier loved best the reassuring landscape of Parisian masonry. We might assume, from its frequent appearance in his lithographs, that his favorite prospect was right outside his front door, where the five arches of the nearby Pont Marie dip into the Seine like the tines of a graceful fork. A corner away, on the ancient rue

Femme-sans-tête was a riverside bistro where ragpickers, barge-men, and river navvies congregated. Daumier, a lifelong sot, often drank with them until he was himself *sans tête*. He did not find it inconvenient that the large wholesale wine market of Paris lay directly across the Seine to the south. He describes lurching home, bottle-laden, along the narrow lanes of the Île, banging his shoulders against the houses on either side. Charles Baudelaire showed that side of him—the Femme-sans-tête, ragpicker side—in a poem the first draft of which he gave Daumier as a present:

> On voit un chiffonnier qui viént, hochant la tête,
> Buttant, et se cognant aux murs comme un poete,
> Et sans prendre souci des mouchards, ses subjets,
> Épanche tout son coeur en glorieux projets.

> One sees a ragpicker coming, bobbing his head,
> Stumbling and knocking against the walls like a poet,
> And, oblivious to police spies, his subjects,
> Pours out his grand designs straight from the heart.

Although Daumier and Baudelaire might appear as two antipo-des of the French cultural globe, it seems likely that Daumier chose his studio on the quai d'Anjou because his friend Baudelaire lived a few doors away at the Hôtel Lauzun. The two differed wildly in appearance. Daumier was large, his face puffed with drink and sausage; only his eyes were said to betray wit and resolve. He was clothed and coiffed in the slightly tatty style of the absolute bourgeois; the photograph by Nadar makes him look like his contemporary Claude Bernard, the self-made professor of physiology, giant of the Collège de France. Baudelaire, pale, intense, and clean-shaven, was either dressed to the teeth in the latest linen of upper bohemia or else disheveled in rags, depending on his fortunes. Daumier's domestic arrangements were tranquil, the poet's life was awash in drugs and disease. Nor could two fictions have been further apart than the bourgeois Robert Macaire of Daumier's cartoons and the jaded *"roi d'un pays pluvieux"* of

NADAR, *Honoré Daumier.*
Museum of Modern Art, New York.

Baudelaire's poem. And what could be more remote from the daily spoofs of *Charivari* than Baudelaire's eternal vision of the poet as dandy? "Le dandysme est le dernier éclat d'heroîsme dans la décadence . . . comme l'astre qui décline, il est superbe, sans chaleur et plein de mélancolie" ("Dandyism is the last flash of heroism amid decadence . . . like a waning star, it is superb, without warmth and full of melancholy"). "Le dandy doit aspirer d'être sublime sans interruption. Il doit vivre et dormir devant un miroir" ("The dandy should try to be sublime without interruption. He should live and sleep before a mirror").

But Daumier and the dandy were lifelong friends and drinking companions. In the early 1840s Baudelaire and his mistress, the "black Venus" Jeanne Duval, frequented Daumier's digs on the rue de l'Hirondelle and in the mid-1850s it was Baudelaire who sat with an anxious Mme. Daumier when the artist was ill. It is also Baudelaire to whom we owe the best contemporary essay on Daumier's caricature: "Quelques caricaturistes." The poet understood that Daumier had seized on the subtle textures made possible by the new medium of the lithograph to gain chromatic effects as rich as those of oil painting. Baudelaire pointed out that Daumier had used black and gray as colors to describe a *physiologie* of bourgeois life: the artist had found a new medium to depict a new class. Daumier's middle-class contemporaries of the 1840s gobbled up innumerable volumes devoted to human *physionomie*, *mimicologie*, and *analyses philosophiques et physiologiques;* the caricaturist offered a convenient guide to their own zoology. Baudelaire spoke of the Daumier bestiary: "Feuilleter son oeuvre, et vous verrez défiler devant vos yeux, dans sa réalité fantastique et saisissante, tout ce qu'une grande ville contient de vivantes monstruosités" ("Leaf through his work and you will find paraded before your eyes, in their striking and fantastic reality, all the living monsters that a large city contains").

Only some of what a large city had to offer in the 1980s was present in Daumier's studio on the night of the concert. But if our sample of the twentieth-century bourgeoisie was short on living monsters, we lacked not for molecular biologists or arthritis doctors. Sons and daughters of the middle classes, we were very tame monsters indeed. Nothing more exotic was on view than the occasional mod haircut of a geneticist or the ostrich boa of an editor. Another stirring Handel aria sprang tunefully from Tobé Malawista's throat: "O sleep, why dost thou leave me?" No such objection arose from the loden-jacketed chap before me; his unlit pipe hung precariously from his lips. He resembled the youthful self-portrait of Gustave Courbet that is often called *The Man with a Pipe* (1848). The half-smiling artist of the portrait has shut his lids as if in drugged rêverie: the pipe dangles from his lips. The picture is not of a tobacco smoker.

By the time Daumier had established his atelier on the quai d'Anjou, Baudelaire, Gautier, and Courbet had been introduced to an artificial paradise three doors away. The wealthy *patron* of the Hôtel Lauzun, Émile Boissard de Boisdevier, was a sometime Salon painter (1835) who had founded the Club des Haschichins. The French at the time ruled much of North Africa, and the favorite weed of the dark continent ruled the Île St.-Louis. Boissard's soirées at the Hôtel Lauzun attracted much of the avant-garde of the day, and his visitors became subjects for nightly experiments in intoxication by wine, hashish, or discourse. The laboratory

G. COURBET, *The Man with a Pipe.*
Wadsworth Atheneum, Hartford.

notes of these experiments were kept by Baudelaire: *The Artificial Paradise* contains an almost clinical description of the isolating effects of cannabis compared to the socializing graces of alcohol. The distinction has not been better drawn since. The dandy before the mirror has watched his mind inflate, he has performed experiments at the back of his skull: "L'homme n'échappera pas à la fatalité de son tempérament physique et moral: le haschich sera, pour les impressions et les pensées familières d'homme, un miroir grossissant, mais un pur miroir" ("Man cannot escape the fate dictated by his physical and moral temper: hashish will [be found to] be an enlarging mirror for man's familiar thoughts and fancies, but a clear mirror").

Daumier and Baudelaire—caricaturist and dandy, cracked mirror and enlarging glass, bourgeois and bohemian—had more in common than their biographies suggest. One need not look very far to find the dandy in Daumier: one finds it in the cadenzas of crayon that define the flutter of a lawyer's robe, in the quivering jowl of a connoisseur, the undulating cravat of a doctor. But his dandiest creation was his extravagant police spy, M. Ratapoil, stool pigeon for the emperor: one of the *"mouchards, ses sujets."* The flair of Ratapoil's moustaches, the ruined finery of his morning coat and high *chapeau* brought out virtuoso passages of crayon calligraphy. In Ratapoil, the draftsmanship is in the service not only of character but also of self-display.

Nor is the sound of the city missing from the seductive throb of *Les Fleurs du mal.* Baudelaire appears to have set the urban stage for those dandies who followed his lead: the brothers Goncourt, Oscar Wilde, our own Tom Wolfe come to mind. In the works of the dandy, concern with silk and self shares the page with beggars and madhouses, thieves and jails, whores and hospitals, *"où toute énormité fleurit comme une fleur"* ("where every outrage blossoms like a flower"). The dandy is, of course, the ultimate realist of city pleasure. In this he differs from the Romantic, whose major allegiance is to the countryside. Thoughts of the Romantics came to mind as the soprano recital continued. A group of Schubert songs began with the rich warble of Heine's "Das Fischermädchen."

ACTUALITÉS.

AUX CHAMPS-ÉLYSÉES.

Ratapoil — Par suite d'une délibération philantropique du Comité du **dix Décembre**,
à deux sous les gourdins......à deux sous!.......

H. DAUMIER, *Ratapoil*. Musée d'Orsay, Paris.

In the background, the piano rumbled its wavelike comment on the lyrics: The poet invites a young fishermaiden into the ebb and flow of his heart. As this *Lieder* sequence went on, I reckoned that a good many of the scientists in the room had worked with another sort of leader sequence: that run of DNA which dictates the ebb and flow of gene transcription in man and microbes.

Microbes reminded me why Romantic fishermaidens would not have favored the ebb and flow of the Seine in Daumier's day. The river was used as a commercial waterway, a public bath, a stable, a laundry—and a sewer. Parisians of the mid-century saw no connections between their use of the water and the spread of disease. Gustave Geffroy (1878) describes the Seine beneath Daumier's window:

> La Seine devient une paisible rivière de campagne bordée d'arbres, avec un large greve. . . . Au loin, des chalands dorment sur une eau verte. . . . Les chevaux que l'on baigne, solides bêtes de travail, émergent de l'eau en massive sculptures. Des enfants courent, jambes nues; les pécheurs à la ligne sont immobil. Des blanchisseuses pliants sous le faix remontent les escaliers de pierre. Des ouvriers et des bourgeois, coude à coude, regardent les remous et ses sillages. Tout cela sur un fond des maisons blanches, rousses et grises du quai, au toits inégaux, aux fenêtres irrégulières.

> The Seine becomes a peaceful country river with large banks bordered by trees. . . . In the distance, barges rest on green water. . . . The horses, solid beasts of labor, rise from the water after their bath like massive statues. Children run by bare-legged; the fishermen are immobile at their lines. The washerwomen, listing under their burdens, climb back up along stone steps. Workers and bourgeois, side by side, look at the swirling water and its wake. All

this against a backdrop of white, rust, and gray houses of
the quay, with their uneven roofs and irregular windows.

But the horses, children, fish, and laundry were doused by a
river fed by open sewers: five miles of open effluent. I do not
believe it an accident that the years of civil revolt in France
(1830-2, 1848-50) coincided with peaks of cholera epidemics in
the summers. The June revolution in the cholera summer of 1848
was a more desperate affair than the fraternal uprising that toppled Louis Philippe in February. By June, the workers ran not
only to the barricades. The ensuing short-lived republic (1848-51)
was also threatened by unrest and disease. Tocqueville pointed
out that in June of 1849 "civil war, always a cruel thing to
anticipate, [was] much worse combined with the horrors of the
plague. For cholera was then ravaging Paris. . . . A good many
members of the Constituent Assembly had already succumbed."

Many of those who could escaped from Paris. Daumier's
friend Millet (*The Man with the Hoe*) fled with his family to set
up his studio in the country, and it is a footnote to the period that
the Barbizon School was founded in response to cholera. In June
1849 Courbet was stricken by the disease and after his recovery
returned to his native Ornans, where he painted his masterpiece
The Burial at Ornans. Again I doubt it a coincidence that his
magnum opus depicts a funeral in which black pigments dominate an icon of rural death.

Indeed, it might be said that the obligatory black costume of
the nineteenth-century bourgeois served as a metaphor of death
by infection. Marxist historian T. J. Clark has presented a remarkable analysis of *The Burial at Ornans* in which he argues that
Courbet used black costumes, social groupings, and other icono-
graphic devices to demonstrate—among other things—that the
Courbets of Ornans were not simple peasants but members of the
rural bourgeoisie. One definition of a bourgeois was that unlike a
worker, peasant, or bohemian he could afford to pay for his own
funeral, and Baudelaire himself pointed out that the black day-

G. COURBET, *The Burial at Ornans*. Musée d'Orsay, Paris.

dress of the bourgeois made him look as if he were perpetually attending someone's funeral. Before the 1830 outbreak of cholera, which spread from Provence to the capital, the *habit noir* was uncommon; by the 1848 epidemic it had become battle dress on the boulevards. Baudelaire's bourgeois was busy attending the funerals of cholera victims.

During the February revolt Baudelaire urged Republicans to the barricades; gun in hand, he called for the death of General Aupick, hero of Waterloo and head of the elite École Polytechnique. The gesture, worthy of Mark Rudd or Oedipus, was not often repeated after the cholera days of June. By summer's end, Baudelaire, who happened to be the stepson of General Aupick, had left for the clean air of the country. Only Daumier remained in Paris throughout the cholera summers. His print of cholera—in the black and white of an etching, not the grays of lithography—shows deserted streets with an emaciated dog, a pair of stretcher-bearers departing, a victim in black dying in the gutter, a passing hearse with two in train.

The poor fought the new bourgeois republic as they fought disease, and they equated the two. Clark has translated the complaint of a M. Dupont, ally and friend of Baudelaire:

La Réaction sur nos murs
Étale son aile livide;
Chassons les miasmes impurs
Dégageons le marais putride.
Nous nous plaignons du choléra
Il nous guette dans notre gîte:
Un coup de vent le balaira
Hurrah! les morts vont vite!

Reaction spreads its livid wings
Over our walls;
Let's chase away the dirty specters,
Drag ourselves from putrid swamps.
We may complain about cholera
It's waiting in our homes:
One whiff of fresh air will clear it away.
Hurray! The dead go quickly.

Predictably, the middle classes took a different view of cholera. A popular engraving of the time entitled *Two Scourges of the Nineteenth Century, Socialism and Cholera* shows a wraith reading Proudhon's socialist newspaper, while at the foot of the guillotine cholera plays a flute carved of human bone. A friend of Daumier, Vetex, was commissioned by the Republic to cast a statue when the epidemic had waned; nowadays it sits in an alcove of the Salpêtrière. It shows an overwrought—and underdressed—figure of Paris thanking God for saving the city from cholera. Intervention by the deity was not very effective: 75,000 Parisians died, the bulk of those in the poorer quarters of the town.

Haussmann's urban renewal during the Second Empire included reconstruction of the city's sewer system. Thus when cholera next threatened the capital from Baltic and Mediterranean ports, Paris was spared. Not only improved sanitation but also strict quarantine measures saved the city. The disease was not, however, on its way to elimination until Robert Koch isolated the causative microbe (a vibrio) in 1894 and rediscovered its water-borne route of transmission. Footnotes to literary history tell us that Émile Zola's father, a civil engineer, died before he could finish building a clean water system for the city of Avignon in the wake of the 1830 epidemic, and that Marcel Proust's father, a public health doctor, played a major role in the sanitary reforms that kept cholera from French borders. We might conclude that literature is the child of hygiene.

Clean water and literature, if not hygiene, were on our minds as Tobé swung into the last song before intermission. Appropriately enough, it was Poulenc's "Air champêtre" set to a fey ode by Jean Moréas. The symbolist poem addresses itself to a gurgling country stream:

> O nymphe à ton culte attache
> Pour se mêler encore au souffle qui t'effleure
> Et répondre à ton flot caché . . .
>
> O nymph, I would join your cult,
> To mingle again with the breeze that caresses you
> And to respond to your hidden waters . . .

There are no nymphs in Baudelaire, no running brooks in Daumier. Between the Romantic ebb of Heine and the symbolic flow of Moréas, a generation of Parisian realists and dandies defined the space of urban art, a culture of the new based on observation. In Daumier's art, the observations were most acute when his medium was that of graphic journalism: its fluent sketches, impromptu poses, multiple copies. His paintings, on the other hand, were patterned after an older vernacular of easel painting. He had looked long and hard at the Old Masters in the Louvre and learned his lessons from the savviest printmaker of them all, Rembrandt. The chiaroscuro of Rembrandt's canvases agreed with the Dutch passion for etching; Daumier based his smallish oil paintings on the journalistic conventions of lithography: the close-up grimace, the backlit figure, the fuzzy corners. Daumier, the caricaturist, never quite got the hang of all that grand painting, of how to fill each meter of canvas in the conventional manner of the Salon painter. Delacroix accused him of having "trouble finishing," and indeed, Daumier never quite completed the few major pieces commissioned from him by the Republic. In most of Daumier's oils, the process of painting remains undisguised; the image remains almost unfinished. Black, lithographic lines trail off in crayonlike fashion over scrumbled washes of ocher, umber, and buff.

Daumier's experiments in oil seem to work best when their subject matter matches that of his daily work for *Charivari:* the people of Paris. For me the most perfect of Daumier's paintings is the little *Washerwoman* in the Musée d'Orsay. Immediately to the left of the tricky entrance to the museum is a room devoted to Daumier; his small paintings and clay figurines are eclipsed by the giant spaces of the former train terminal. But the washerwoman manages to hold her own against all the arches and statuary. She is brushed in dense lithographic strokes and seems as solid as the masonry of the quai d'Anjou on which she treads. She and her child are shown climbing up to the street from the riverbank below. As in a print, the figures are posed in silhouette against the creamy houses of the right bank; they are framed by the stone walls of the *quai.* Indeed, since the oil is almost exactly the size of a lithographer's stone (49 × 33 cm), mother and child may be said to have stepped from the artist's stone to the pavement of the street. We do not see the river: we infer its presence from the geometry of the site. The composition may derive from Baudelaire's comment to Daumier after a day in the country: "L'eau en liberté m'est insupportable; je la veux prisonnière aux carcans, dans les murs géométriques d'un quai" ("I find free-flowing water insufferable; I want it imprisoned, yoked by the geometric walls of a quay").

Since the site described by both painter and poet was the

H. DAUMIER, *The Washerwoman*. Musée d'Orsay, Paris.

quai right outside the studio where the concert was held, I resolved to look at it during the short intermission. Ample halftime applause now rewarded Tobé and Mme. Aïtoff her accompanist. There was much moving about as several rounds of amiable greetings and general introductions were exchanged. We were assured that a first-rate collation would be served at the end of the concert; there wafted from the kitchen scents that would have troubled the *physiologie* of M. Brillat-Savarin himself. I threaded my way through the bustle to a window overlooking the quai d'Anjou. The streets were well lit and the Seine sparkled from a hundred lights: a few cars scuttled along the motorway across the river. The Pont Marie was there on the left—just as in Daumier's lithographs—and here, just in front of the studio, was the little break in the quayside wall that marked the beginning of the stone staircase down to the river. Here the washerwoman and her child had climbed up and down, dawn and dusk. Here Daumier had caught them once and for all. Here Baudelaire had seen the same scene, and he wrote verses as free of sentiment as the streets of Paris:

> L'Aurore grelottante en robe rose et vert
> S'avançait lentement sur la Seine déserte.
> Et le sombre Paris en se frottant les yeux
> Empoignant ses outils, veillard laborieux.
>
> Dawn, quivering in robes of rose and green,
> Crawls slowly over the empty Seine.
> And Paris, rubbing her eyes in the dark,
> Picks up her gear like an old workwoman.
>
> ("Le Crépuscule du matin," 1857)

It struck me that both Daumier and Baudelaire were not simply observing the Paris scene in *Washerwoman* or "Le Crépuscule du matin." Their observations had been modified not only by the conventions of art but by the social concerns of the new realism.

Realism in its urban phase was a meliorist experiment in the sense that city life itself was an experiment in nineteenth-century Paris, or in any other city for that matter. Across the river, in his *Introduction to the Study of Experimental Medicine*, their contemporary Claude Bernard had proclaimed that: "L'observation est l'investigation d'un phénomène naturel, et l'expérience est l'investigation d'un phénomène modifié par l'investigateur" ("Observation is the investigation of a natural phenomenon, and an experiment is the investigation of a phenomenon modified by the investigator").

Looking from Daumier's studio over the dark river to the gleaming motorway, seeing trim new buildings squeezed between floodlit landmarks of the old Marais, watching the lights of a *bateau-mouche* play on ancient façades of the Île St.-Louis, hearing strains of Charles Trenet from a transistor by the river-side, I had the impression that the city experiment had worked. Experiments of French art and science had not been the only successful efforts of the last century. That evening, Paris itself might be said to have been a successful experiment, an experiment carried out not only by the likes of Bernard or Daumier but by the French people whose sense of order sometimes coincides with the goals of equality and fraternity. The city since Daumier seems to have survived cholera and revolution, war and famine, occupation and betrayal, structuralism and nouvelle cuisine. I hoped that one day the unfinished experiment of life in urban America might conclude with as much success as the Paris of that evening. An ocean away from the Manhattan of crack and crime, I was less certain than usual that modern city life was a fatal disease that required empathy rather than intervention on the part of the doctor. I was buoyed by this optimism as my host approached.

As we looked over the river, the view of water prompted me to remind Steve that my wife and I expected the Malawistas to visit our house at Woods Hole next summer, and that we would all be having dinner together within a month by the East River in New York. Steve was going to lecture on Lyme disease in a postgraduate course that I conduct each year; he had first given us a talk on Lyme arthritis in 1977. He told me he would be presenting a new aspect of the disease that should be of interest to me. A Harvard entomologist, Andrew Spielman, claimed that Lyme disease had originated on Naushon Island in Massachusetts. Since Naushon is separated from Woods Hole only by a narrow channel that joins Vineyard Sound to Buzzards Bay, and since I remembered that the tick that harbored the spirochete of Lyme disease was carried by deer, I asked Steve how the disease would have arrived on the mainland.

"Well, I guess the deer must have swum across the Hole."

Further conversation was interrupted by the flicking of lights, which signaled the end of the *entr'acte*. We resumed our seats as Tobé and her pianist were received with another friendly round of applause. The next two songs were by Benjamin Britten and were chirped in the staccato of folk tunes: "Oliver Cromwell is dead!" we were told, and bell-like chords echoed, "Haw-haw." Next came a song from Somerset, "O Waly, Waly." Its lyrics continued the aqueous motifs of earlier songs:

> The water is wide, I cannot get o'er,
> And neither have I wings to fly.
> Give me a boat that will carry two,
> And both shall row, my love and I. . . .
> A ship there is, and she sails the sea,
> She's loaded deep as deep can be.
> But not so deep as the love I'm in:
> I know not if I sink or swim.

Thinking about Steve's remark, I wondered whether the Naushon deer sank or swam. I had only recently learned that deer could swim at all. In fact, Prosser and Deedee Gifford, who live near us at Woods Hole, had assured us that they had seen deer swimming across the channel between Woods Hole and Naushon Island. Gothamite that I am, I was in no position to doubt the proposition that deer can swim—or fly, for that matter. Having been brought up as city-bound as Daumier or Baudelaire, I'm always ready to believe any countryman's tale of sea and forest; I'm a sucker for the tall stories in *Smithsonian* or *National Geographic* with all their wisdom of the wild. My thoughts wandered to the only deer Paris had shown me: the deer of Courbet's canvases on the level above the Daumier room at the museum across the river. Seated by the gleaming Seine that evening, with Britten's "O Waly, Waly" in my ears, I fancied that small herds of white-tailed deer might—well, why not?—have dipped their gawky limbs into the waters off the Île St.-Louis. As dawn quivered in rose and green, they had made their way downstream to the Musée d'Orsay. They had emerged, those graceful creatures, to shake the Seine off their antlers and stepped ashore to settle on the Rive Gauche. The distance they would have had to travel and the strength of current they would have encountered are roughly similar to those between Naushon Island and the Woods Hole mainland.

Deer, of course, not only can but *do* swim. And while it is not certain that deer carried the tick that carries Lyme disease from Naushon to the mainland it *is* certain that where there are no deer there is no Lyme disease. We now know that the tick (*Ixodes dammini*) spends its winters embedded in the deep fur of the white-tailed *Odocoileus virginianus*. Bambi, in Latin. The deer tend not to get the disease but they harbor all stages of the *I. dammini* tick, and therefore, in the words of Andrew Spielman, "their presence is prerequisite to the maintenance of infections transmitted by this vector."

Naushon and some of its sister islands off the eastern mainland served as wooded, brush-filled sanctuaries for deer in the three centuries during which the creatures fell prey to Indians and settlers. On the mainland, trees and deer disappeared as red man and white used them for fuel, food, and shelter. Importation of iron tools and iron weapons played a major role in leveling the land and destroying its wildlife. The scribe John Brereton, who accompanied Bartholomew Gosnold on his voyage of discovery in New England in 1602, described the landscape of the offshore islands as filled with "an incredible store of Vines, as well in the woodie part of the island; where they run upon every tree, as on the outward parts, that we could not go for treading upon them. . . . Here also in this island, great store of Deere, which we saw and other beasts as appeared by their tracks . . . " But by 1640 deer were already on their way to destruction and, again according to Andrew Spielman, the last deer on Nantucket Island was eaten in the middle of the nineteenth century. Pictures of Woods Hole of the last century show the low coastline scalped of trees and bare of wildlife.

Only Naushon remained a deer preserve, because of the stewardship of its private owners: Presidents Ulysses S. Grant and Theodore Roosevelt visited the island and shot deer for sport. Wealthy Americans tend to favor trees on their estates; deer parks are the proper preserve of the mighty. Deer did not repopulate the mainland until the 1960s; by then, large areas of Cape Cod and the Massachusetts shore had become reforested as a result of general prosperity and the advent of the summer home. Properly zoned, much of the area had become filled with the kind of dense underbrush that resembled the landscape of the offshore islands before man and iron had changed the New World. It is therefore not surprising that deer and the deer tick first spread disease in affluent communities of the Northeast. From Ipswich in Massachusetts to Lyme in Connecticut to Shelter Island in New York, a reforested landscape had been permitted to assume its original parklike aspect. The victims of Lyme disease have been winter residents and the folk of summer who dwell in spacious homes among the trees, the shrubs, the lawns. In our epidemic, editors and agents, artists and models, writers and dandies have become victims. Cholera may have spread along the Left Bank by the water of the Seine; Lyme disease has flourished along the seacoast of upper bohemia.

Two songs by Fauré with texts by Sully Prudhomme were next on Tobé's program. More water! Repetitions of *"L'Eau murmure, l'eau murmure"* in "Aux bords de l'eau" were followed by dream-like ruminations which seemed to promise release from the troubles of the world. "Ici-bas" also came out in favor of flowers and the sun. The music was as charming as the lyrics were banal; Tobé's warble rolled over Fauré like a harp. After a forgettable bauble of Stravinsky's, she launched into a *berceuse* by Tchaikovsky. The lullaby is set to a text by Maikov in which the wind, obedient to the poet's fancy, responds to his good mother's question:

> " . . . Qu'as-tu fait pendant
> Ces trois jours? As-tu balayé les étoiles?
> As-tu repoussé les vagues?"
> "Non, Maman, j'ai bercé un petit enfant."
> > "Dors, mon petit."

> " . . . What have you been doing for
> Three days? Have you blown away the stars?
> Have you pushed back the waves?"
> "No, Mother, I have rocked a small child to sleep."
> > "Sleep, little one."

Lyme disease was discovered in the United States thanks to some good mothers in Connecticut. Mrs. Judy Mensch, who lived in a large house surrounded by woods, first encountered what was to be called Lyme arthritis in November 1975. Her eight-year-old daughter, Anne, came down with a swollen knee, which her doctor treated as "osteomyelitis." But when the symptoms persisted and the diagnosis was changed to "juvenile rheumatoid arthritis," the good mother began to suspect something wrong. Three other children on the same street had gotten severe arthritis within a year and a half; the girl next door needed a wheelchair after her third attack, and a boy around the corner and another little girl down the street were also afflicted. Mrs. Mensch began to call her neighbors and soon came up with a dozen other victims. She telephoned the Connecticut State Department of Health and spoke with Dr. David Snydman, who had just come to the state from the USPHS Centers for Disease Control (CDC) in Atlanta.

Dr. Snydman had also received a call from a Mrs. Polly Murray, whose husband and two teenage sons had come down with arthritis sufficient to put them all on crutches at the same time. Mrs. Murray lived a few miles north of Mrs. Mensch; the house was surrounded by woods. Snydman drove to Lyme to investigate, called up doctors, checked hospital records, and obtained lists of other victims, who by now seemed to exceed a dozen or so. He came up against a puzzle. Many of the cases, especially in children, seemed to fit into the clinical picture of juvenile rheumatoid arthritis, a rare and disabling chronic disease which, paradoxically, sometimes afflicts adults, but which differs from the more common, adult form of rheumatoid arthritis in not tagging its victims with a positive test for rheumatoid factor in the blood. Juvenile rheumatoid arthritis is therefore considered one of the rarer "seronegative" diseases of joints, and finding a dozen or so cases clustered in space and time was unheard of. Or was it?

Dr. Snydman put in a call to his friend Allen C. Steere, who had also just come from the CDC to Connecticut. Steere was a first-year fellow in rheumatology at Yale, and Steve Malawista was his chief. Steere's training had been in epidemiology, and Malawista urged him to get some experience at the laboratory bench. The project Malawista had set Steere when he arrived as a novice in July 1975 was to study the roles of cyclic nucleotides and microtubules in the inflammatory properties of human white cells; Steve's lab and mine have been friendly competitors in this sort of research for decades. Allen Steere was just getting started on white cells when fate beckoned.

Steere and Malawista agreed that there was something going

on at Lyme that warranted dropping the white cell project. They presented their proposal to the Yale Human Investigation Committee, and with Snydman's help brought in all the known or suspected cases and performed every conceivable clinical and laboratory test. They studied the case histories and epidemiological evidence; they scoured the records and local street maps. Their original study, presented for the first time at a meeting of the American Rheumatism Association in Chicago on June 10, offered a new name: "We think that the Lyme Arthritis is a new clinical entity," the abstract concluded. By July 1976, a front-page story in *The New York Times* broke the news to the public. Written by a crack science writer, Boyce Rensberger, it gave a complete account of the ongoing study at Yale and was illustrated with a photograph of young Steere "checking a patient's knee for 'Lyme Arthritis' at Yale University School of Medicine as Dr. Stephen E. Malawista, rheumatology chief, observes." "Lyme arthritis" was in the lexicon for good.

The full manuscript of Steere and Malawista's study was published in *Arthritis and Rheumatism* as "Lyme Arthritis," subtitled: "An Epidemic of Oligoarticular Arthritis in Children and Adults in Three Contiguous Connecticut Communities"; Steere, Malawista, and Snydman were at the head of the list of authors. I have been told that Allen had originally proposed the subtitle as the full title of the article, but that Steve with his didactic flair insisted on the eponym. Be that as it may, the paper is a classic of clinical science. Differentiating the disease clearly from other known types of arthritis, the authors pointed out that "its identification has been possible because of tight geographic clustering in some areas, and because of a characteristic preceding skin lesion in some patients." The skin lesion, present in 25 percent of the fifty-one patients, was correctly identified as *erythema chronicum migrans*, an expanding red nubbin of a rash that had been identified at the turn of the century in Sweden. The skin lesion had not previously been associated with arthritis, but as Steere, Malawista, et al. pointed out, fever, malaise, headache, and neurological symptoms were all part of the syndrome. The Yale group correctly deduced that "although the prevalence of *erythema chronicum migrans* in the three communities reported here is not known, it is doubtful that it is so common that one quarter of the patients with arthritis would have the skin lesion just weeks before the arthritis by chance alone. Thus the authors think that both symptoms may be manifestations of the same illness." They also correctly deduced from the clustering of the disease in more sparsely settled, heavily wooded areas rather than in town centers—and the absence of a common source of transmission such as water—that "the epidemiology fits best with an illness transmitted by an arthropod vector." They had reasoned from the first that a tick might have transmitted the disease.

Whatever else the investigation led to, whatever else developed, to my mind this first description of a new disease, this exercise of reason to produce a new bit of knowledge, is an example of what we mean when we speak of imagination in science. It has given us the sensation of the new. As one rereads the article, one can hear echoes of Baudelaire's hymn to the imagination:

Mystérieuse faculté que cette reine des facultés. Elle touche à les autres; elle les excite, elle les envoie au combat. Elle leur ressemble quelquefois au point de se confrondre avec elles, et cependant elle est toujours bien elle-même, et les hommes qu'elle n'agite pas sont facilement reconnaissables à je ne sais quelle malédiction qui dessèche leurs productions comme le figuier de l'Évangile. Elle est l'analyse, elle est la synthèse. . . . Elle a créé, au commencement du monde, l'analogie et la métaphore. Elle décompose toute la création, et avec les matériaux amassés et disposés suivant le règles dont on ne peut trouver l'origine que dans le plus profond de l'âme, elle crée un monde nouveau, elle produit la sensation du neuf.

How mysterious is imagination, that Queen of the Faculties! It touches all the others; it rouses them and sends them into combat. At times it resembles them to the point of confusion, and yet it is always itself, and those men who are not quickened by it are easily recognizable by some strange curse which withers their productions like the fig tree in the Gospel. It is both analysis and synthesis. . . . In the beginning of the world it created analogy and metaphor. It decomposes all creation, and with the raw materials accumulated and disposed in accordance with rules whose origins one cannot find save in the furthest depth of the soul, it creates a new world, it produces the sensation of the new.   (*The Salon of 1859*)

Imagination in science is the faculty that permits the investigator to reassemble those snippets of fact—the spreading rash, the swollen knee, the wooded lot—according to rules that are by no means hidden in the furthest depth of the soul. We tend to use that part of our nature to give us not the rules but the courage to break them.

Within the next few years, Steere and Malawista were joined by two other young stars of Yale medicine, John Hardin and Joseph Kraft, and went on to study the disease prospectively. This time they knew where and when to look: in the Lyme area, and in the "high" season of the malady, in summer. On the basis of 314 new cases, they defined the clinical spectrum of what by 1979 was coming to be called Lyme *disease* rather than Lyme *arthritis*. The illness turned out to be more serious than originally described in 1977, but the first full description, published a decade ago, has not required significant change. Stage one of the disease is the rash, *erythema chronicum migrans*, accompanied at times by symptoms of "summer flu" with headache and fever. These symptoms and the rash itself usually go away. Stage two follows within several weeks to months. About 15 percent of patients develop neurologic problems: strange transient paralyses, confusion, and such serious consequences as Bell's palsy or meningitis. In 8 percent, the second stage of the illness involves disorders of the heartbeat; in some cases the whole heart is inflamed (myocarditis) and deaths have been reported. Arthritis—stage three—follows in 60 percent. Developing as early as a few weeks to as late as two years after the rash, the joint disease can lead to destruction of cartilage and bone. The Yale group identified markers in the serum (cryoglobulins, IgM antibodies) that predicted which patients would go on to complications and, more important, discovered that prompt antibiotic treatment at the stage of the rash would stop the disease in its tracks. Long courses of intravenous antibiotics were effective at the later stages.

Having described the disease and its treatment, and having presented good epidemiological evidence that some sort of tick living on the back of some sort of animal was the vector of some sort of microbe, the Yale group by 1979 was left with the questions of *which* specific tick, feeding on *which* animal "reservoir," carried *which* microbe that caused Lyme disease. By 1982 the answers were in. The tick, a new species of *Ixodes dammini*, was named by Andrew Spielman; the main animal reservoirs—also uncovered by Spielman and his coworkers—were the white-footed mouse and white-tailed deer; and the microbe was a spirochete that resembled the causative agent of syphilis. The spirochete, first recovered from the mid-gut of ticks, was named *Borellia burgdorferi*, after Willy Burgdorfer of the Rocky Mountain Laboratories of the USPHS. Cats and dogs may carry the tick, birds may spread their nymphs and larvae, but if the mice or deer are killed off, there is no disease. Each of these findings required another exercise of the scientific imagination, another "observation modified by the investigator"; each produced its own sensation of the new.

Tobé had now launched into the last two songs of her recital; both the "Coucou" and the final "Oublier si vite" were by Tchaikovsky.

The first of these, programmatic to a fault, fulfilled our expectations of an ode dedicated to a mistake of the avian class. The last song was lush and sentimental, and Tobé sang it in waves of lyric delight. The poem by Apukhtin mourns: *"Oublier si vite tout le bonheur vécu dans une vie"* ("To forget too soon all the happiness of one's life").

One forgets too soon in the course of a life in science those happy, rare moments when the imagination takes over and one makes a discovery. Too often they are buried in an avalanche of disputes, of claims and counterclaims. Who had the idea first? Who did the work? Was it luck? Was it really new? Too soon one realizes that one has simply rediscovered an old observation in a new setting. Some of this happened with Lyme disease. It turns out that in 1970, a Wisconsin dermatologist named R. J. Scrimenti had reported the coincidence of *erythema chronicum migrans* with neurological symptoms in a fifty-seven-year-old doctor. Persuaded by Scandinavian reports that the rash was carried by an *Ixodes* tick that might transmit a spirochete, Scrimenti looked for a spirochete in his patient and correctly treated him with penicillin (*Archives of Dermatology*, 102 [1970], 104–5). Indeed, E. Hollstrom had already pointed out in 1958 that *erythema chronicum migrans* would respond to penicillin.

The unique spirochete was first identified by Burgdorfer after a painstaking search for a microbe in the mid-guts of ticks harvested at Shelter Island. Much of the field work in the course of the Long Island epidemic was done by a group of practitioners, pathologists, and public health doctors from New York State and from SUNY, Stony Brook. These doctors, especially Jorge Benach, Bernard Berger, and Edgar Grunwaldt, have been amply celebrated by Berton Roueché in his *New Yorker* reminiscence of the tick disease.

But the Yale group put it all together first, and got it almost all right at the very beginning. They also paved the way for a remarkable analysis of how Lyme disease is an accident of ecology and entomology. This has been brought to our attention by

Andrew Spielman, who began his work with ticks in a search for the vector of an entirely different disease.

In 1969, an elderly woman who lived on a moor on Nantucket Island experienced a malarialike infection due to a tick-borne parasite called *Babesia microti*. This rare case was followed by a second one, in an acquaintance of the old woman, who had been spending the summer in a nearby Nantucket village. After six more cases of babesiosis were identified on Nantucket in 1975, other cases popped up on Shelter Island. As had the Yale group with Lyme disease, Spielman at Harvard decided that "the geographical clustering of human infections helped establish the venue for epidemiological studies."

By 1976, Spielman's group had found that white-footed mice were the major reservoir for *B. microti* and the search was on for an insect vector. A tick was suspected, but the *Ixodes* ticks found on the mice seemed to belong to a species (*I. muris*) that previously had never attached to humans. A splendid job of systematic taxonomy led Spielman and his group to conclude that the *Ixodes* tick species "collected from Naushon Island as well as most other sites located along the New England coast and on eastern Long Island proved to be a new species, later designated *I. dammini*." (Gustav Dammin was a coworker of Spielman's.) When Lyme disease and babesiosis were linked epidemiologically by their clustering in time and space, and later by their coincidence in the same patients, their shared mode of transmission via the deer tick (which harbored both microbes) became clear. Burgdorfer's identification of the spirochete in *I. dammini* followed in 1982, and soon after, there appeared in *The New England Journal of Medicine* an article entitled "The Spirochetal Etiology of Lyme Disease." Allen Steere was the first author and Steve Malawista the last; Willy Burgdorfer was among the others. The spirochete had been found in the blood, skin lesions, and spinal fluid of three patients with Lyme disease and in twenty-one ticks found in areas of Connecticut endemic for Lyme disease. It had taken from the summer of 1975 to the spring of 1983 to describe a new disease, to find out what caused it, and to learn how to treat it. Steere et al. pointed out the implications: Since Lyme disease and syphilis were both caused by a spirochete, and since syphilis was the original "great imitator" of other diseases, the later manifestations of Lyme disease may mimic other conditions (heart attacks, nerve palsies) while live organisms take up residence in the spleen. In this paper, which represented the apex of their science, they did not remind their audience that Baudelaire reached the heights of his art in "Spleen."

Can we prevent Lyme disease? Spielman thinks that the best way to go about it is to get at the mice. But—sad to say—one can do this job just as well by killing off all the deer. At the request of the residents of Great Island off Cape Cod, all but one or two of the thirty-five deer that inhabited the island were shot during a two-year span. In the third year after deer were eliminated from Great Island, "the human population of that site largely became protected against infection. Whereas the 200-odd summer residents of this island previously had suffered four to eight Lyme disease infections annually, none were reported thereafter." Spielman doubts that these measures would work "when practiced in a portion of a continuous land mass." But I wonder what we will do about the deer if the epidemic of Lyme disease keeps mounting, like AIDS?

Sitting in the urban nest of Daumier's studio as Tobé came to the end of her recital I thought back on the elaborate machinery of nature and nurture that makes a microbial disease possible. For *B. burgdorferi* to make a living as a pathogen in Lyme, Connecticut, Gosnold had to have charted the Cape and Naushon Island; settlers and Indians had to have cleared the Northeast of forests and deer; Naushon had to have served as a private deer sanctuary; deer had to have swum or roamed back to the mainland of New England; mice and ticks had to have found themselves in a landscape with deer; and the economy of the United States had to have flourished enough to permit its middle classes the luxury of winter and summer homes in parklike settings. Those geographic considerations reminded me that diseases—like Daumier's art—are complicated products of civilization. Not only artists dictate the style of their time: not only microbes dictate who gets sick and from what. The canon of our new molecular biology agrees with that of the older literature: It takes a lot of global luck and human collusion for a bacterium or virus to become an agent of disease.

The intricate tricks of biochemistry required of a microbe to set up shop as a pathogen guarantee that not each microbe will have an equal chance of hurting every human. In that sense, if not with respect to its fury, Lyme disease may be said to be the AIDS of the affluent. Nowadays, while the sad rules of the human immunodeficiency virus have been explained to alert members of the gay community, the HIV epidemic in America affects chiefly black and Hispanic abusers of intravenous drugs. Those folks will never meet a deer or be bitten by *Ixodes dammini.* Nor is it likely that the residents of Lyme, Connecticut, will have to peddle crack or heroin for a livelihood. But although we know enough about the epidemiology of AIDS and Lyme disease to limit their relentless spread, few of those at high risk for either disease seem ready to change their social habits in the near future. The slum dweller is not likely to abandon the drug culture simply on doctor's orders; the summer resident of Cape Cod or Shelter Island is unlikely to give up his pet cat or dog. Certainly, as Steve Malawista has pointed out, no one will sign up to kill Bambi. We should probably not feel superior to the Parisians bathing in the polluted Seine. When Haussmann hacked out the sewers he did so over great opposition. Cholera was defeated because the fears it aroused were greater than the "rules" of social arrangements then current. When we become afraid enough of Lyme disease, we may be moved to greater action. I, for one, worry about the later—as yet unknown—consequences of the disease for those now treated simply with a fast course of antibiotics. We have a lot to learn.

As the rhythmic applause ended the concert in Daumier's

studio, and our comfortable crew of upper bohemians headed for
a splendid feast, the skylights and windows reflected our party
finery. Through the glass of the window, we must have looked
like the bourgeois doctors of Daumier's caricatures. So be it, I
thought. Dominant over Western culture for a century and a half,
the bourgeois, meliorist movement we represented seems to have
gotten *some* things right. We may not have built the City of God,
but we have gotten good at treating sewage. Our social arrangements may not be in better array than those of the Second Empire,
but we can drink water from a tap. Our painting and poetry may
not be more sublime than those of the Second Republic, but we
can now kill Baudelaire's spirochete and cure a blind Daumier.
Cholera is gone, and we are busy clearing up our new epidemics.
Thanks to scientists from the Institut Pasteur we have pinned
down the virus of AIDS, and thanks to our host, Steve Malawista,
and to Allen Steere, we can identify and cure Lyme disease.
Thanks to the Burgdorfers and Spielmans we have learned how
woven into the fabric of natural history is the health of a people.

I'm persuaded that work of this sort in the sciences requires
leaps of the imagination no less thrilling than Daumier's prints or
Baudelaire's verse. For way down there, in the furthest depth of
the soul, the imagination lurks in artist and scientist alike, itching
for its chance to astonish us all.

"It decomposes all creation, and with the raw materials
accumulated and disposed in accordance with rules whose origins one cannot find save in the furthest depth of the soul, it
creates a new world, it produces the sensation of the new. Since it
has created the world (so much can be said, I think, even in a
religious sense), it is proper that it should govern it." Would that
it were so, *cher maître*, would that it were so.

14

To the Nobska Lighthouse

The Nobska lighthouse stands guard over shoals at Woods Hole where the Atlantic runs between Vineyard Sound and Buzzards Bay. The bluff on which the lighthouse sits is the highest on that stretch of the coast and on fair days yields splendid views of upper Cape Cod and its islands. The prospect is never fairer from Nobska point than on early mornings in October, when—in the words of Justice Oliver Wendell Holmes—"the wind blows from the west and the air is clear." Recently, such a morning found me running uphill to the Nobska lighthouse. A plangent sea was on my left, thickets of wild grape and bittersweet were on my right. In the distance across the sound, the highlands of Martha's Vineyard flashed pink in the dawn. Nearer by, the hillocks of Naushon Island flickered mauve and green. A few cirrus clouds were backlit on the eastern horizon, the sky above was clear. On the crest of the hill the westerly breeze rustled low conifers and floated a strike force of gulls. Breathless, I stopped at the top of the bluff, convinced that the shores of Arcadia could offer nothing so bracing as this New England sunrise.

The Nobska light station is placed on a tidy promontory seventy-six feet above sea level. Its lawns are closely mowed and its hedges tightly clipped, its buildings display the prudent ordinates of Yankee architecture. The horizontal axis is defined by the keeper's house: twin, gabled saltboxes joined into a single cottage. Modest vertical accents are provided by three chimneys, a steel radio antenna, and a signal tower from which small-craft warnings flutter on stormy days. The chief vertical axis is announced by the monumental shaft of the lighthouse, a tapered tower some forty feet high made of whitewashed steel-encased brick. The tower is topped by a black lacework cupola in which the light source is housed behind a ten-sided cage of window panes. A single 150-watt bulb refracted by a cunning Fresnel lens generates 7,000 candlepower and can be seen for more than ten miles.

With stars and stripes fluttering from a freestanding flagpole, with deep shadows cast by morning light under the cottage eaves, the scene was an Edward Hopper canvas brought to life. Other themes sprang to mind. I had read that the lens of the lighthouse had been ground in 1828 by New England craftsmen from designs by Augustin-Jean Fresnel (1788–1827). Fresnel was a Jansenist from the Vendée who in the post-Napoleonic restoration pursued his optical theories while on tours of duty with the civil service. He was convinced that light was a wave rather than a particle, as Newton had taught. The young Frenchman arrived at his equations in settings fit for making waves of light: the Lighthouse Commission and the *Corps des Ponts et Chausées* (Bridge and Road Corps). His more practical work resulted in the replacement of mirrors by lenses in lighthouses the world over. Fresnel's early death from tuberculosis ended a blossoming reputation not only in physics but also in moral philosophy; he had become a keen apologist for the puritanical doctrines of his sect. He might have been pleased to know, were he among the elect, that for more than a century and a half his lens had cast light over waters that the stern Pilgrims had mastered. He might also have subscribed to the closing sentiments of "Fair Harvard":

> *Let not moss-covered error moor thee by its side,*
> *While the world on truth's current glides by;*
> *Be the herald of light and the bearer of love,*
> *'Til the stock of the Puritans die.*

Reasoning that I had been diverted from matters Arcadian to refrains academic by the anoxia of uphill running, I started downhill with relief. Arcadia had waited. Nobska beach, in the cove below the lighthouse, was at low tide. Its sands reflected the morning sun and the breeze played with tendrils of seaweed at the tidemark. By the roadway, bracken on the low dunes glowed in autumn paisley. The beach was empty, the only artifact visible an old Corvair parked some thirty yards away. The single object in motion was on the water: the first ferry to Vineyard Haven had rounded the point of Woods Hole harbor. It made a dashing sight, with its white hull, black smoke, and frothy wake against a turquoise sea. Exhilarated, I kept running along the short length of the beach back to the center of town.

I had almost left the Corvair behind me when I noticed a striking bumper sticker placed prominently on the flivver's rear. It showed the abortion rights symbol, a black coathanger on which the red international logo for "prohibited" had been superimposed. NEVER AGAIN was the legend, and NARAL (the National Abortion Rights Action League) was noted as the sponsor. The car was empty and bore no other identification except its Massachusetts plate. At that moment, I spied what must have been the owner of the car emerging from behind a bend of the cove. At that distance I could see she was a fit, middle-aged woman with short gray hair, dressed in khaki shorts and a blue denim work shirt. She was busy gathering seashells: stopping, stooping, starting, she looked like a busy shore bird. Suddenly she halted and, shielding her eyes, looked straight out at the sea and the passing ferry. Her trim form echoed the vertical of the lighthouse above; the sun caught her face and was reflected by the galvanized tin bucket she had put down beside her. Solitary against the beach, her Keds in the sand, she could have served, I thought, as a model for a low-keyed statue of Reason.

The woman in her Keds, the NARAL logo, the lighthouse—the Enlightenment?—spurred associations that turned the rest of my outing into a rumination on the days of the rusty coathanger. My mind was, literally, jogged back to Bellevue Hospital in 1959 and the era when abortion was illegal. Coathangers, rusty or not, were not the chief instruments of botched home abortions. The victims treated by my generation of house officers had been invaded by knitting needles, rat-tailed combs, and—sad to say— the metal probes used by plumbers. It is not true that only poor women bore the brunt of injury; fear of parents, fear of their partners, and fear of professional abortionists often brought daughters of the middle class to the emergency room. Rich and poor alike were at risk for the major complications of all that clumsy instrumentation: bleeding and sepsis, frequently both. For reasons not hard to imagine, the patients arrived most often at midnight and too often in shock.

Sometime after midnight on a warm Labor Day weekend thirty years ago, the Keds that I remember to this day were neatly stowed side by side under the bed of a young woman who lay febrile, breathless, and barely conscious in the emergency ward of Bellevue. One white sneaker was immaculate, the other was stained by two splotches of blood that had soaked into the canvas uppers and dried on the rubber of the instep. Most of what I recall of the larger scene was also in primary colors. The three doctors and two nurses at the bedside were in white, as were the curtains around the bed, the sheets, and the patient's gown. The blankets alone were gray, city issue, but the young woman had flushed, freckled cheeks and flame-red hair. Her lips were blue and her temperature was 104. Trying to rouse her, the nurse called her Kate; I have forgotten her last name. She was a nineteen-year-old nursing student from the school across the street and had been brought in after a fumbled attempt at self-abortion. I was the chief medical resident of Bellevue Hospital and all of ten years older than the patient. I ordered some epinephrine, diluted it, and injected a tenth of a cc in her skin.

"We're going to look for the Thomas lesion," I said, as I pointed to the pale forearm taped to a plank with white gauze. "If there is endotoxin on board, that little spot should be necrotic in a few hours." First white, then red, then black; color and then the absence of color.

The human details of the case are less clear in memory than the stark tableau of the emergency room. I seem to recall that

Kate was a farm kid from Dutchess County. She had missed a period, turned positive in a furtive rabbit test of the day, and tried to instrument herself with the help of a friend late on Saturday night. The procedure would have involved a hand mirror, some stolen local anesthetic, and a steel knitting needle sterilized over a candle. But it hadn't worked, all that happened was a cervical tear and diffuse bleeding, which the kids tried to stop with gauze. Shaken and afraid, Kate had gone to ground in the student nurses' dorm all day Sunday. By Sunday night she was again oozing large amounts of blood and had developed shaking chills. She was brought to the receiving area of Bellevue by her friend, who also provided all the details of Kate's history. By the time I saw her early on Labor Day morning, she should have been better. The gynecologists had typed, cross-matched, and transfused three pints of blood, performed a dilation-and-curettage, and sutured her cervical wounds to stop the bleeding. But complications arose. Her temperature climbed, her white cell and platelet counts dropped, bleeding started again from every needle and suture site. Suspecting that their patient was bleeding from disseminated intravascular coagulation due to gram-negative sepsis—a disorder of blood clotting caused by bacterial endotoxin—the surgeons paged the medical resident on call. He in turn knew that I was in the house, that I was working with bacterial endotoxin, and that I was up to date on gram-negative shock. I had been briefed by an expert, Lewis Thomas, our chief of service.

So there we were, like doctors before us and after, up to date but quite at sea, at the bedside of a sick young woman, searching in the only way known at the time for endotoxin in blood. We gave her more blood transfusions, intravenous broad-spectrum antibiotics (Aureomycin? Chloromycetin?), and prayed that her kidneys wouldn't shut down. I forget now what bug it was that grew out of her blood cultures the next afternoon, *Aerobacter* or *Pseudomonas*. I do remember that by then things could not have gotten worse. Her kidneys had failed, she never brought her oxygen up, she kept bleeding. We could not pull her out of shock and she died before we found out whether the Thomas lesion had turned positive.

I also remember meeting her parents the next day in the squalid waiting room of the old hospital. A postmortem examination by the Office of the Chief Medical Examiner, which was mandatory in such cases, had shown that she had died of septic shock with bilateral renal cortical necrosis and pulmonary edema with blood in the lungs. The parents appeared grief-stricken but not entirely surprised by the news that their daughter had died from a fumbled abortion. They were stern fundamentalists, American Gothics, and deep in their rustic hearts they seemed to have expected that sin would catch up with Kate, who was the "fastest" of their three daughters. She had broken their hearts when she had run away to the big city to become a nurse; the profession in those days was tainted by a touch of the profane in the minds of small-town folk. As we spoke of their daughter's death, they looked at me as coldly as if I myself had raped and killed her. In cool fury, directed at cities, hospitals, doctors, nurses, women—who knows what—the father permitted himself to say, "God punished her. She must have deserved it. She's better off this way." He took his wife's hand, asked the way to the mortuary, and left the building. Through the glass-paneled door I saw him stop, carefully fit a black felt hat to his pate, and proceed up East Twenty-sixth Street with his wife in tow.

Absorbed in those ancient recollections on my morning ramble I almost failed to notice that I had come abreast of another Woods Hole landmark, the seaside Church of the Messiah. Its new copper gutters shone in the glory of fall. Morning light also caught the salmon and gray of its cemetery stones; the green lawns had not yet been cleared of overnight leaves. I reckoned that poor Kate had been born a generation too soon on two counts: these days abortion is legal, and we know much more about the cause and treatment of endotoxin shock. Young women like Kate need not die. She would have been forty-nine by now; I imagined her standing under the Nobska light, her Keds in the sand, her Corvair parked down the road. More power to NARAL. But as I looked up at the New England steeple, it struck me that the Puritan fathers would have been as stern on abortion as Kate's father. I'm not sure how they would feel about endotoxin.

The meliorist path of our secular republic is not the road mapped out by the elders of Plymouth. The Yankee patriarchs found it easy in the name of their God to blame His victims and easier still if their names be women. Dr. Cotton Mather would have been pleased by President George Bush's veto of a bill permitting the use of federal funds to pay for abortions of indigent women who have been the victims of rape or incest. Governor Bradford of Plymouth Colony might have gone a touch further. On September 8, 1642, some thirty miles north of the Church of the Messiah, a sixteen-year-old youth named Thomas Granger was convicted of unnatural sexual acts and executed by order of the magistrates of Plymouth. According to Governor Bradford's journal of the event, *Of Plymouth Plantation 1620–1647*, the lad had been

> detected of buggery, and indicted for the same, with a mare, a cow, two goats, five sheep, two calves and a turkey. . . . A very sad spectacle it was. For first the mare and then the cow and the rest of the lesser cattle were killed before his face, according to the law, Leviticus xx.15; and then he himself was executed. The cattle were all cast into a great and large pit that was digged for the purpose of them, and no use made of any part of them.

No mention is specifically made of the turkey, but Bradford tells us that the elders were worried that innocent sheep might be slaughtered. They forced young Granger not only to confess, but to identify his former playmates: "And whereas some of the sheep could not so well be known by his description of them, others with them were brought before him and he declared which they were and which were not."

The Pilgrims' attention to details of sexual conduct was coupled to a strict regard for biblical authority. Shortly before Granger's execution, Bradford asked three local divines to find legal and scriptural precedents for the death penalty in cases of sexual deviance. He asked several specific questions related to offenses of sex and received appropriate answers in which no graphic detail of plumbing was omitted. As one might expect from a future president of Harvard, Charles Chauncy's reply had more citations in Latin and English than the other two responses, and the most from the Old Testament. His answer was also the strongest in rhetoric, the freest of sentiment, and the sternest in tone.

The Answer of Mr. Charles Chauncy

An contactus et fricatio usque ad seminis effusionem
sine penetratione corporis sit sodomia morte plectenda?

Question: The question is, What sodomitical acts are to be punished with death, and what very fact committed (*ipso facto*) is worthy of death, or if the fact itself be not capital, what circumstances concurring may make it capital? The same question may be asked of rape, incest, bestiality, unnatural sins, presumptuous sins. These be the words of the first question. The answer unto this I will Lay down (as God shall direct by His Word and Spirit) in these following conclusions.

Chauncy answered that the Mosaic laws are "immutable and perpetual" and grounded on the law of nature, indeed, that all the sins enumerated are punishable by death. Quoting extensively from Luther, Melanchthon, Calvin, and other fathers of the Reformation, he reassured the governor that

Then we may reason . . . what grievous sin in the sight of God it is, by the instigation of burning lusts, set on fire of hell, to proceed to *contactum et fricationem ad emissionem seminis,* etc. and that *contra naturam,* or to attempt the gross acts of unnatural filthiness. Again, if that unnatural lusts of men with men, or woman with woman, or either with beasts be to be punished with death, than *a pari* natural lusts of men toward children under age are so to be punished.

These themes, and their canonic variation, were also sounded by the two other elders of the Church, Mr. Rayner and Mr. Partridge. The Old Testament called for the death penalty for "unnatural vices" or offenses to God, and the Puritan preachers found ample precedent in Mosaic law for divine retribution. But a closer reading of Charles Chauncy's reply to Governor Bradford yields a remarkable passage, which must contain the first—and most severe— American argument for the prohibition of abortion. The "pro life" movement may be said to have begun in 1642; it was announced in concert with a call for death:

> In concluding punishments from the judicial law of Moses that is perpetual, we must often proceed by analogical proportion and interpretation, as *a paribus similibus, minore ad majus,* etc.; for there will still fall out some cases, in every commonwealth, which are not in so many words extant in Holy Writ, yet the substance of the matter in every kin (I conceive under correction) may be drawn and concluded out of the Scripture by good consequence of an equivalent nature. *As, for example, there is no express law against destroying conception in the womb by potions, yet by analogy with Exodus xxi.22, 23, we may reason that life is to be given for life* [italics mine].

Perhaps Chauncy's doctrine that life is to be given for a life found its highest expression in the era of the rusty coathanger. Social historians have traced some of the prohibitions against abortion in the days before *Roe v. Wade* to the severe Mosaic laws of Plymouth Plantation. Puritan values and Catholic teaching made Massachusetts the last state in the Union to permit doctors to prescribe birth control for married women (1966). The prohibition of unpopular private behavior has a long history in New England; not only sodomized cattle have been sacrificed in Massachusetts. The Puritans' preoccupation with sexual offenses, their obsession with anal coitus and seminal emissions, their fear of filthiness and the unnatural have set the darker themes of political and religious discourse in America for more than three centuries. H. L. Mencken defined Puritanism as "the haunting fear that someone, somewhere might be happy." A more dynamic interpretation of the excess attention paid to pudenda by the Pilgrims might explain why the life that was to be given for a life was invariably a woman's.

More agreeable aspects of the Puritan legacy came to mind as I loped the last mile home. My path took me to the back of Eel Pond, a natural marina around which the village is disposed. The last yachts of the season and assorted skiffs were berthed in the small harbor; its periphery was ablaze with autumn elm and maple. Cormorants ruffled the pond. Across the water, the sun shone on the colonial cupola of the Woods Hole Oceanographic Institute (WHOI). A flag snapped in the breeze above the pediments of the Marine Biological Laboratory; the early sun was reflected from windows of its library. The hum of machinery which carried softly from the labs reminded me that both of those scientific institutions are in their halcyon days. That summer, deep-water submersibles from WHOI had found the battleship *Bismarck* at the bottom of the Atlantic, while with the spiffiest of new microscopes scientists of the MBL had discovered the molecular motors of mitosis. The morning panorama of a maritime campus, neat and shipshape, already busy at work, was a hard-edged illustration of Puritan values. Bradford and Winthrop would have approved: their land still housed heralds of light and bearers of love; truth's current had not passed Woods Hole by.

Governor Winthrop expressed a millennarian vision of the New Jerusalem when he spoke of the colony "as a City upon a Hill, the eyes of all people are upon us." The eyes of all people were no less important to the elders than the ears, for the Puritan leaders were preachers of the Word. But above all, they were men who worshipped ideas. "Every man makes his God," wrote Dr. Oliver Wendell Holmes to Harriet Beecher Stowe; "the South Sea Islander makes him out of wood, the Christian New Englander out of ideas." Holmes—son of a Cambridge minister, professor of anatomy at Harvard, and father of the Supreme Court justice— knew that he and his kind, the sons of the Puritans, could never "get the iron of Calvin out of our souls." The other sentiment he could not erase was a Calvinist sense of the elect, of belonging to an elite whose sainthood was made visible by the products of mind.

Historians of the Puritan revolution teach us that a ministry of educated men was required in order to replace the sacramental priesthood of the Roman Church. Education based on the Word of the Bible, and not the authority of a church, was expected to assure the victory of Puritan mind over papal matter. What was less expected was that biblical education, especially in the New World, would also lead to a democratic, individual response to society: all this and the rise of the middle class. Friedrich Engels, writing in 1892, pointed out that Calvin's creed was one fit for the most advanced bourgeoisie of the Puritans' time and that Calvin's constitution was "thoroughly democratic and republican." Almost a century later, the historian Michael Walzer has described the Puritan clergy in England and America as "educated (or self-educated) and aggressive men who wanted a voice in church government, who wanted a church, in effect open to talent. . . . Decisions would be made by prolonged discussion and natural criticism, and finally by a show of hands. Somber, undecorated clothing would suggest the supremacy of the mind. . . . The Puritan ministers provide perhaps the first example of 'advanced' intellectuals in a traditional society. . . . Its first manifestation was the evasion of traditional authority and routine."

A disproportionate number of these advanced intellectuals came to New England; between 1629 and 1640 some one hundred Cambridge men arrived in America. Charles Chauncy would have returned to a chair by the Cam, in England, had not the new Cambridge made him its master. One suspects that Chauncy, like other intellectuals since, may have evaded traditional authority and routine in order to impose an authority and routine of his own.

Traditional authority and routine do not rule Woods Hole today. From the Nobska lighthouse to Eel Pond, moss-covered error keeps no one at its side; the Yankee landscape and the learned institutions throbbing by its sea bear witness to the nobler side of the Puritan effort. From the Charles to the Housatonic, New England considers itself, perhaps rightly, as the intellectual arsenal of our democracy. The darker side of the Puritan endeavor—patriarchal, bigoted, severe—seems for the moment to be under wraps. Indeed, even the history of Puritan terror, the tradition of Chauncy, Cotton Mather, et al., are in good hands these days. Historian Gordon Wood, writing in *The New York Review of Books*, contends that the two leading scholars of Puritan life and letters, successors to such Puritan stock as Perry Miller and Samuel Eliot Morison, are Sacvan Bercovitch (Harvard) and Andrew Delbanco (Columbia). From Bercovitch and Delbanco one gathers that the Puritan terror was at least in part a response to the alienating experience of absolute power in the face of absolute wilderness. Those scholars remind us that the men who hanged witches in Salem also founded Harvard. Nowadays that university is neither bigoted nor severe. It remains a place for the worship of ideas, and in that sense its scholars are all sons of the Puritans.

A future historian may judge that our era, with its free-and-easy social arrangements, our uncommitted youth, casual sex, foul manners, terrifying streets, our infatuation with the gaudy, the rich, the drugged, the besotted, the violent—our culture of Lawrence Taylor, Mick Jagger, and Donald Trump—is not a happier place than the strict New England of 1642. Young men have died for sodomy in both societies, young women have been murdered then and now. If the traditions of Chauncy and company were distantly responsible for the death of Kate in the Bellevue of 1959, one might ask what religious or secular orthodoxy is responsible for deaths at Bellevue in 1990, for the victims of rape, murder, addiction, and AIDS?

Looking at the peaceful scenes of New England, I thought of the new Bellevue, where I work most of the year. An unshaven derelict named Steven Smith, discharged after "treatment" for violent behavior, "dressed like a doctor" in a scruffy scrub suit, put a stethoscope around his neck and roamed around the hospital at will. On Saturday night, January 7, 1989, he raped and murdered a young pathologist who was working late in her office. I was reminded at the time of the death of young Kate thirty years earlier: a life for a life. Kathryn Hinnant was also pregnant. For whose life did she pay? Steven Smith's? That same future historian might find that we are unknowing accomplices in Kathryn Hinnant's death as Charles Chauncy was in the execution of Thomas Granger. He might, if conservative, argue that Dr. Hinnant died for our liberal creed. He might be able to find evidence that our closed asylums, our practice of permitting the mad and violent to prowl the streets, had results more lethal than the Puritan terror.

Saturday nights in Bellevue Hospital were less hazardous for young doctors in my day. The chief resident, like all house officers, lived in the house staff dormitory; if lucky, one saw one's family on alternate evenings. This arrangement gave one a goodly amount of time in the hospital and made it possible not only to follow patients but also to do simple research. In the summer and fall of 1959 one of my projects was to study how epinephrine caused necrosis of skin in rabbits treated with endotoxin. Lewis Thomas had established a small animal room on the sixth floor of the old Bellevue, and there he put me to work measuring fever in rabbits—another bioassay for endotoxin. The procedure involved the frequent insertion of small thermosensitive probes into the rectums of bunnies; I am persuaded that my postdocs who do density gradient experiments with clean gloves have a better deal these days.

In the event, the epinephrine project was part of an effort to find out the mechanism of the Shwartzman phenomenon, the thorough exploration of which had made my mentor's scientific reputation. Here is his account of the *local* phenomenon in *The Youngest Science:*

> A small quantity of endotoxin is injected into the abdominal skin of a rabbit, not enough to make the animal sick, but just enough to cause mild, localized inflammation at the infected site, a pink area the size of a quarter. If nothing else is done the inflammation subsides and vanishes after a day. But if you wait about eighteen hours after the skin injection, and then inject a small non-toxic dose of endotoxin into one of the rabbit's ear veins, something fantastic happens: within the next two hours, small, pinpoint areas of bleeding appear in the prepared skin, and these enlarge and coalesce until the whole area, the size of a silver dollar, is converted into a solid mass of deep-blue hemorrhage and necrosis.

Kate, the nursing student, had died of the *generalized* Shwartzman phenomenon, in which two appropriately timed injections of bacterial endotoxin produce bilateral renal cortical necrosis, pulmonary edema, and—too frequently—death. Whether local or generalized, the Shwartzman phenomenon leads to the clumping of platelets and especially neutrophils within the circulation. These tend to become sequestered in the small capillaries of kidney and lung or to attach to the sticky walls of blood vessels of the prepared skin site. By 1959 Thomas and coworkers knew that if white cells were removed from the equation, the lesions did not develop. A few years before, he had discovered that small amounts of adrenaline—epinephrine—which alone had little effect, would cause hemorrhagic necrosis in the skin of rabbits prepared with a previous injection of endotoxin. His younger disciples, and soon the whole house staff of Bellevue, came to call this lesion "the Thomas test" since we applied it to humans to judge whether they had endotoxin in the circulation. Ironically, on the night Kate was admitted I had returned to Bellevue to check on the skin of some rabbits whose "Thomas lesion" had been abrogated by endotoxin tolerance.

Nowadays, thanks to a generation of investigators, but especially to Drs. Timothy Springer, Ramzi Cotran, Michael Gimbrone, and Michael Bevilacqua of the Harvard Medical School, we have a pretty good notion of why exactly the Shwartzman phenomenon comes about. Indeed, we know so many of the proteins and genes involved that we are at the point of dotting the *i*s in iC3b and crossing the *t*s of its TATA box (these are abbreviations for the relevant molecules). When endotoxin is injected, the walls of blood vessels (endothelial cells) are made receptive and sticky, because the endothelial cells display specific adhesive molecules for white cells. In turn, white cells display specific adhesive molecules which permit them to stick to each other and to blood vessel walls (iC3b). In the process, molecules such as interleukin 1, tumor necrosis factor, and complement split products are let loose in the circulation, with consequences described earlier in these pages. Those gymnastics of cell regulation produce the effects that Lewis Thomas knew by 1959:

> In the Shwartzman phenomenon, cell death is caused by a shutting off of the blood supply to the target tissue. After the second injection, the small veins and capillaries in the prepared skin area become plugged by dense masses of blood platelets and white cells, all stuck to each other and to the lining of the vessels; behind these clumped cells the blood clots, and the tissue dies of a sort of strangulation. Then the blood vessels suddenly dilate, the plugs move

away into the larger veins just ahead, the walls of the
necrotic capillaries burst, and the tissue is filled up,
engorged by the hemorrhage.

We never did figure out how epinephrine worked. But when, at
the end of my Woods Hole run, I thought about poor young Kate
and her botched abortion that Labor Day weekend in 1959, I had
an idea for an experiment. What if endotoxin were to increase the
number of epinephrine receptors on the surface of endothelial
cells, as it increases the number of adhesive molecules? What if
that poor young woman died because the blood vessels of her
kidneys closed in an overeager response to epinephrine? What
if ... ?

Looking at the gracious landscape of the Puritans, I realized
that the pursuit of ideas in that university seventy miles to the
north—by Bevilacqua, by Holmes, and yes, by Chauncy—had provided the facts I needed to ask those questions. Not only Fresnel
lenses project light. I also realized, of course, that I was looking
for a scientific solution to a social problem. The Kates of today
need not die, because abortion is still legal, and as a doctor I
strongly resent those movements that would permit return of the
rusty coathanger. I have no idea when life begins, but I am sure
when it ends. Absent a new Puritan terror, young women—children,
indeed—will become pregnant. Absent recourse to safe abortion,
some of those, and mainly the poor, will die in blood and pain.
Liberal programs, when they go wrong, may disrupt social *order*.
But the error that fundamentalists make is to value creed over
social *justice*. Mosaic laws are laws for old men. In the slogans of
the campaign against legal abortion, I hear echoes from the
Plymouth of 1642: A life for a life is a call for revenge by elders on
the bodies of young women.

In advocating the cause of keeping abortion legal and safe, I
am drawn to the finer side of the Puritan temper. Dr. Oliver
Wendell Holmes, after an apprenticeship in Paris, brought home
not only a French microscope but also the enlightened Gallic

habit of clinical investigation in urban hospitals. Discovering that young Boston mothers died of puerperal fever because doctors carried the infection from bed to bed, he defined the problem, described the obvious solution, and was roundly denounced by the traditionalists. In 1855 Holmes replied to his elders on behalf of the young women of Massachusetts much as I would speak on behalf of those who will surely die if *Roe v. Wade* is further diluted: "I am too much in earnest for either humility or vanity, but I do entreat those who hold the keys of life and death to listen to me also for this once. I ask no personal favor; but I beg to be heard in behalf of women whose lives are at stake, until some stronger voice shall plead for them."

Sources

Introduction

Cennini, C. *The Craftsman's Handbook*, trans. D. V. Thompson. New Haven, Conn.: Yale University Press, 1933.

Connolly, C. *The Unquiet Grave* (reprint of 1945 ed.). New York: Viking Compass, 1957.

Goldwater, R., and M. Treves. *Artists on Art*. New York: Pantheon, 1945.

Meiss, M. *The Painter's Choice: Problems in the Interpretation of Renaissance Art*. New York: Harper & Row, 1967.

Orwell, G. *Decline of the English Murder and Other Essays*. London: Penguin, 1965.

Snow, C. P. *The Two Cultures and the Scientific Revolution*. London: Cambridge University Press, 1959.

Watson, J. D. *The Double Helix*. New York: Atheneum, 1968.

1. The Doctor with Two Heads

Baldick, R. *The First Bohemian: The Life of Henry Murger*. London: Hamish Hamilton, 1961.

Cantor, N. F. *Twentieth Century Culture*. New York: Peter Lang, 1988.

Collins, L., and D. La Pierre. *Is Paris Burning?* New York: Simon & Schuster, 1965.

Combat (Paris), no. 3 (May 1942).

Combat médical (Paris), no. 2 (March 1944).

Frizell, B. *Ten Days in August*. New York: Simon & Schuster, 1956.

Garnot, N. S. F. "L'Architecture hôpitalier au XIX siècle: L'Exemple parisien," *Les Dossiers du Musée d'Orsay;* no. 27 (1988).

Gramont, S. de. *The French*. New York: G. P. Putnam's Sons, 1969.

Guerard, A. *France: A Modern History*. Ann Arbor: University of Michigan Press, 1959.

Hillairet, J., and P. Payen–Appenzeller. *Dictionnaire historique des rues de Paris*. Paris: Les Éditions de Minuit, 1972.

Magraw, R. *France 1815–1914: The Bourgeois Century*. London: Fontana, 1983.

Marx, K., and F. Engels. *Basic Writings on Politics and Philosophy*, ed. Lewis Feuer. New York: Doubleday/Anchor, 1959.

Monod, R. *Les Heures décisives de la libération de Paris*. Paris: Éditions Gilbert, 1947.

Le Petit Journal (Paris; illustrated supplement), February 27, 1898.

Seigel, J. *Bohemian Paris*. New York: Elisabeth Sifton Books, 1986.

Simon–Dhouailly, N. *La Leçon de Charcot: Voyage dans une toile*. Paris: Musée de l'Assistance Publique, 1986.

——. *Musée de l'Assistance Publique de Paris* (catalogue). Paris: Musée de l'Assistance Publique, 1987.

Zeldin, T. *France 1848–1945* (3 vols.). Oxford: Oxford University Press, 1979.

Zola, É. *Le Docteur Pascal*, in *Oeuvres complètes*. Paris: Cercle du Livres Precieuses, 1960.

2. Titanic *and* Leviathan

Ballard, R. *Discovery of the Titanic*. London: Hodder & Stoughton, 1987.

Bradford, W. *Of Plymouth Plantation 1620–1647*, ed. S. E. Morison. New York: Alfred A. Knopf, 1952.

Gay, P. *Sigmund Freud*. New York: W. W. Norton, 1988.

Marshall, L. *The Sinking of the Titanic and Great Sea Disasters*, ed. L. Marshall. Philadelphia: J. C. Winston, 1912.

Melville, H. *Moby-Dick; or, The Whale*. New York: Heritage, 1943.

Oceanus, 28 (Winter 1986–7; *Titanic* expedition issue).

Russell, T. H. *Sinking of the Titanic*. New York: L. H. Walter, 1912.

Wade, W. C. *The Titanic*. New York: Penguin, 1986.

3. Wordsworth at the Barbican

Hartman, G. H. *Wordsworth's Poetry 1787–1814*. Cambridge, Mass.: Harvard University Press, 1971.

Nicolson, M. H. *Newton Demands the Muse*. Princeton, N.J.: Princeton University Press, 1946.

Ozick, C. "Science and Letters: God's Work—and Ours," *The New York Times Book Review*, September 27, 1987.

Vane, J. R. "Inhibition of Prostaglandin Synthesis as a Mechanism of Action for Aspirin-like Drugs," *Nature, New Biology*, 231 (1971), 232–4.

Wordsworth, W. *Poems*. London: J. M. Dent, 1920.

4. The Treasure of Dongo

Behrman, S. N. *Portrait of Max*. New York: Random House, 1960.

Bellini Delle Stelle, P. L., and U. Lazzaro. *Dongo, ultima azione*. Milan: Mondadori, 1961.

Brooke, R. *The Poetical Works of Rupert Brooke*, ed. G. Keynes. London: Faber & Faber, 1946.

Cornford, F. *On a Calm Shore*. London: Cresset, 1960.

Delzell, C. E. *Mussolini's Enemies: The Italian Anti-Fascist Resistance*. Princeton, N.J.: Princeton University Press, 1961.

———, ed. *Mediterranean Fascism 1919–1945*. New York: Harper & Row Torchbooks, 1970.

Forgacs, D. *An Antonio Gramsci Reader*. New York: Schocken, 1988.

Marshall, J. *The Castle Keep: The Villa Serbelloni in History*. Bellagio: privately printed, 1970.

Orwell, G. *Homage to Catalonia*. London: Victor Gollancz, 1938.

Payne, R., ed. *The Civil War in Spain 1936–1939*. New York: G. P. Putnam's Sons, 1962.

Stansky, P., and W. Abraham. *Journey to the Frontier*. London: Constable, 1966.

———. *Orwell: The Transformation*. New York: Alfred A. Knopf, 1980.

Thomas, H. *The Spanish Civil War*. New York: Harper & Row, 1962.

5. Losing a MASH

Hoffman, S. *Under the Ether Dome: One Doctor's Apprenticeship at Massachusetts General Hospital*. New York: Charles Scribner's Sons, 1987.

Klass, P. *A Not Entirely Benign Procedure: Four Years as a Medical Student*. New York: G. P. Putnam's Sons, 1987.

Konner, M. *Becoming a Doctor*. New York: Elisabeth Sifton Books, 1987.

Le Baron, C. *Gentle Vengeance: An Account of the First Years at Harvard Medical School*. New York: Richard Marek, 1981.

Orwell, G. *Homage to Catalonia*. London: Victor Gollancz, 1938.

6. Gertrude Stein on the Beach

Brinnin, J. M. *The Third Rose*. Boston: Addison-Wesley, 1959.

Cohen, S. "Some Struggles of Jacques Loeb, Albert Matthews and Ernest Just at the MBL," *Biology Bulletin*, 168 (1985), 127–36.

Curtis, W. C. "Good Old Summer Times at the MBL," *The Enterprise* (Falmouth, Mass.), August 12, 1955.

Freud, S., and J. Breuer. *Studies in Hysteria* (reprint of 1895 ed.), in *The Standard Edition of the Complete Psychological Works*, ed. J. Strachey and A. Freud. London: Hogarth Press, 1966.

James, W. *Essays on Faith, Ethics and Morals*. New York: New American Library, 1974.

Lewis, S. *Arrowsmith*. New York: Harcourt, Brace, 1924.

Loeb, J. *The Mechanistic Conception of Life* (reprint). Cambridge, Mass.: Belknap Press of the Harvard University Press, 1965.

————. *The Organism as a Whole: From a Physico-Chemical Viewpoint*. New York: G. P. Putnam's Sons, 1916.

McGrath, W. J. "Peter Gay: *Freud*," *The New York Review of Books*, August 12, 1988.

Pauly, P. J. *Controlling Life: Jacques Loeb and the Engineering Ideal in Biology*. Oxford: Oxford University Press, 1987.

Skinner, B. F. "Has Gertrude Stein a Secret?," *The Atlantic Monthly*, April 1935.

Solomons, L. M., and G. Stein. "Normal Motor Automatism," *Psychological Review*, 2 (1896), 492–512.

Stein, G. *The Autobiography of Alice B. Toklas*. New York: Harcourt, Brace, 1933.

————. *How to Write*. Paris: Plain Editions, 1931.

————. *Lectures in America* (reprint of 1935 ed.). Boston: Beacon Press, 1985.

————. *Paris, France* (reprint of 1939 ed.). New York: Liveright, 1970.

————. *Picasso*. London: B. T. Batsford, 1938.

————. *Selected Writings*. New York: Vintage, 1972.

Steiner, W. *Exact Resemblance to Exact Resemblance: The Literary Portraiture of Gertrude Stein*. New Haven, Conn.: Yale University Press, 1978.

7. Inflammation: From Khartoum to Casablanca

Abramson, S., and G. Weissmann. "Current Comment: The Mechanisms of Action of Nonsteroidal Antiinflammatory Drugs," *Arthritis and Rheumatism*, 32 (1989), 1–9.

Bowle, J. *The Imperial Achievement*. Boston: Little, Brown, 1974.

Ford, F. M. *Parade's End*. New York: Alfred A. Knopf, 1922.

Gide, A. *Journals, IV. 1939–1949*, trans. J. O'Brien. New York: Alfred A. Knopf, 1951.

McFarland, J. "Inflammation," in *Cyclopedia of Medicine, Surgery and Specialties*. Philadelphia: F. A. Davis, 1941.

Metchnikoff, É. *Immunity in Infective Diseases* (reprint of 1905 ed.). New York: Johnson Reprint, 1968.

Reibman, J., H. M. Korchak, L. B. Vosshal, et al. "Changes in Diacylglycerol Labeling, Cell Shape, and Protein Phosphorylation Distinguish 'Triggering' from 'Activation' of Human Neutrophils," *Journal of Biological Chemistry,* 263 (1988), 6322.

Smith, L. R., K. L. Bost, and J. E. Blacock. "Generation of Idiotypic and Antiidiotypic Antibodies by Immunization with Peptides Encoded by Complementary RNA: A Possible Molecular Basis for the Network Theory," *Journal of Immunology,* 138 (1987), 7–9.

Thomas, L. "Adaptive Aspects of Inflammation," in B. K. Forscher and J. C. Houck, eds., *Immunopathology of Inflammation.* Amsterdam and New York: Excerpta Medica, 1971.

Weissmann, G., ed."Advances in Inflammation Research," vol. 1 (1979), 1–64.

———, ed. *Mediators of Inflammation.* New York: Plenum Press, 1974.

West, E. *The Night Is a Time for Listening.* London: Victor Gollancz, 1966.

8. Hay on the Vineyard: The American Revolution in Art

Allen, G. *Life Science in the Twentieth Century.* New York: John Wiley, 1975.

Breton, A. *Surrealism and Painting,* trans. S. W. Taylor. New York: Harper & Row, 1972.

Brinton, C. *The Anatomy of Revolution.* New York: Prentice-Hall, 1952.

Craven, T. *Modern Art: The Men, the Movements, the Meaning.* New York: Simon & Schuster, 1934.

Flint, J. *The Prints of Louis Lozowick.* New York: Hudson Hills, 1982.

Fruton, J. S. *Molecules and Life: Historical Essays on the Interplay of Chemistry and Biology.* New York: John Wiley, 1972.

Goodman, C. *Hans Hofmann.* Cambridge, Mass.: Harvard University Press, 1986.

Groce, N. E. *Everyone Here Spoke Sign Language.* Cambridge, Mass.: Harvard University Press, 1985.

Lew, J. *Arshile Gorky.* New York: Harry N. Abrams, 1966.

Motherwell, R. *Reconciliation Elegy.* Geneva: Skira, 1980.

Nachmansohn, D. *German-Jewish Pioneers in Science.* Berlin and New York: Springer, 1979.

Sandler, I. *The Triumph of American Painting: A History of Abstract Expressionism.* New York: Praeger, 1970.

Schapiro, M. *Modern Art, 19th & 20th Centuries: Collected Papers.* New York: George Braziller, 1978.

Stella, F. *Working Space.* Cambridge, Mass.: Harvard University Press, 1986.

Tashjian, D. *William Carlos Williams and the American Scene 1920–1940.* Berkeley: University of California Press, 1978.

9. Haussmann on Missiles

Giedion, S. *Space, Time and Architecture*. Cambridge, Mass.: Harvard University Press, 1952.

Gooch, G. P. *The Second Empire*. London: Longmans, 1960.

Haussmann, G. E. *Mémoirs* (3 vols.). Paris: Hermann, 1890–3.

Horne, A. *The Fall of Paris*. New York: Viking, 1965.

Pinckney, D. M. *Napoleon III and the Rebuilding of Paris*. Princeton, N.J.: Princeton University Press, 1971.

10. Gulliver in Nature

Barre–Sinoussi, F., J. C. Chermann, F. Rey, et al. "Isolation of a T–Lymphotropic Retrovirus from a Patient at Risk for Acquired Immune Deficiency Syndrome," *Science*, 220 (1983), 868–71.

Diderot, D. "Encyclopedia," trans. Jacques Barzun in *Rameau's Nephew and Other Works*. New York: Doubleday/Anchor, 1956.

Gallo, R., S. Z. Salahudding, R. Popovic, et al. "Frequent Detection and Isolation of Cytopathic Retrovirus (HTLV–III) from Patients with AIDS and at Risk for AIDS," *Science*, 224 (1984), 500–2.

Loeb, J., and R. Beutner. "On the Nature of the Electromotive Force in Plant Organs," *Science*, 37 (1913), 672–3.

Swift, J. *Gulliver's Travels*. London: Penguin, 1967.

Wall, R., and L. Strong. "Environmental Consequences of Treating Cattle with the Antiparasitic Drug Ivermectin," *Nature*, 327 (1987), 418–21.

Watson, J. B., and F. H. C. Crick. "A Structure for Deoxyribose Nucleic Acid," *Nature*, 171 (1953), 737–8.

11. The Age of Miracles Hadn't Passed

Englebert, O. *The Lives of the Saints*. London and New York: Thames & Hudson, 1951.

McGinley, P. *Saint Watching*. New York: The Viking Press, 1969.

New York University Medical Center. *University Hospital Reimbursement Rates and Expected Lengths of Stay*. New York: Anther, 1988.

Ober, W. M. *Bottoms Up!* Carbondale: Southern Illinois University Press, 1987.

12. A Slap of the Tail: Reading Medical Humanities

Ayer, A. J. *Wittgenstein*. New York: Random House, 1985.

Barzun, J. *A Stroll with William James*. Chicago: University of Chicago Press, 1983.

Brody, H. *Stories of Sickness.* New Haven, Conn.: Yale University Press, 1987.

Cronin, A. J. *Shannon's Way.* Boston: Little, Brown, 1948.

de Kruif, P. *Microbe Hunters.* New York: Harcourt, Brace, 1926.

———. *The Sweeping Wind.* New York: Harcourt, Brace and World, 1962.

Flexner, A. *Medical Education in the United States and Canada* (reprint of 1910 ed.). Salem, N.Y.: Ayer, 1972.

James, W. *The Principles of Psychology* (2 vols.). New York: Henry Holt, 1890.

Lewis, S. *Arrowsmith.* New York: Harcourt, Brace, 1925.

Matthiessen, F. O. *The James Family.* New York: Alfred A. Knopf, 1947.

Medawar, P. *Pluto's Republic.* Oxford: Oxford University Press, 1982.

Merton, R. K. *On the Shoulders of Giants.* New York: Free Press, 1965.

Ober, W. M. *Bottoms Up!* Carbondale: Southern Illinois University Press, 1987.

Pasternak, B. *Dr. Zhivago*, trans. M. Hayward and M. Harari. New York: Pantheon, 1958.

Sacks, O. *Awakenings.* New York: Summit, 1987.

Weissmann, G. *The Woods Hole Cantata.* New York: Dodd, Mead, 1985.

Zinsser, H. *Rats, Lice and History.* Boston: Little, Brown, 1935.

13. Daumier and the Deer Tick

Banville, T. de. *Petites études: Mes souvenirs.* Paris: G. Charpentier, 1882.

Baudelaire, C. *Les Fleurs du mal,* ed. J. Crépet, A. Blin, and C. Pichois. Paris: Galimard, 1968.

———. *Les Fleurs du mal,* trans. Richard Howard. Boston: David Godine, 1982.

———. *Oeuvres complètes,* ed. Y. G. Le Dantec and C. Pichois. Paris: Galimard, 1961.

Bernard, C. *Introduction to the Study of Experimental Medicine,* trans. H. C. Green. New York: Henry Schuman, 1949.

Brock, R. *Robert Koch.* New York: Springer, 1988.

Brookner, A. *The Genius of the Future.* London: Phaidon, 1971.

Burgdorfer, W., A. G. Barbour, S. F. Hayes, et al. "Lyme Disease—A Tick-borne Spirochetosis?," *Science,* 216 (1982), 1317-9.

Clark, T. J. *The Absolute Bourgeois.* London and New York: Thames & Hudson, 1973.

———. *Image of the People: Gustave Courbet and the 1848 Revolution.* London and New York: Thames & Hudson, 1973.

Faunce, S., and L. Nochlin. *Courbet Reconsidered.* Brooklyn, N.Y.: The Brooklyn Museum, 1988.

Geoffroy, A., quoted in P. Adhemar, *Daumier.* Paris: Pierre Tisne, 1954.

Goncourt, E. and J. *Gavarni.* Paris: Plon, 1954.

Lassaigne, D. *Daumier,* trans. E. B. Shaw. Paris: Hyperion, 1938.

Malawista, S. E., J. M. Oliver, and M. Rudolph. "Microtubules and Cyclic

Nucleotides: On the Order of Things," *Journal of Cell Biology,* 77 (1978), 881–6.

Malawista, S. E., A. C. Steere, and J. A. Hardin. "Lyme Disease: A Unique Human Model for an Infectious Etiology of Rheumatic Disease," *Yale Journal of Biology and Medicine,* 57 (1984), 473–7.

Malawista, T. "Programme, février 1988." Paris: Privately printed, 1988.

Montgolfier, B. de. *Île St.-Louis* (catalogue). Paris: Musée Carnavalet, 1980.

Nochlin, L. "The Development and Nature of Realism in the Work of Gustave Courbet: A Study of the Style and Its Social and Artistic Background," Ph.D. dissertation, New York University, 1963.

———. *Realism.* New York: Penguin, 1971.

Rensberger, B. "A New Type of Arthritis Found in Lyme, Conn.," *The New York Times,* July 18, 1976.

Roueché, B. "The Foulest and Meanest Creatures That Be," *The New Yorker,* September 12, 1988.

Spielman, A. "A Changing Landscape and the Emergence of Lyme Disease in North America." In press.

———. "Prospects for Suppressing Transmission of Lyme Disease," *Annals of the New York Academy of Science,* 539 (1988), 212–20.

Starkie, E. *Baudelaire.* London: Penguin, 1971.

Steere A. C., T. F. Broderick, and S. E. Malawista. "Erythema Chronicum Migrans and Lyme Arthritis: Epidemiological Evidence for a Tick Vector," *American Journal of Epidemiology,* 108 (1978), 312–9.

Steere, A. C., M. S. Grodzicki, A. N. Kornblatt, et al. "The Spirochetal Etiology of Lyme Disease," *The New England Journal of Medicine,* 308 (1983), 733–40.

Steere, A. C., S. E. Malawista, J. A. Hardin, et al. "Erythema Chromicum Migrans and Lyme Arthritis: The Changing Clinical Spectrum," *Annals of Internal Medicine,* 86 (1977), 685–98.

———. "Lyme Arthritis: An Epidemic of Oligoarticular Arthritis in Children and Adults in Three Contiguous Connecticut Communities," *Arthritis and Rheumatism,* 20 (1977), 7–17.

Telford, S. R., T. N. Mather, S. I. Moore, et al. "Incompetence of Deer as Reservoirs of the Lyme Disease Spirochete," *American Journal of Tropical Medicine,* 39 (1988), 105–9.

Tocqueville, A. de. *Recollections,* trans. G. Lawrence. Garden City, N.Y.: Doubleday, 1970.

Zurier, R. B., G. Weissmann, S. Hoffstein, et al. "Mechanisms of Lysosomal Enzyme Release from Human Leukocytes II: Effects of cAMP and cGMP, Autonomic Agonists and Agents Which Affect Microtubule Function," *Journal of Clinical Investigation,* 53 (1974), 297–309.

14. To the Nobska Lighthouse

Bevilacqua, M. P., S. Stengelin, M. A. Gimbrone, and B. Seed. "Endothelial Leukocyte Adhesion Molecule 1: An Inducible Receptor for Neutrophils Related to Complement Regulatory Proteins and Lectins," *Science*, 243 (1989), 1160–4.

Boutry, G. A. "Augustin Fresnel: His Time, Life and Work," *Science Progress*, 36 (1948), 587–604.

Bradford, W. *Of Plymouth Plantation 1620–1647*, ed. S. E. Morison. New York: Alfred A. Knopf, 1952.

Delbanco, A. *The Puritan Ordeal*. Cambridge, Mass.: Harvard University Press, 1989.

Marx, K., and F. Engels. *Basic Writings on Politics and Philosophy*, ed. Lewis Feuer. New York: Doubleday/Anchor, 1959.

Mencken, H. L. *Letters*, Selected and annotated by Guy J. Forgue. New York: Alfred A. Knopf, 1961.

Morse, J. T. *Oliver Wendell Holmes: Life and Letters*, 2 vols. Boston and New York: Houghton Mifflin, 1896.

Thomas, L. "The Physiological Disturbances Produced by Endotoxins," *Annual Reviews of Physiology*, 16 (1954), 467–78.

———. *The Youngest Science: Notes of a Medicine Watcher*. New York: The Viking Press, 1983.

Walzer, M. *The Revolution of the Saints: A Study in the Origins of Radical Politics*. Cambridge, Mass.: Harvard University Press, 1982.

Weissmann, G., and L. Thomas. "Studies on Lysosomes I. The Effects of Endotoxin, Endotoxin Tolerance and Cortisone on Release of Acid Hydrolases from a Granular Fraction of Rabbit Liver," *Journal of Experimental Medicine*, 116 (1962), 451–66.

Woods, G. S. "Struggle over the Puritans," *The New York Review of Books*, 36, 17 (1989), 26–34.

Illustration Credits

A NOTE ABOUT THE AUTHOR

Gerald Weissmann, M.D., is the author of two previous collections of essays, *The Woods Hole Cantata* and *They All Laughed at Christopher Columbus*. He is professor of medicine at New York University Medical Center in Manhattan and spends part of each year doing research at the Marine Biological Laboratory in Woods Hole, Massachusetts. Dr. Weissmann is a columnist for *Hospital Practice* and editor in chief of *M.D. Magazine*. He has contributed to *Discover*, *The Sciences*, *The New York Times*, and the Washington *Post*.

A NOTE ON THE TYPE

The text of this book was set in Walbaum, a typeface designed by Justus Erich Walbaum in 1810. Walbaum was active as a type founder in Goslar and Weimar from 1799 to 1836. Though letterforms in this face are patterned closely on the "modern" cuts then being made by Giambattista Bodoni and the Didot family, they are of a far less rigid cut. Indeed, it is the slight but pleasing irregularities in the cut that give this face its human quality and account for its wide appeal. Even in appearance, Walbaum jumps boundaries, having a more French than German look.

Composed by Superior Type,
Champaign, Illinois

Printed and bound by Fairfield Graphics,
Fairfield, Pennsylvania

Designed by Valarie J. Astor